4

BLOOD+

01

FIRST KISS

I HAVE NO CHOICE BUT TO FIGHT

Through an encounter with a stunning young man named Hagi, Saya Otonashi, a typical high school student, becomes wrapped up in a battle with the horrendous Chiropterans. What is this curse from her past, and can the answers be found to save her future?

# BLOOD+

# BLOOD+

## FIRST KISS

VOLUME ONE

original concept by **Production I.G** • **Aniplex**
*a novel by* **Ryo Ikehata**
*Illustrations by* **Chizu Hashii**

*English translation by* **John Thomas**

Milwaukie

**SAYA OTONASHI**—Okinawa high school student. The adopted daughter of the Miyagusuku household, she is well cared for by this loving family, but has no memories of anything beyond the past year.

**HAGI**—A handsome cello player. Believing he knows about Saya before she lost her memory, this young man takes her fate into his hands.

**KAI MIYAGUSUKU**—The eldest son in the Miyagusuku clan. He is strong and quick in fights, but his heart is tender and nothing means more to him than his family.

**RIKU MIYAGUSUKU**—The youngest son in the Miyagusuku family. Unlike his older brother, Riku has a good-natured and kind character, and takes care of much of the cooking and cleaning around the house.

**GEORGE MIYAGUSUKU**—Father to Saya, Kai and Riku. Retired from the U.S. Army, he now runs a pub. He is old friends with David.

**DAVID**—A member of Red Shield, an organization with the aim to exterminate the Chiropterans. He has been secretly observing Saya for some time.

LOUIS—A member of Red Shield and a colleague of David's. Louis is an expert in intelligence gathering. He is a cheerful type who never turns down a hearty meal.

JULIA—An acquaintance of George, she is Saya's physician. She is actually on Red Shield's medical team, and is a colleague of David's.

CLARA—A member of Red Shield's Elite Forces. A fan of large-scale machine guns, Clara is a brave female soldier.

SPENCER—A member of Red Shield's Elite Forces. Spencer is a short and happy-go-lucky type, but like Clara, is an adept soldier.

McCOY—A member of Red Shield's Elite Forces. This giant of a man quietly carries out his duties.

ROGERS—A member of Red Shield's Elite Forces. Rogers's trademarks are his goatee and sunglasses.

KAORI KINJOU—A classmate of Saya's and a fellow member of the track team. She does what she can to support Saya, who has lost much of her memory, and they are close friends.

MAO JAHANA—A junior at Saya's school. She is a strong-willed young woman who has her sights set on Kai.

AKIHIRO OKAMURA—A reporter for the *Ryukyu Daily Newspaper.* He is especially interested in the Chiropteran incident at Koza Commercial High School and is beginning to investigate on his own.

MIN—A boarding school student at Lycee du Cinq Flèche in Vietnam. She is a bright girl who likes to share gossip with her friends.

ANNA-MARIE—A student at Lycee du Cinq Flèche. This beauty is considered the queen of the school.

MS. LEE—Teacher and dormitory head-mistress at Lycee du Cinq Flèche. Ms. Lee is known for her rigidity and strictness.

MUI—A young girl living in a juvenile protection institution in Vietnam. She will become chums with the likes of Riku and Kai through a shared love of baseball.

VAN ARGENO—An employee of French drug company Cinq Flèche Pharmaceuticals. He supplies the U.S. Army with certain needs.

KARL—The head of the Vietnam branch of Cinq Flèche Pharmaceuticals as well as the head of the board of Lycee du Cinq Flèche.

SOLOMON—The youthful CEO of drug company Cinq Flèche Pharmaceuticals. He is a serene and handsome young man.

Book design by Heidi Whitcomb
Cover and interior illustrations by Chizu Hashii
English translation by John Thomas

Special thanks to Philip Simon, Michael Gombos, and Camellia Nieh for editing consultation.

Published by Dark Horse Books
A division of Dark Horse Comics
10956 SE Main Street
Milwaukie, OR 97222

darkhorse.com

Library of Congress Cataloging-in-Publication Data

Ikehata, Ryo.
  [Fasuto kisu. English]
  First kiss / written by Ryo Ikehata ; illustrations by Chizu Hashii ; English translation by John Thomas.
      p. cm. -- (Blood+ ; v. 1)
  "First published in Japan in 2006 by Kadokawa Shoten ..., Tokyo"--T.p. verso.
  ISBN-13: 978-1-59307-898-0
  I. Hashii, Chizu. II. Thomas, John. III. Title.
  PL871.5.K44F3713 2008
  895.6'36--dc22
                        2007048513

Dark Horse Books First Edition: March 2008
ISBN 978-1-59307-898-0

Printed in the United States of America

10 9 8 7 6 5 4 3 2 1

# CONTENTS

BLOOD+01

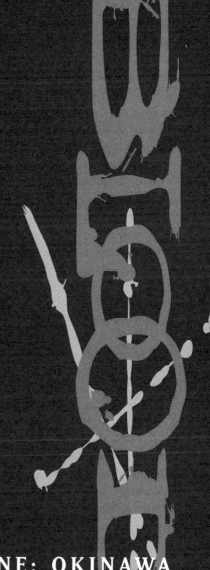

BOOK ONE: OKINAWA

THE BLUE FLOWED across the sky, and for a moment all sounds seemed very far away.

Below her floating body, her tailbone scarcely touched the bar. She was flying.

Just as that thought crossed through her mind, she felt something hard under her back.

Shoosh—her body sank into the mat.

"Almost had it!"

She could hear Kaori's voice and saw her push back her ponytail as she helped her up. The bar that had fallen to the ground looked to her like a rare desert snake, its body rigid as if it were readying a strike on its prey.

The shadows spread across the ground were dense. Today was another hot day.

After adjusting her tank top, Saya hopped off the mat. Her hair wasn't long, typical of schoolgirls her age, and she wiped the sweat off her brow with her fingertips.

"Too bad. You were that close! Oh well. It's nothing to get discouraged about. I mean, if you would have made it, that's like national meet level."

"That's not it."

"Hn?"

There was a gurgling sound, like something was being squeezed.

Noticing that Kaori's eyes had moved to her stomach, Saya smiled, revealing her white teeth.

"I'm starving."

Kaori's expression shifted to a look of "this again?"

This pattern had repeated over and over, but because it was her own body, Saya had grown used to it.

Like most other high schools, the edges of the sports grounds at Koza Commercial High School were lined with plants and trees. Ferns with leaves the size of hand-held fans and flower petals reflecting primary colors displayed the native nature of Okinawa. A high school student from another part of the country might see this as curious, or even exotic, but since Saya had never been off this island it was just the normal, everyday scenery to her.

With the humidity as high as it was, the shade from any tree was a source of cool relief.

Sitting down on the grass next to Kaori, Saya took a bento box from her gym bag and using both hands placed it next to Kaori's.

"Time to eat!"

Before the words had left her mouth, Saya's plastic pink chopsticks began to move on a collision course with her lunch. With her sports drink bottle frozen at her lips, Kaori stared at Saya's lunchtime ritual. It was like one of those nature shows. After tracking the gazelle, the cheetah makes its attack straight for the throat. Kaori was fascinated by this up-close display of the effect of appetite on the behavior of animals.

Naturally, Saya was used to Kaori's glare as they ate together.

"That's just like you, Saya—getting so hungry that it slows you down."

"Well, there's that, too, but it's like my body doesn't want me to give it my all . . . it's hard to explain."

"If it wasn't for that you could make it to nationals."

Kaori pouted her lips in mock resentment.

"And how is it that you can eat that much and never gain an ounce?"

"Co-come on. How should I know?"

"Here I am all worried about my diet, too. You make me crazy sometimes," said Kaori. "Watch your lunch!"

Suddenly Kaori grabbed Saya by the shoulders and, pushing the weight of her slender body against her friend (Kaori didn't need to worry about diets), pulled Saya back-first onto the grass. As if her life depended on it, Saya held her bento box out level in order not to spill its contents.

At that moment Saya's gaze was distracted by something up in the sky.

From behind the school building appeared a giant metal bird, its thunderous roar shaking the ground as it tore straight across the sky.

It was a large-scale airplane dropping a giant shadow that skated through the sports fields and finally out of Saya's field of vision.

"What a huge airplane."

"That was a bomber."

"A what?"

"A bomber. It's an airplane that drops bombs. The American military is always going to wars from Okinawa. Even during the Vietnam War they flew their planes from here. My mom knows about this stuff because she works at the base. I can't stand them, but she says it's thanks to the U.S. Army base that we have food to eat."

"I . . . don't really know about this stuff."

"Right. Of course you don't, Saya. You have . . ."

Kaori bit her lip before the next words came out.

Saya had no recollection of any event in her life that had occurred more than one year ago.

Simply labeling it amnesia seemed too exaggerated, and for the most part her day-to-day life wasn't all that inconvenienced by it. However, it was times like this that she did feel a sense of loss for the memories she no longer had. The worst part about it was feeling like she didn't know who she really was.

"Saya!"

Saya turned toward the voice to see a uniformed boy standing on the stairs leading from the field to the school.

He had red highlights in his brown hair, and his face had an attractive, but rough look.

"Time to go to the clinic!"

"All right!"

Even though she knew she had to go, Saya couldn't seem to stop the movement of her chopsticks into her lunch. She stuffed pieces of omelette and fried shrimp into her mouth all at once, and then packed her cheeks with the remaining white rice. She put away her chopsticks and lunch box as she chewed the remains of her food.

"That's so cool that Kai-sempai takes you."

"You think so?" is what Saya wanted to say, but with a mouth crammed with food, she couldn't get the words out. After helping her put her things in her gym bag, Kaori touched Saya's cheek with her right hand.

It seemed a piece of rice was stuck right next to Saya's mouth.

"I mean, he was a baseball ace. Even now there are a ton of girls who like him."

"Hmph. What do I know?"

The very porcelain-toned Saya watched the piece of rice go from Kaori's light-cocoa-colored tanned hand to disappear between her plump lips.

"We got that meet in the morning. I need all the nourishment I can get!" The city-sponsored track-and-field meet being held the following day was a precursor to the all-prefecture meet.

It would have a big influence on who would be selected to participate after the seniors graduated. Just looking at her numbers, anyone could guess that Saya would be one of those chosen to compete.

"Ha ha. Okay. See you tomorrow!"

Stuffing her bag under her arm, Saya stood up, gave a little wave, and ran off.


After changing back into her school uniform in the locker room, Saya ran to the opposite side of the baseball field to find Kai waiting for her, sitting coolly on the front edge of the seat of his motorcycle.

"Sorry I'm late."

"Yeah, yeah."

"I'll take a bus home today to make it up."

"Hn. Here."

Putting on the motorcycle helmet Kai tossed her way, Saya extended one long leg over the seat of the bike and got on behind Kai. She wrapped both arms around his waist.

"Kai, you used to play baseball, right?"

"I quit before you came to live with us."

There was no nostalgic or emotional tone in his answer. Rather his feelings about the question seemed to come out in the spit of the bike's exhaust pipe as it took off with a start.

Pressing her head into Kai's back, Saya avoided the whip of the wind.

"It's been a whole year since Father took me in, but there is still so much I don't know about."

"The past doesn't matter. You heard Dad say that. We're a family. Maybe not the same blood, but now we're family."

"I guess . . . you're right."

A small amount of sweat formed on Kai's back. The warm sensation that came through Kai's shirt felt like an oasis as the wind blew loudly on either side.

In the last year, how many times had she heard words of encouragement while riding on the back of this bike?

At the beginning, without memory, all her experiences were like that of a baby (she was even surprised she could form her thoughts into words), and that's when she was adopted into the Miyagusuku family.

As could be expected, Saya didn't remember very much of those first few days. However Kai, his younger brother, Riku, and his father, George, were nothing but kind and supportive to the sudden new member of the clan.

That being said, Kai's choice of words tended to be rough, and George couldn't be described as having the longest fuse, so arguments had happened. But there had been ten times as many happy times as tense ones since Saya's arrival. The accumulation of being together with these three men, whether it be sharing a meal, going out for groceries, or just discussing the finer points of whatever television show was on at the moment, had made Saya feel like in her heart she was part of a real family.

Riding on the highway near the sea, the smell of salt filled the air.

Beyond the highway rested a white sandy beach and an unbroken sea the color of a polished turquoise stone which extended as far as the eye could see. White splinters of reflections from the sun flashed in the slowly rolling waves.

Saya loved this view of the sea.

Gazing upon the carefree rock crag jutting out into the open ocean gave her a strange sense of comfort. Constantly washed in the spray of the waves, that rock never moved, was always there.

Kai knew this, and that's why he chose to take this route.

"Thank you," Saya whispered into her big brother's back.

+

*"Our next story is a follow-up on the recent string of murders in the Nago region. According to local police, it appears that a sharp-edged blade was used by the attacker to murder his female victims, but the lack of blood at the scenes of discovery suggests that the murders must have taken place elsewhere, and the bodies were then moved—"*

"How are you feeling, Ms. Otonashi? Is anything coming back?"

The curtain slid open and a crisp, white doctor's robe appeared.

Staring at the cream-colored ceiling, Saya had vaguely noticed the news on the radio playing somewhere in the background. Being careful of the intravenous drip in her right arm, Saya slowly lifted herself up to a sitting position.

"No. Nothing yet."

"Right. Just rest until we are done today."

"Okay."

A female doctor smiling sweetly as she compared the remainder of an I.V. drip with her watch wasn't anything surprising in Okinawa, but this doctor was a young Caucasian. The glasses on such a beautiful face created a certain distance, a coldness. Reinforcing Saya's impression, the doctor turned without another word and stepped back, closing the curtain behind her. Saya could hear the sound of her flat heels walking away from her bed.

Saya only knew that the doctor's name was Julia.

She was acquaintances with her foster father, George, and was supposedly a good physician. Putting his trust in Julia, George chose this little clinic over the much bigger Sogo Hospital to treat Saya. With her regular appointments set in advance, Saya almost never saw any other patients when she was there. The neighborhood didn't really seem like a place that could support an exclusive doctor or clinic.

And for Saya, all the efforts to unbury her lost memories had been fruitless. Was the drug in the I.V. drip having any effect at all? After her long commute to the clinic, her appointments consisted of a prick in the arm from the needle, a little catnap on the bed, and then a brief exchange with Julia. It had become a routine. It felt like the cycle would never end . . .

But, it doesn't matter, thought Saya.

*I just gotta do whatever it takes to get better.*

The sky was still bright blue as Saya left the clinic.

Being in the southernmost region of Japan, and close to the equator, the feel of summer lasted longer than in other places, even though it was technically autumn.

"Saya-chan."

As she stepped off the bus at her stop, she heard a voice call out from behind her.

She turned around to see Riku jogging toward her from the shopping street with a convenience store vinyl bag hanging from one hand.

Sometimes mistaken for a girl, Riku had gentle facial features, silky cheeks, and chestnut-colored hair that mussed in the slightest breeze.

Fitting with his appearance, he had kindly come to meet his big sister at her bus stop.

"What's that? Some snacks?"

"Yup. Dad asked me to get some. Are you just coming back from the hospital?"

". . . Hm. Yeah." Her answer was distant as her consciousness focused on her sense of hearing. A graceful tune had floated through the humid air into Saya's ears and straight to her heart.

It was coming from the neighborhood where the bus had come through, where there were few cars and little bustle, so the music could strike its target with ease. The orchids and lilies set out in front of the florist seemed to soak in the music, letting out a deep and fragrant sigh.

Her sense of vision was a half-second behind her hearing, and her eyes began scanning for the moving strings creating the gorgeous music, drawing her view to the sidewalk on the other side of the street.

Through a space in the crowd of people she could see the form of the musician.

Dressed in a dark suit, this tall man sat among the flowers near the trees lining the road. He had the face of a musician. He must have been in his late twenties. He was definitely a Westerner, but there was something different about him from the Americans she was used to seeing. His noble and graceful look came from the long slits he had for eyes and the high bridge of his nose.

*That isn't a violin?* she thought. He played a larger looking stringed instrument which sat across his chest and reached the ground at an angle. The bow in his right hand deftly drifted over the strings, but it looked painful. You wouldn't have guessed just by listening that his hand was wrapped in a thick bandage.

"What is this? . . . strange."

It could not be called music that calmed the soul. Yet it somehow was engaging, alluring . . .

Without even noticing, Saya's eyelids fell closed.


Darkness—

A light flickered through the navy blue darkness, thick as seawater.

Following the comforting sounds of the waves, a faint scene began to spread out.

This was someplace never before seen.

A corridor, and an arched exit up ahead. The walls on either side were ancient and majestic looking. They were centuries old and in places patches of ivy grew.

From somewhere came music from a cello.

Its sound became the guide. A bright light.

The stone wall opening had iron bars inserted in it. Can fit through. To the other side.

The air was chilly. A damp smell. Somewhere water was dripping.

Up a spiral staircase. Up. Up.

Among the ruins was a door.

The thick door was reinforced with rusted metal bindings. Hand stretched out to it.

—No use.

Don't open it.

Thin outstretched hand reached for the handle. A metallic squeal.

"No!"

The vision had suddenly disappeared. Saya's eyes flew open as her hands were frantically grabbing at something, but found nothing but air. Pulled by the momentum of her reach she fell face first into a flowerbed.

The weak young girl crumbled like a house of cards.

"Are-are you okay?" asked her brother.

". . . Ye-yeah."

Riku pulled Saya up out of the flowers, and as she wiped the leaves off her uniform she could feel her ears turn red with embarrassment.

"What just happened? I mean, all of a sudden—"

"Nothing. Let's just go."

Her response was loud. Almost a shriek. Even people on the other side of the street looked over at her, giving questioning and disapproving glances.

Had she interrupted the performance? Saya's conscious was overwhelmed with the fact that the musician's bow had stopped moving, and his eyes were pointed straight at her. She turned and made a running exit back the way she had come.


OMORO was the name of the shop. It was a pub that took up the ground floor under the Miyagusuku family residence.

But since who-knows-when all the regulars and locals had called it "George's Place." Even though everyone knew who owned the shop, Saya always pondered why "Owned by George Miyagusuku" was written under the name "OMORO."

Naturally, the sign on the shop had been there long before Saya had arrived. The only reason she could come up with was that the cheerful, but egotistical George liked seeing his name written in big letters above the entrance. No doubt he had already had the sign planned out before he even knew what kind of shop it would be.

Kai probably said to George it looked too vain and embarrassing to write that above the door, and that complaint was more than likely answered with a flying spoon to the head. Or it might have been silenced with a nice and simple sleeper-hold.

When it came to Okinawa shopping areas, every place pretty much looked the same as anywhere else, but shops with things like "BAR & RESTAURANT & COFFEE" written on them in English catered to customers from the U.S. military base. Since George's retiring from the military, the ratio of American military and base workers who were customers at OMORO was incomparable to other restaurant-pubs in the area.

Parked in front of the little park which rested across the street from the pub was a sedan that Saya had seen before.

Avoiding the glance from the large black man behind the steering wheel eating a round pastry, Saya grabbed the door handle and let herself in the shop.

"I'm home!"

"Oh, Saya! And Riku, too?"

"I met her at the bus stop. Here you go."

"Thanks."

Taking the bag from Riku and laying it on the counter, George turned to the sink. From the sack he pulled out a yellow sponge made to look like a panda's face, and then made a strange expression.

"What the heck is this? I asked for a kitchen sponge."

"That's all they had."

From the stool he sat on Riku put a cup under the customer's filtered drinking water tap.

"Well, if that's all they had . . ."

Not wanting to act like a crybaby soldier, George hunched his muscular back and squeezed soap into the panda-faced sponge. His hair was just beginning to turn gray, but his huge shoulders and arms looked like those of a strongman decades younger. Even the most alcoholic regulars knew not to hit up George for a last nip, or else they would be sent home quicker and in more pain than if they had just kept walking. Saya had no guess as to how many men had lost fights to her father, George. She hadn't actually seen any of them.

"You must be hungry, Saya," George said, turning his dark and weathered face her direction. "I'll get dinner cooking."

"Hn? Wait a sec . . ."

After Saya set her gym bag on the counter and removed her lunch box her face turned white.

"My track shoes! I must have left them at school!"

"Tomorrow's the meet, right? Why not grab them on the way?" asked George.

"And wake up early? Saya will never be able to do that," Riku replied quickly.

"Cram it."

Spinning on her stool, Saya lightly kicked her little brother, and then jumped off when she was pointed at the door she came in.

"I'll grab them and come back!"

"Now?"

"I'll be right back, so don't start dinner without me."

"Hmph. Just be careful."

"Wait for me, all right?"

As Saya turned to push open the door her head plunged into something dark.

A business suit. Her eyes drove straight into chest of the matte black jacket.

"Kya!"

She had walked out at the same moment a customer was trying to enter. She caught herself just before she fell over backward.

He was a tall man. The collar of his white business shirt was buttoned snugly to the top and was barely covered by a tightly knotted necktie. Above the necktie rested a face that looked as if it was made of iron, and it was now glaring sternly down at Saya.

His eyes were scary. After a moment Saya realized she had stopped breathing.

". . . Uh, Come in, David-san."

". . ."

Without saying a word, David continued to glare down at Saya. Saya didn't move either. Her legs were frozen in place.

"Do you have some business with my daughter, David-san?"

George's voice melted the ice in her legs.

With one elbow on the counter, George's distasteful look was not one he would ever use when greeting a customer. George had never addressed David in this way. The formality in the addition of "san" sounding menacing, in a way.

"We need to talk."

If his face was iron, then his voice sounded like stones being rubbed together.

"Riku, go upstairs and watch TV."

"Okay."

Hopping off the stool, Riku's slow stride communicated frustration as he walked to the door in the rear of the shop.

Saya could relate to that feeling.

She had heard that David and George were old friends, but what was so great about hanging out with David was a complete mystery.

It wasn't that he was lewd or obnoxious, it was more his attitude, and the air about him. It just didn't feel like he lived a very normal life.

She must have had a concerned look on her face. George forced a smile.

"Didn't you forget something at school? Hurry on back, or we'll start dinner without you."

"Oh . . . yeah . . . be right back."

They say summer days are long, but by eight o'clock, the sky has turned to nighttime colors.

Just as could be expected, the school gate was locked.

It was well past the end of the school day, and all the sports practice sessions were finished by this hour.

"Sheesh. I should have known it'd be closed. Now what am I going to do . . ." Saya mumbled to herself and glanced up and down the street in front of the school.

All clear. No one was around.

Saya mustered all the courage she had and pulled herself over the metal-barred gate.

"Forgive me," she apologized to no one in particular as she stood in the schoolyard she had left only a few hours earlier.

To the right beyond the gate was the visitors' entrance to the school. The large teachers' office was further past that.

From looking at the window of the office Saya could see that the lights were still on.

Her track shoes must have been left in the sports club equipment room. It was going to be a real pain if she was wrong, thought Saya as she nimbly walked past the teachers' office and in the direction of the small sheds next to the sports field used as clubhouses and storage. She went up the short flight of stairs and was quietly passing under the second-floor passageway between the library and school building when it happened.

Saya's knees went stiff.

In front of her she saw a person's shadow move. Because it was almost dark, the shadow seemed to appear from out of nowhere.

It wasn't a teacher.

The clothes he wore were the color of the night sky. He had beautiful long locks and an elegant pale face. Where had she seen him before? Ah, yes. He was the cello player.

"Finally, we meet."

He spoke quietly, but at the same time with a soft tone of anticipation realized. Saya's eyes were glued to his bandaged hand.

Something glinted white. A blade. He held a knife.

An electric current ran up her spine, and her breath was stuck in her throat.

*It appears that a sharp-edged blade was used by the attacker to murder his female victims . . .*

The radio news broadcast she heard earlier sprung back into her ears, and then faded into a painful ringing.

The sound of his shoes walking across the dirt brought Saya back to her senses.

She was too scared to scream, but her body was in motion. Saya spun around in a snap and took off running.

She was suddenly aware of the intense beating of her heart. She needed to find somebody. Anybody. For help.

With every ounce of energy she had, Saya ran until she slammed into the glass of the visitors' entrance door. She banged on the glass with both hands.

"Hello? Anybody . . ."

Her voice was hoarse. She had trouble catching her breath.

She felt something on her shoulder and her heart almost burst out of her body.

"No!"

"Whoa there!"

From behind the withering Saya stood a man pulling back his right hand as if he had touched a hot frying pan. He was in prime shape.

He didn't teach her grade, but he was definitely a teacher. On his sweatpants was a small nametag with "Inamine" written on it.

"Se-sensei . . ."

"You don't need to scream. What are you doing out here at this hour?"

"Sensei! There was a strange . . . a suspicious man . . ."

"Suspicious man?"

"That way. By the fields."

"Got it. Wait here."

It sounded like he wanted her to wait for him in the teachers' office, but since there were no other teachers or anyone there, sitting alone in the big empty room seemed even more frightening. She didn't want to run into the guy with a knife again, but being alone seemed like a bad idea.

In the end, Saya chose to stick close to the able-bodied adult.

Saya slid behind Mr. Inamine's back and they returned the way Saya had come.

They slowly walked through the elevated path, but now there was no one. Making it under the passageway between the library and the main school building, they could see no indication of anyone else being out there.

"Just as I thought. There's no one here."

The circle of light from Mr. Inamine's flashlight swept across the ground.

Mr. Inamine leapt straight up.

Just as he stood there, he disappeared right in front of Saya's eyes.

He hadn't bent his knees and jumped up. It was if he was sucked straight up into the night sky.

Just before he vanished Saya saw what looked like an arm reach over from the rooftop and grasp Mr. Inamine by the head.

Was that even possible?

Crack. Splat. The sound of something thick and wet being torn apart could be heard.

Coming from above her head. Something.

"Sen . . . Sensei?" Saya spoke timidly after gulping to clear her throat.

There was no answer, but the teacher did return.

But he wasn't the same as he was a moment before.

Having fallen flat on the ground, Mr. Inamine lay sprawled out stomach-down, but his head was loosely attached and twisted completely around, and was now looking up at Saya.

"Aa . . ."

It was like her vocal cords forgot how to form words.

Saya's vision became foggy, and gravity began to act strange. It was more than the lack of balance and the fall backward from her legs buckling that shook Saya; rather it was the feeling of the cold ground after she landed on her tailbone that jostled her.

Right then something black fell over the dead body of the teacher.

For a moment it looked like a big fur-skin pelt had come from the roof of the passageway. She thought it was trying to hide the body.

When it moved she realized that this wasn't the case.

It turned its head and it looked as if it had human features.

It was bigger than any man, and clearly had the body of a beast.

Its large and muscular shoulders and extremely long arms were more than enough to lift a full-sized man off the ground to the roof above by his head.

The creature's profile looked a little like a primitive ape, but its sharp fangs were definitely carnivorous. Yet, like some reptiles, its eyes were bright red.

A monster.

After that, where Saya ran to get away was a complete blur.

All she knew was her two legs brought her back to the visitors' entrance. Unconsciously she must have run toward the light.

Once Saya got a grip on the glass door the still of the night exploded.

"Gra . . ."

Her ears went deaf. That's how unbearable the sound was. She felt the fabric of her uniform vibrate. A blast of air that felt strong enough to carry her.

It was a howl. The shriek of that demon.

As if it was vibrating like the prongs of a tuning fork, the glass of the door resonated and in the blink of an eye was completely pulverized. Saya fell backward through the glass opening she had been leaning on.

The yell of the monster had stopped, but still reverberated through Saya's head and her ears throbbed with pain.

"Oww . . ."

Standing up, Saya's eyebrows knotted from the pain in her right leg.

From the hem of her skirt a red streak of blood ran down her thigh. She must have been cut by a shard of glass. It didn't appear to be that deep of a cut, but the polka-dot stains of blood on the floor made Saya a bit queasy.

With this, she would surely be out of tomorrow's track meet.

Those kinds of thoughts ran through Saya's head.

But only for a moment.

There wasn't time to be thinking about the meet or for getting first aid for her cut.

Through the now meaningless frame of a door wriggled the matte black shadow.

Its blood-colored eyes beamed straight at Saya.

Putting pressure on her wound with one hand, Saya ran into the teachers' office.

Darting through the air-conditioned office, Saya flew through the door to the classrooms. Behind her she could hear the crunch of the office's steel door being crushed and the sound of the teachers' books and papers being thrown from their desks.

After turning the corridor, Saya made it for a few steps before she stopped, petrified where she stood.

At the end of the dark corridor she could see the shadow of a tall man standing.

The moonlight coming in through the window revealed his beautiful pale face.

It was the same man from the bus stop, and then from the school grounds moments earlier. The coffin-shaped box he carried on his back must have held his musical instrument.

From his right hand the blade of his dagger shone in the moonlight.

"..."

Despite the intensity of the circumstances, several seconds went by.

In front of her eyes, the serial slasher, and behind her a man-eating monster was closing in.

Saya felt like now she understood the true meaning of helplessness.

The floor shook with a boom.

There was no time to look. She could sense a giant mass and the stench of blood told Saya the ferocious beast had found her.

It was so close, it was almost towering above her.

It was at that instant that the tall man's bandaged right hand flashed.

The silvery light grazed Saya's right ear.

There was no way she could react fast enough to avoid it.

Surprised to hear a deafening shriek, Saya turned around to see the beast had thrown his head back. Blood poured out of its left eye socket, which now had the dagger's handle poking out of it.

A normal animal, like a lion or a shark, would avoid such a painful situation, but that wasn't the case with this monster. It stood its ground, and swung its arms in such strong anger the wind fluttered Saya's hair.

The long and sharp talon-like nails of the beast took a slice out of the concrete wall as if it was made of tofu.

Unexpectedly, the wall came falling down, and in a daze, Saya stepped backward just as the tall man slid between her and the monster.

At almost the same moment the next swipe of its claws came swinging forward.

The young man didn't move.

It wasn't pretty, but somehow the slender man was able to stop the log-sized arm flying at him with his right hand.

Seeing the monster's hand strike the bandaged hand left Saya dumbstruck.

Upon the strike the bandage covering the man's right hand had been cut, and a serpentine appendage was loosened and uncoiled toward the floor. What was revealed under the cloth was a beast-like hand with dark-brown skin that looked as hard as armor.

"What . . . what . . . is that?"

The question that stammered out of Saya's convulsing lips represented her complete mental state.

And what was that? What was this monster and also, who was this man?

These two were enemies, and their battle was not yet over. With one hand bound by the tall man, the monster took a swipe with its free hand at the face of the opponent.

There was the sound of a heavy thud as the cello case was knocked off the man's back. Beneath his skin there must have been a layer of metal. That's how tough he looked.

Faster than the eye could see, the tall figure of the man spun and wrapped his right leg around the beast's flank. At first glance it looked like a light and simple kick, but as powerful as an axe on a seedling, it brought the large frame of the monster to the floor.

As the giant rolled down the hallway, the tall man turned and came back up the hallway toward Saya.

"This way."

"Huh?"

There was no time for protests or questions. He came close to her and leaned down. Before she knew it, he had lifted her up with both arms as if she weighed almost nothing.

The next time Saya's feet hit the floor was inside the third-floor biology lab.

On the shelves were specimens of formerly living creatures in large jars. A formaldehyde-dyed mammal fetus shone in the moonlight next to a white-colored reptile floating listlessly in the next container. There were also insect samples and stuffed animals frozen in position, sitting silently on the classroom shelves.

What had broken that silence was a whimper from Saya.

"That . . . that thing . . . what . . . what was that?" Saya had half-collapsed in the shadows of the specially painted science lab desks.

"A Chiropteran," he answered indifferently. Like he had done it a thousand times before, the tall man wrapped a handkerchief around Saya's cut.

"A Chiropteran . . . ?"

"A beast that drinks blood from the living."

"Beast . . . ?"

And this was coming from someone that had the same sort of hand as the beast he described.

Moments ago the Chiropteran, as he called it, and this guy got in a fight, and then he flew up two flights of stairs carrying Saya and his cello case like they weighed nothing. Saya quickly reached the conclusion that he was not any normal human being.

The tall man used his right hand to unlatch the lock on the cello case. It opened in a cross shape, like a bird spreading its wings, and the instrument underneath the lid was visible. Its ceramic amber was beautifully polished to a shine.

Saya had no knowledge of classical music or the instruments played, but could still tell that she was looking at something special.

Rather than touching the instrument, the man placed his hand onto the inside of the lid. With a swish, that section of the case opened up. From inside its velvet interior several ornamental charms fell into view.

What was it that he had stored in there? A katana—?

It didn't seem proper for a bloodthirsty weapon to rest so close to such a beautiful and feminine musical instrument.

There were laws in this country on carrying fixed-length blades. At least that was what she had heard. That must be why he had it hidden away.

The tall man nimbly removed the sword from its sheath.

He then wrapped the palm of his monster-like right hand around the blade of the sword.

"Wha-what are you doing?"

Sliding his palm sideways across the glass-like blade he then let go, allowing a blackish-red stream to flow from the cut he had inflicted on himself.

As the red drops speckled the floor below, he brought his right hand closer to Saya.

"What . . . ?"

Someone who cuts their own hand couldn't be normal. Especially cutting so deeply as to allow that amount of blood to flow. What could he have been thinking?

Saya stared at him in terror.

Without a word the man brought his red-soiled fist closer to Saya's face.

Blood dripped onto her uniform blouse.

What stopped his hand from reaching her face was not Saya, herself, but an ominous shriek from the hallway.

The tall man's calm eyes moved to the entrance of the classroom.

The door blasted inward to the room, and the monster from below, the Chiropteran, entered shoulder-first.

The dagger had been pulled from its left eye. It should have been a deep and debilitating injury, but the monster appeared to have forgotten any pain.

Or it never was in any pain. Yet Saya could see the muscles and skin around the deep wound were boiling in reaction. It reminded her of the video they saw on fungi reproduction she had been shown in this very classroom.

As she watched, the damaged area of the eye regenerated itself, and finally a new eyeball broke through the membrane and turned to focus on her.

Just as Saya gulped in surprise, the monster leapt into the air.

As the giant creature's back scraped the ceiling, it was able to cross the classroom in one bound and land with a loud crash.

Desktops cracked into splinters, and the shaking of the room knocked all the jars and vials off the shelves to crash into pieces onto the floor.

Realizing that if the tall man hadn't swept her aside before the monster had landed that she would have been crushed along with the desks gave Saya a chill.

As the creature tilted forward from its landing, its upper body turned toward her. Their eyes met. But it was not an emotional meeting of the minds. She saw the creature looking at her as food, as nourishment, and nothing more.

Got to get away! This thing was deadly!

From her position flat on the ground, Saya looked straight up and her mind was focused only on getting up and out.

Rising, she had forgotten about the man covering her that had pulled her out of the monster's path.

"Saya."

He spoke in nothing more than a whisper, but Saya's gaze was immediately drawn to his eyes.

His warm hand swept across her cheek and then lifted up her chin.

After bringing his right hand to his mouth, his face came close to Saya's. Once she realized what was going on, it was too late.

Her very first kiss tasted like blood.

As his lips left hers, he said her name again.

"Saya—"

In a state of shock, Saya swallowed the blood that remained in her mouth. Why wasn't she able to spit it out? The liquid mass felt like it leapt down her throat and then spread throughout her body to the tips of every limb.

"—Fight."

Her heart throbbed in her chest.

She could feel the blood flow through her veins under the surface of her skin.

In an instant, a flood of memories opened up all at once.


After stopping his motorcycle in front of the school gate and pulling out the key, Kai heard what sounded like the roar of a large animal.

The shrill shriek sounded loud enough to shatter layers of glass, and repeated several times.

"What the—"

Hanging his helmet on his handlebars, Kai Miyagusuku's brow wrinkled in concern. It wasn't common for homeless dogs or wild birds to stray onto the school grounds. Something wasn't right.

Kai had a pretty good intuition for dangerous situations.

In other words, he could smell violence. When he sensed that sort of atmosphere, naturally he defended himself, and often found the best defense was to go on the offense. Just like in baseball, victories were won or lost on reflexes and guts.

Kai never intended to get into trouble, but it just seemed like he often found himself mixed in with a rough crowd.

Even today, on the way back from dropping Saya at the clinic he got a call from Kakimoto (and it had sounded like he was in real trouble), and he'd had to go and try and clean up that mess. If George hadn't called him asking him to go pick up Saya at school, he would probably still be in that alleyway trying to get things settled. Solving disputes not with words, but with fists was a trait that must have been handed down from his father.

But instead, here he was to try and find Saya. Apparently Saya had thought she had left her track shoes at school and had come back to find them, but in the meantime Kaori had dropped them off at the shop. George said if Kai didn't get Saya home for dinner she would be looking for those shoes at school all night, and by George's command, Kai had unwillingly come back to school on his motorcycle.

It should have been an easy-enough task, but at this hour something about the school was strange.

It was easy for Kai to hop over the locked school gate, yet he hesitated.

As he ran from the visitors' entrance to the teachers' office, Kai had a hunch of what was to come. On the floor he saw glass shards scattered about along with what looked like fresh blood.

"Saya!"

With his shoes still on, he rushed into the teachers' office. There was no one there.

He ran through the ramshackle teachers' office and toward the classrooms. He had just started to run down the hallway when he heard the echo of iron being torn apart, causing his legs to stiffen.

Again, he heard the roar of a large creature. Without thinking he slapped his hands over his ears and looked up at the ceiling, to locate the sounds of equipment and furniture being destroyed on one of the floors above him.

"Did a gorilla escape from the zoo?" mumbled Kai as he raced up the stairway.

Arriving at the corridor on the third floor, the shards of glass glittering on the floor acted as a jeweled signpost showing the way. He stood in front of the sign saying "Biology Lab."

Kai stepped over the door, which was now flat on the floor, and jumped into the classroom, only to be completely taken aback at the scene before him.

In the back of the room in the shadow of splintered desks he saw the shape of a man holding a woman in his arms.

"Saya—Fight!"

It sounded like a young man's voice, but that is what he said.

"Saya?"

Kai squinted his eyes to get a better look, but couldn't be sure who was there. What was more important was the other occupant in the classroom.

Kai saw the gigantic figure turn his way.

"What in the hell . . ."

This was no gorilla. What was a creature like this doing inside of a school?

As its head turned, Kai couldn't think of any animal it looked similar to. It was more like some kind of mix between a monkey, a wolf, and a bat.

From the finger-length fangs threads of saliva dripped to the floor.

The monster, not completely focused on Kai, stepped toward him.

Kai stared at the creature, his limbs slumped frozen in place.

*Boom. Boom.* The floor shook with each step, and the monster's thick arms came down on Kai as it closed in.

"Yaah!"

Such a pitiful voice had never left his lips before. Teeming with fear, Kai mustered his strength and rolled back into the hallway as the creature swung, tearing a hole in the wall above him. Still sitting with his back to the wall Kai looked up into the eyes of the monster.

The hair on the back of his neck stood on end, and every sweat gland on his body opened up. This is what is felt like to be killed.

What happened?

Just as the monster had Kai cornered and ready to kill, it suddenly lost all interest in him.

The scarlet eyes of the beast were now focused on the girl standing in the rear of the classroom.

Saya.

But was this the same Saya that Kai knew? Her often-complimented jet-black hair now had blondish highlights, or was that the reflection from the moonlight pouring in through the window?

But on top of that, the hard expression on her face didn't look like Saya. Her face appeared as if it had been chiseled from a block of ice. Kai couldn't decide which was more shocking, the look on her face or the color of her eyes that were—the same color as the monster's, wet with the color of twilight and blood.

"Sword."

Saya's low mutter in English sounded like command from a member of royalty speaking to a servant.

The tall man presented her a long sword still in its scabbard, which she accepted with her slender left hand.

That is when the beast began its strike.

It seemed less a run at victory, and more like a risky defensive attack.

As it rushed at Saya, it swung its giant arms over its head, smashing shelves as if they were Styrofoam in the process. Tens-of-thousands-of-years-old fossilized shellfish and vegetation broke into pieces and boxes displaying insects pinned onto boards smashed apart, freeing their long-dead prisoners.

Avoiding the shower of glass, wood splinters, and butterfly wings, Saya slid backward.

The monster scooped up a desk in its empty claw.

Without missing a beat, Saya landed in the back of the classroom. With her back to the rear blackboard she spread her feet and lowered her hips closer to the floor. She freed the sword from its scabbard.

Its blade was shaped differently from a typical Japanese katana. Just past the hilt and guard was a sharp L-shaped bend in the blade. Saya pressed her thumb on the rear edge of the bend and blood began to flow. Along each side of the blade was a groove, and Kai could clearly see the red line of blood flow straight up the side of the sword.

The monster came straight at Saya for a second time.

Its knife-like claws sliced through the air.

Saya shifted her head as smoothly and lightly as leaves blown by the wind. The exposed claws caught nothing but a few strands of hair.

At the same time, Saya had driven forward on her right leg.

"DYAAA!"

Her battle cry was enough to crush the courage of any enemy in ear's reach. It was much more massive than could be expected from her small frame.

The silver flash from below cut up from the right side of the beast's abdomen to the left side of its collarbone clean through, bisecting the monster.

Her blade stood perfectly still at the point where the sharp strike was completed. Drops from the massive eruption of blood hit Saya on the cheek. Unblinking, Saya's eyes remained wide open.

Kai then saw the two halves of the monster's remains transform. The red-colored exposed meat of the beast where the cross-section was made gradually changed color.

It was blood. Similar to what water looks like when it freezes, the coagulating blood was crystallizing into stone. The hardening of the blood and the open wound advanced faster, quickly transforming the entirety of the remains. The blood inside had essentially petrified the body tissue.

It was a difficult spectacle to believe. It was hard for Kai to comprehend anything that had happened in this room over the past few minutes.

"Saya . . ."

Without even thinking about it, Kai muttered his sister's name.

The expression on her face as she looked over at him made his spine go cold.

It was the look of anger and hatred only someone who had killed could express.

Then it suddenly dissipated.

Saya turned and stared at her reflection in the window to the hallway. Kai carefully watched Saya's state as she stood there, rigid. It seemed like she was paralyzed.

The sword in her right hand fell victim to gravity, and hit the floor with a clang.

"No!"

Seeing her blood-splattered face and hands, Saya screamed out.

The color of murder drained from her eyes, and her body became listless. From out of the shadow the tall and darkly dressed man reverently put his arms behind her shoulders to break her fall.

"Not yet?"

As the man carefully held the unconscious Saya in his arms, from his profile Kai could see a person who looked very melancholy, very lonely.

"Hey! Hey, you!"

Kai didn't know who this man was, but Kai was about to find out.

"What the hell is going on? What do you think you are going to do with Saya?!"

Kai's legs were still a little unsure, but his pride would not allow him to show any weakness. As a bluff, his tone was more aggressive than needed.

"Hey! Listen to me when I'm talking!"

Like a graceful woman, the young man didn't pay any attention to Kai, and instead looked out the window onto the school grounds.

"Hey, freak! What is with you . . . and your monster?!"

Chances are the last part of his angry tirade wasn't heard by the man.

The night air was battered with the unique sound of rotors along with violently bright spotlights pouring down onto the school grounds.

Kai had seen these fly across the sky countless times. They were American military helicopters.


One would think the sofa arranged for visitors in a military base's top general's office would be of a high quality, but once sitting down, this one wasn't comfortable at all.

He wasn't thinking it needed to be a Stark or a Noguchi, but something more ergonomically designed, or at least made of leather was a must. These were the thoughts of Van Argeno.

For the sake of the visitor, wasn't it worth going the extra mile, even splurging just a little? Alas, the choice of furnishings no doubt fell under the jurisdiction of the master of this room, the middle-aged man sitting with a sullen look at the desk by the window. His first job was to make a product that fit the value and function the Army was looking for.

"So it should be wrapping up soon, I would expect."

Wearing a cream-colored Armani suit, Van fiddled with a pawn on the chessboard sitting on the table.

Dressed in a short-sleeved uniform, the reply from the top brass of Kadena Base came in the form of silence and a bitter glare. Van couldn't help but give a snide sneer.

"It's not like you will personally suffer any damage. I hope that's not what you are worried about."

"The ones responsible for capturing the 'mouse' are American soldiers. We are not your tools."

What a serious tone.

What he needed was, oh yes, right here—a black candy.

Japan had all kinds of varieties and flavors of sweets, as well as a long history of production. Above all, the Japanese have always loved the large drops made with black sugar. The color of coal, their simple sweetness coupled with just a slightly salty taste blended into a subtle and satisfying treat.

On top of that, black sugar was an export of Okinawa. To not take advantage of being assigned so close to such a delicacy would have been nothing less than a travesty.

Van pulled out another fresh piece from the bag of black candy he'd bought at the airport duty-free shop. As he untwisted the paper wrapper the wireless radio on the table began to chatter.

"Target objective completed."

"Mm. Faster than I expected."

"Any damage?"

"Unit damage is zero. We have what appears to be one school employee casualty, most likely Japanese, and one beast casualty. Besides that, zero. No one else present."

"So the 'mouse' is dead?"

Van's perfectly sculpted eyebrows shuddered nervously. Yet behind the clear lenses of his glasses and under his non-folded eyelids was a razor-sharp gleam.

He had a different theory.

He thought surely half of the soldiers dispatched, maybe a couple less, would be coming home in body bags.

The commanding officer had the same expectation, and that's why his face showed concern.

Van definitely wanted to see the body of the "mouse" for himself.

While being stared at with a blame-casting gaze, Van continued to fiddle with the chess pieces. Finally there was an end to this silent standoff.

Van's feminine hand placed a round piece of black candy into his mouth.

American troops stationed in Japan were, indeed, soldiers from the States dropped onto this island far from home and were often ridiculed and chided by the locals. Yet somehow this particular job was finished remarkably clean and fast.

Within an hour of the stone-like body of the "mouse" recovery from Koza Commercial High School, it sat in a U.S. Army base anti-bacterial clean room.

Van looked down from the behind the glass in the observation room.

"So, the 'mouse' was cut in half by a single slice of a long blade. Are you telling me there are still samurai warriors running around this country?"

With the "mouse" lying on the operating table, somehow he couldn't resist making a joke at its expense. As he had said, the crystallized monster had indeed been separated into two, and cast no shadow under the bright lights of the room.

"Well, where is the other one?"

"We are still searching for it."

The researcher answered inside from the other side of the glass, inside the operating room, and he turned to continue investigating the body of the "mouse."

The curt answer emoted a desire to not be interrupted during work.

"I heard stories of it slicing marines into mincemeat, but never imagined seeing one come back like this. It truly is bizarre. Don't you think so, too?"

"I am in the middle of an operation. Please keep unnecessary questions and comments to yourself, Mr. Argeno."

"Oh, I made him angry!"

Joking with the high-ranking researcher in the room with Van, he turned the hard candy in his mouth over with his tongue.

"But seriously, who did this? Who could do such a thing to our precious 'mouse'?"

When she opened her eyes, all she saw was ceiling.

"Saya."

She felt a sharp pain in her arm as her name was softly spoken.

From the tiles on the ceiling she slowly turned her head toward the voice, discovering George sitting on a chair close to her bed, his back hunched over leaning toward her.

"Father . . ."

"Are you all right?"

"Yesterday . . . I forgot something . . . I went to school . . . to get it . . . and then . . ."

And then.

She couldn't remember clearly. She had jumped the gate. She sort of remembered being on the school grounds, but everything after that was gone. It was like watching a movie and the film just cut off in the middle.

"You fainted at school."

"Really . . ."

Saya wasn't in as much shock as someone else in the same situation might be.

Saya was used to lapses in memory. She only possessed memories of one year of her entire life. Considering the ten-plus years she had already lost, what difference would a dozen hours here or there make?

"You are still a little groggy, huh? Now it's just temporary, but . . . it might take a little more time for your memory to return."

Calmed by George's businesslike tone, Saya gradually noticed the female doctor standing behind him taking notes.

As always, with her long blond hair pulled back in a ponytail, she observed the situation, giving her patient a sense of trust through her encouraging smile.

So this must have been her clinic. Saya was used to getting treated in an examination room on the first floor, but this was probably an in-patient room on the second floor.

"No sign of fever. Pulse is normal."

She held one beautifully textured hand on her forehead while the middle finger of the other hand checked her heart rate on her wrist.

Saya remained quiet during these tests.

"I was worried that in her state of shock her body had experienced some sort of anomaly, but there don't seem to be any other symptoms to support that. But she does need some rest."

After carefully listening to Julia's diagnosis, George turned back to Saya, his mouth open as if he had a response, but he changed his mind.

"After you went back to school Kaori-chan came by with your track shoes."

"Did she? . . . I wanted to be in the track meet . . ."

"There's always next time. And I'll bring a bento and cheer you on."

"'kay"

Her father's warm words swept away any lingering regrets.

Saya flashed a white grin as her stomach growled for attention.

Her eyes opened wide, but it didn't quell her hunger.

Embarrassed, Saya pulled the sheets up to her eyeballs.

George's short whiskers shook as he laughed.

Holding a fist to her mouth to block any sign of a smile, Julia's face soon returned to its usual seriousness.

"A mental shock can cause irregularities in the body's system."

"Ha ha . . . Sensei, is it all right if I cure this ailment?"

"Yes, I suppose."

Showing true consideration, Julia bid Saya good health and left the room.

George enthusiastically picked up a plastic bag off the table and extended it to Saya.

"When I got the call that you had fainted, I hurried right over. I didn't have a lot of time to be choosy, but I figured you'd be hungry when you woke up."

The convenience store bag fell open and a variety of *onigiri* spilled out on to the bed. Pickled plum, salmon, *konbu* seaweed, leaf mustard, pork and egg, chicken, beef rib, Okinawa's own *goya champuru* (which wasn't the best), all in different colored packages.

"Thank you, Father. I can't wait."

After Saya picked up a rice ball and peeled off the vinyl wrapper, a knock at the door got George out of his seat.

"Yes?"

"We need to talk."

It was a low, almost toneless male voice.

From her bed, Saya was just barely able to see the face of the man in the hallway over George's shoulder.

That combed-down blond hair, that intrepid and rigid expression—David!

"Saya, Dad is going to talk downstairs. Now eat those all up, all right?"

"'Kay."

Sensing David's glance, Saya stared at George's giant back as she chewed her fancy *onigiri*.

She usually had no interest in adult conversations, but this time something piqued her curiosity. George didn't seem interested in what David had to say.

With all the regular customers, like the always-laughing Forest, and his other old army buddies, George joked around and treated them like brothers. But George talked to David as if there were a transparent wall between them. At least that's how Saya saw it.

How did they call themselves friends? They must have gotten along in the beginning.

But it wasn't Saya's place to speculate on stuff like that, as her supply of *onigiri* was depleted. In thirty minutes the cache of rice balls had turned into a pile of plastic wrappers.

"Oh well, I am stuffed."

Letting out a satisfied sigh, Saya fell back diagonally onto the bed. It was then that her school uniform lying on the shelf caught her eye.

"Oh yeah. I need to get changed."

The clock on the wall said it was already past 10:00 AM. She could still make it to her afternoon classes. It wasn't that in her weakened state her love of learning was more important to Saya than physical health. Actually, she wanted to hurry up and see Kaori to give her thanks.

Saya jumped off the bed and slipped out of the patient pajamas and put on her short-sleeved white shirt and navy pleated skirt, finishing the ensemble with her red ribbon tie.

Making sure everything was on straight, she looked at herself in the mirror.

It was just when she was fixing the bed-head protrusions in her hair that it happened.

The face of the girl in the mirror was covered in a red wine-colored stain, and her crimson eyes scowled back at Saya.

"—huh?"

Stepping back in surprise, Saya blinked and looked back at the mirror again. The face that looked back at her was her own. There were no streaks of blood.

Right at that moment a strike of pain crashed through her head.

The synapses in her brain were arcing electrical bursts of information, and visions started to play back before her eyes.

Sensei . . . right. Inamine-sensei was dead. His bones were crushed, leaving him looking like a broken plastic doll.

The monster had red eyes.

And that tall man. He had helped somehow. Who was he?

A reflection in the glass. A face covered in blood. A bloody sword-bearing woman named Saya.

What was that? What just happened? What did Saya see?

Saya crossed her arms across her chest so hard she almost pulled herself in half. A cold sweat ripped through her pores and she looked down at her sweaty palms

Her hands weren't covered in sweat. It was blood.

"No . . . !"

That was enough. She didn't want to see anymore. Yet, even though she willed her eyelids to stay closed, they still kept timidly blinking open.

She opened up her balled fists, yet now there was no blood.

Was everything she just saw a hallucination?

"At school . . ."

Something must have happened. Something bad.

"Father."

Feeling so panicked she was about to cry, Saya left the room.

It was a small-scale two-story hospital. It took her no time to find George. At the bottom of the stairs in front of the receptionist's window sat her father and David sitting side-by-side on a sofa in the waiting area. Saya recognized his back, even though he wasn't facing her way, but she couldn't call out to him.

From the tension she observed between them in their conversation, interrupting seemed like a bad idea.

"What are you hesitating for? You will return Saya to us."

"I don't think Saya will be happy about that."

"Happy?"

David repeated angry George's word choice.

"Have you forgotten the reason for her existence? She fights them, and she is the only 'weapon' of her kind in the world. Nothing more and nothing less."

"In the past year she became my daughter . . ."

George's head hung low as he stared at his reflection in the floor, like a frail old man, yet his voice remained as hard as steel.

"Don't tell me you have forgotten already. The Christmas bombings in the North. How long do you think you can be Saya's pretend family?"

The walls and everything around her suddenly felt like they were sucked away, leaving Saya standing alone.

Pretend family.

Those two words shot from David's mouth like a beam into the center of Saya's brain.

"Since she has been under your watch have you developed feelings for her? Saya lives to fight and to fight and to fight. That will never change. That is Saya's fate."

Having taken on a markedly bitter tone, there were a few seconds of silence after David's last sentence.

"I'll be the one to tell her."

George stood up from the sofa.

"So stay away from Saya."

". . . Understood."

As David remained seated and looked up at him, George turned away.

His grim expression stiffened as he looked in Saya's direction.

Not wanting to see his saddened face, Saya did a disoriented about-face.

She also might not have wanted her face to be seen.

"Saya!"

Even after storming out the rear entrance, George's cracked voice echoed in her ears.

The bright sunlight was painful on sleep-deprived eyes.

It was too early to be out of school, but this day classes were canceled.

Like many others, Kai had left for school before getting the call from the class phone tree telling him that school was closed today. So students were returning home in two and threes.

Since the night before, the American Army had put blockades around the school, and even to this moment nobody, including school officials or the Okinawa police, was allowed in.

Even though the school was blocked off, the baseball field was in a separate location, and was still accessible. Kai was in his usual spot in the back of the baseball field crouched down in the shade looking at the road. The round tank and gauges of his beloved Eliminator sparkled in the sunlight.

It was on this bike he had carried Saya's unconscious body to Julia's clinic the night before.

He took her there partially because it was closer than the big hospital in the city, but also his body probably chose the route it was most used to taking.

Leaving Saya's health in George's and the familiar Julia's hands was, in the end, the right decision. George immediately came running when he heard what had happened.

Hearing of Saya's safety from Julia, was a relief, but in his heart remained a heavy black lump.

"Dad, Saya was . . ."

He had to tell about what he had seen. That decided, he started speaking to his father, who then placed his large hand on top of Kai's head.

"Riku is worrying at home. For now, head back. Take a bath and get some sleep."

Behind his father's forced interruption, Kai could see his father was in pain.

It reminded him of when he threw out the elbow of his pitching arm and found out he had to give up playing baseball. Kai was violent and depressed and throwing things, but the usually talkative George patted him lightly on the head and spoke to him like everything was okay, in short, choppy sentences. *Don't think about today. Just go to bed.* Like that.

But in this case he wasn't able to forget what happened by sliding into bed.

"What's wrong? What's with the serious face?"

Kai stood up, and stepped away. Indifferent to the voice, he suddenly felt the weight of the young girl jump onto his back. On his shoulder he felt a pointy chin and turned to see the face of his classmate, Mao Jahana looking back at him. She had beautiful long brown hair and he could smell perfume rising from her collar.

"Knock it off! You're heavy."

"I am not! Where are you going?"

Her skinny legs landed on the concrete, and like a baby fawn, she pranced as she tried to keep up with him.

"Shouldn't you be home by now?"

"I called for a car to pick me up, but it hasn't arrived yet."

It was these kinds of statements that made Mao come off like a princess.

She was the only daughter of one of the wealthiest and most powerful families in the city. She really got the royal treatment, and had luxury cars to come pick her up and drop her off where she wanted. She was so rich that she had no idea where the money came from. It was because Jahana Industries was a synonym for the Yakuza.

"Sayyy, Kaiii." She had a habit of stretching her words out. Her perfectly formed nose turned toward the school gate. "All the big news stations are here. If they don't get the guy it'll be a big deal, huh."

It had been that way all morning.

Kai thought back to the news reporter that he had seen on the road in front of the gate on his way to school. With his back to the gate the reporter spoke boisterously to a camera facing the school.

He said the remains of a teacher, Inamine, were discovered at the school and the murder was being blamed on some drug addict private in the U.S. military. He said that the suspect had been detained by the American forces, but a request to extradite for trial in Japan had been denied.

This was no joke.

Even if he was an acid-dropping jarhead, a human life was a human life. The thing he saw at school the night before was no human.

"It's so messed up. The American Army guys won't even let the Japanese police go into the school. They say a teacher is dead, so then they can just take over our school. It's like we live in a military state or something."

Barely listening to Mao's political rambling, Kai straddled his motorcycle.

He put on his helmet and was turning the key when he felt the handlebars dip.

Looking over his shoulder he saw Mao sitting right behind him with a smug look of victory on her pretty face.

"Hey!"

"So, where are we going?"

". . ."

Kai often skipped class with Mao, and along with Kakimoto and Kato they'd kill time having meaningless conversations about nothing. He understood that she was the complete opposite of him is so many ways, but this pushy tendency was difficult for Kai.

Kai considered a few ways to get her off his bike, but then decided to ask her a question.

"You seen that big box in the music room?"

"Yeah. You mean the organ, right?"

"Nah. The box that the big-looking violin goes into."

"Oh, you mean the cello case. Why? Are you going to start playing cello?"

"No . . . a cello, huh?"

The guy with the long hair who was with Saya carried a box that looked just like the one in the music room. He must have been carrying a cello, too.

After everything had happened Kai had stared in a stupor at the army helicopters and the American soldiers that slid down the ropes one-by-one into the schoolyard before the man made him go to the edge of the school grounds.

It was then things got fuzzy. In reality when the man dashed off, Kai was in such a daze he was half-unconscious, like when a kitten is drinking warm milk. Like they were bungee jumping in the dark, Kai remembered a sensation of floating through the air before they found themselves on a store rooftop one street over from the school.

When he finally came to his senses he found that it was just the unconscious Saya and Kai left alone under the night sky.

Kai had the unnerving feeling the man had vanished like a ghost, but also realized that not only had he carried that big cello case, but also two people like they were nothing all the way to the top of that roof. There was no way to conclude he was a normal human being.

"If you want to see a cellist there is one on Park Avenue."

"Cellist?"

"You know. A person that plays a cello. He's good-looking, too."

"What do you mean?"

"He's a foreigner. He's tall and has long hair and I think he was hurt. His right hand was wrapped in a bandage."

All the things Mao described fit exactly with the image Kai remembered of the young man from the night before. A tall white guy with styled long hair and a bandaged right hand—there was no mistake.

"That's him!"

The bike suddenly was in motion and Mao almost slipped off the back.

"Oh my, Kai!" said Mao in a strangely sexy voice as she wrapped herself around his back.


In a hurry, one could make it from Koza Commercial High to Park Avenue in less than ten minutes.

Since it was still the middle of the morning, the shopping arcade wasn't particularly crowded. It was past the time people are heading to work or school, so the bus stop was completely empty.

This was the closest stop to their home, so Kai figured it must have been the bus stop Saya was always using.

"You sure this was where you saw him?"

"That's what I said, isn't it? I am not going to forget where I saw a good-looking guy like that."

Mao was confident she was right.

With the sound of the bike's exhaust filling his ears, Kai went around the block, but saw no sign of anyone like the person Mao described.

"Dammit. He isn't here."

"He's always here in the late afternoon. How about we go to that café and wait for him? Wait. I have a better idea. Let's go see a movie to pass the time. Oh! Oh! This one! I've been wanting to see this!"

Mao had jumped off the motorcycle and was pulling on Kai's sleeve with one hand while pointing to a poster hanging in a used CD shop window.

The poster was for a low-budget indie movie titled *Squid Wrestler vs. Shrimp Boxer*.

". . . You seriously want to see this?"

"Whatever is fine, right? C'mon, let's go."

"I don't feel like it."

"Whaaat? Spoilsport! You want to look for that cellist? What will you do if you find him?"

"You know. I have my reasons."

"Your reasons? Excuuuse me? This has to do with her, doesn't it?"

"Her?"

"'Her' meaning Saya!"

". . . She has nothing to do with it."

No matter how hard Kai tried to wave the idea away with his hand, Mao's teasing and smiling face had disappeared.

Seeing her with a serious expression, it was clear from her eyes that Mao was no dummy.

"No way . . . Kai, remember when you had to quit playing baseball and started hanging out with us and would glare all scary-like? But ever since she moved in with you, something changed, you know?"

What changed certainly wasn't his gruff way of communicating.

"What do you think about her?"

"What do I think? I think she came to my house a year ago, and I thought I knew her pretty well. But after seeing her yesterday, I don't know what to think."

Even Kai didn't know why he was expressing these ideas to Mao. Kai thought he was good at keeping his feelings to himself, but that might have just been wishful thinking.

The things he saw yesterday were weighing down on him, and somehow they had to come out, or else he might have lost it.

Mao's response to this was extremely brief.

"Stop being an idiot."

". . . idiot?"

"I don't know what happened, but this isn't the Kai I know. Kai wouldn't worry about the little details, just shoot first and ask questions later. That's what I like about—"

"—That's right!"

Kai had listened intently to Mao's speech, and suddenly lit up.

"This isn't like me at all!"

This must have been what it felt like when people said a weight was lifted off their shoulders.

Fretting about it meant nothing. Actions, not words, was the way.

Every individual has their own way to go about doing things. Kai Miyagusuku's way was to run at a problem head first.

"Hey, thanks."

As he gave his gratitude to the sullen-faced Mao, he received a call on his cell phone.

"Hello. Oh, Dad?"

George's voice was unusually sharp, and he sounded panicked.

"Saya . . . ?"

George told him Saya had walked out of the hospital.

Before he asked for details, Kai was on his bike.

"What are you . . . ?"

Without responding to Mao's complaint, Kai took off down the street.

The wind stung his face.

Saya must have been feeling pretty confused, too. That was Kai's conclusion. In her case it wasn't just any everyday confusion, either. No doubt she was really distressed about what was going to happen next.


It was already evening.

The water and the clouds shared the same deep copper red tone as the sky.

From the beach the long shadow of the great rock looked incredibly sad.

She had walked all the way here. She hadn't thought about where she was going. Her feet just brought her to this place.

But now she was really tired from walking. Saya sat on the sand with her knees bent. She rested both arms across her knees and laid her head on her forearms. She was exhausted.

*Pretend family.*

Those two words repeated themselves over and over in her head.

Over this past year she had really felt like a member of the Miyagusuku family, but that had only been on the surface. In reality she was just a guest in their home.

She was the kind of guest that had come from somewhere, and slept under the same roof with them for a while, and then she would be on her way.

But from now on where would she be going? Was she to live with David?

The particles of saltwater in the wind gave its echo a fresh and thick sound.

A tune she had heard before.

Saya's head shot up, and she turned around to see the young man sitting higher up the beach on the breakwater wall.

He wore the same dark-colored suit and he leaned back against the concrete. He had the bow in one hand and it slid across the strings of his cello. His hand was, once again, wrapped in the same white bandages.

Saya stood up and walked up to the man as she dusted the sand off her skirt.

"Who are you?"

If his form had been a statue, then his figure would have been worthy of placement in the State Hermitage Museum's main reception hall. His beauty was that stunning.

The young man looked up.

However, he didn't stop playing. The music continued to flow, if only a bit softer.

"Do you know me?" Saya continued.

The sound of the waves mixed seamlessly with the vibration of the strings, and the tune continued.

"If you know what I am, then tell me!"

The bandaged hand holding the bow stopped. All that continued was the sound of the sea.

It felt like a blade cut open the sudden tranquility. This lasted for several breaths.

"If I tell you, then you will lose the now."

"Huh?"

"But if this is what you desire . . ."

"If it's what I desire?"

Saya stared straight into his deep blue eyes, which were surprisingly clear in the twilight.

From the distance she heard the sound of a motorcycle come closer, and then stop just above them on the breakwater.

"Saya!"

She looked up to see Kai practically flying down the concrete stairs of the breakwater bank toward them.

She could see his face was flushed with anger.

"Get away from her, you asshole!"

The young man avoided the throw of Kai's motorcycle helmet with a half-step to the side.

It was like he knew the helmet's path before it left Kai's hand. Kai then dipped low and delivered a practiced right hook.

But, again, the man moved delicately out of the way, and Kai's throw barely touched his collar.

But that didn't stop Kai. As his shoes kicked up sand, Kai moved left and right, sending punch after punch. He looked like a real pro boxer on the attack.

Despite Kai's practice and passion, not a single punch landed on the man. It was as if he was skating on ice around Kai—a superbly graceful display.

"C'mon, jerk!"

Suddenly changing the rhythm of a fight by yelling at your opponent might be an effective strategy, but it didn't seem to work here. Having been on the track and field team, he knew the importance of breathing exercises.

Hitting nothing but air obviously frustrated Kai, and his punches got more reckless, until one was returned, sending Kai doing a full turn in the air.

"Kai!"

He landed face up in the sand.

Saya rushed to his side to help him up. His eyes were closed, but his groan told her he wasn't unconscious. It was a good thing he'd landed on sand.

"It may be best not to move him so quickly. He'll be fine in a few moments."

The young man had already returned his cello to its case.

Saya had a million questions she wanted to ask the man. But at this exact point in time, she had no desire to hear a single one of his answers.

Seeing the tall man walk up the stairs without another word, Saya returned her attention to Kai, whose head was resting on her knees.

She wiped the sand that was stuck to the sweat on his brow away, and then stroked his hair.

"You're so reckless . . ."

She was about laugh, but instead tears started to flow.

She wasn't supportive of the fact that he'd suddenly attacked the man out of the blue, but she knew in her heart that he'd done it to protect her, and despite her words, it made her very happy.

Finding her couldn't have been easy, either. Who knows how many places he looked before finding her here? Yet, he remembered how much Saya liked the view at the beach, so that must have been what brought him here.

"Unh . . . Saya?"

The rain of tears on Kai's face could have been mistaken for a sudden squall.

Kai pulled himself up, though his eyes were only half-open. The fact that he raised his fists ready for the fight to continue was very Kai.

"Where is he?"

"He's gone."

"Gone . . . looks like he got me."

His tone wasn't nearly as self-defeating as she expected. Yet as he moved to sit down beside her, there was a sense of loss. It didn't matter if he won or not, but to be bothered when a fight ended before it was over was a trait that George also carried, thought Saya.

"I think that guy knows something about me."

"Why? Did he say something?"

"No. Not a word."

The sinking sun melted into the orange sea, and the sky fired up like a brilliant bougainvillea blossom.

The brilliant display in the sky coupled oddly, but nicely, with the dull sound of the crashing waves.

". . . What's going to happen to me?"

"Are you worried?"

Saya answered by nodding her head slightly.

"I will always be by your side. Riku and Dad will always be by your side, too. Are you still worried? No matter what happens, Saya, you are you. And you are our family."

"Kai . . ."

The profile of her older brother's face set in front of the sunset painted a picture of a boy that looked much older than his years.

But in an instant that tension flushed away, and he turned back into the Kai she was used to.

"*Nankurunaisa.*"

"*Nankuru—naisa*?"

"It's Okinawa dialect. It means somehow it'll all work out. Dad says it a lot. Like when you came here, and when I quit baseball . . . Let's work through it. It's kinda like a magic spell."

"*Nankurunaisa.*"

"Feels good saying it, huh?"

"Yeah."

Wiping the tears from her eyes, Saya nodded in agreement.

It felt like it had been a long time since the last time she laughed.

But it was more than that. She felt a stress release from her tight shoulders, which was evidenced by the tone of her voice.

It was right then her stomach chose the worst timing to pipe in. Saya's face turned red.

"You gotta be hungry. And Dad is worried. Let's get home."

"Yeah."

Saya grabbed Kai's outstretched hand and he pulled her up.

## 02

IT WAS LATE before Louis got back.

Cramming his big build into the passenger seat, he had more than just information, but some physical evidence to share.

"*Yokorasho*," he sighed in Japanese, as he put his hands on the dashboard covered with junk food wrappers.

Having just ended a call to headquarters on his satellite phone, David glanced over at his partner and kept the several complaints he wanted to say to himself.

Louis's extraordinary appetite was matched only by his intelligence gathering abilities.

But there was another with an insatiable appetite.

David pulled down the photo of a young girl stuck behind the sun visor and stared at the smiling face. Saya Otonashi.

Decades old, the edges of the photograph were worn down.

In the old faded photograph the girl is standing next to a striking young man. "Joel's diary" is also inscribed on it. One of Saya's servants.

"Want one? It's Goya *takoyaki*. I read about it in a magazine. Park Avenue is the only place in the country they sell it."

David took one look at the grilled octopus–filled dough balls shoved his way and waved them away with the back of his hand.

"No thanks . . . what do you have for me?"

"I was able to confirm this. There is one more 'mouse' out there."

"I see."

This was a troubling state of affairs.

Due to this slip-up by his colleagues, it would be nice if he could get it by the tail as it wasn't desirable for the situation to get out of hand. The American military certainly shared his opinion that the biggest fear was not "them" but being scrutinized by the mass media and society as a whole. At any rate, as far as power relationships go, they were in no position to cross swords with the U.S. military.

There was no choice but to continue on nice and smoothly. This was no time to be afraid.

It was time to get armed. With the one-of-a-kind weapon that could slaughter "them."

Looking past the rearview mirror, David saw the entrance open at OMORO, the pub that faced a playground. He couldn't hear the cowbell, but he did see George anxiously hurry out a drunken customer.

David pushed open the driver's side door, exposing himself to the nearly 30° C air outside.

On his way to OMORO David suddenly stopped.

From inside the pub, out walked Saya, dressed in her school uniform. She must have been on her way to school. Neither she nor George had noticed him.

". . . Father?"

"What's the matter? You'll be late. You are starting back at school today, right?"

Likely stiff from standing behind the bar all night, George rubbed the base of his neck with his hand, and gave a puzzled look.

"It's all right for me to be here, right?"

George's profile hardened.

"I'm sorry. Never mind. I'm off!"

Flashing a fake smile, Saya turned and ran off, double-time. From the back she looked like someone trying to escape.

George stood like a stone statue for a few moments, and then turned to go back inside. He looked like a tired middle-aged man.

David saw his chance and called out to him.

"George!"

"Oh, it's you . . ."

There was never a warm reception for David.

It didn't stop David from following George into the shop. George plopped down on a barstool at the counter, but David elected to remain standing.

"You haven't told her yet?"

There was no response. His silence said it all.

"What are you accomplishing by delaying the inevitable? We are out of time and out of choices."

"Weren't we waiting for her to recover naturally?"

"The circumstances have changed. We just found out there is a second one."

David rejected any resistance from this father being forced to hand over his daughter.

"If we could have told her everything from the beginning, don't you think we would have? We learned the hard way after what happened to her in Vietnam."

If what they learned had been accompanied by agony, it would have been the worst pain imaginable.

For both the organization, and for David himself.

"That's why I left everything up to you, and you stopped seeing it in your observations. I don't want us to give her any unnecessary motivations."

After David adjusted his stance, he spoke again.

"I'll give you until sundown. I can't wait any longer than that."


Like well-behaved ants, all the students in the school stood in straight lines in the school gymnasium. However, the principal's long-winded speech was starting to cause boredom among the ranks.

After their short break from school, the first thing on the agenda wasn't classes, but an all-school assembly to mourn the loss of Mr. Inamine, the teacher killed by the drugged-up U.S. Army soldier.

"—And yet, his remains have still not been returned to the grieving family. This regrettable turn of events certainly compounds their grief. Setting aside the horror of the situation that took place, the U.S. Army has told us that it is an emergency situation, yet still, they have gone too far—"

The talk coming through the speakers moved from a farewell to a fallen teacher to a rather unusual rant against the U.S. military. Since they hadn't returned the remains, and also since all communication was one-way, it was understandable that people would get angry.

Because the U.S. military gave no reason why they took Mr. Inamine's body and hadn't returned it, the students were extra sensitive to the mental states of their teachers, and didn't want to do anything to upset them.

As the principal's lengthy talk continued, anti-Army comments were quietly whispered among the students.

"I can't stand this," muttered Kaori into Saya's ear from right behind her. "My mom said it's really tense at the base, too, and everyone is in a bad mood . . . Hey, are you listening?"

"Huh? Yeah."

It seemed like she had spaced out for a minute.

"—We will now observe one minute of silence, in order to pray for our teacher, Mr. Junichi Inamine's safe journey to the next world."

As Kaori cutely zipped her lip, everyone in the gymnasium sent their eyes to the floor upon the principal's command.

A hush fell over the gym. Only the cicadas continued their buzzing.

After the assembly was over it was back to classes, as if nothing had happened.

It was right after a murder at school, but teachers had work to do, and students had tests to take and classes to pass.

Even when someone is very close to a tragic or abnormal event, the security in the routine of everyday life is a strong emotional protector which is tough to crack. It is because life continues one step at a time, and one second at a time, on and on forever.

However, Saya was feeling helpless and alone.

Saya didn't have a concrete past like Kaori and her other schoolmates. She felt it would not be strange at all if her normal everyday life ended at any moment.

During a break, Saya went to the biology lab, but every trace of the events of that night had been completely wiped away. The destroyed desks and blackboard, as well as the contents of the display cases had all been replaced.

The tear in the first-floor hallway was gone, and the broken window in the teacher's office was also brand new.

*They can make it go away. Eventually what happened that day will completely disappear.*

Saya was a part of that event, and she became aware of the possible instability of her own existence. The hole in the wall was refilled and repainted to hide what had happened, and then no one had to know.

What was true? What was the right thing to believe?

Walking though the main gate after school, Saya's legs still felt heavy.

"Hey, you're all hunched over!"

The voice as lively as a little bird flapping its wings, and the slap on her shoulder blade caused Saya to suddenly pop her head up.

"Ka-Kaori."

Kaori, carrying her gym bag, gave a cheerful grin that was a little too bright for Saya at that moment.

"The mood at school is so gloomy, so, c'mon, cheer up!"

"Yeah . . ."

"Hold on a second . . ."

Kaori sped up to get a close look at Saya's face. Her facial expression looked like a policeman trying to find flaws in a suspect's alibi.

"Wha-what?'

"Did you eat a proper breakfast this morning?"

"Today . . . no, I didn't."

"I knew it! I thought you seemed pretty drained."

"No, I mean, that's not it . . ."

"I got it! Let's go to the *okonomiyaki* restaurant. We haven't been there in forever."

Just as the great detective made her final judgment, Saya's stomach rumbled in agreement.

". . ."

Saya's cheeks turned red, despite the fact that she was on regular speaking terms with the talkative monster that lived in her belly.

"See? See? The body doesn't lie. C'mon, let's go!"

"Hol-hold on."

Kaori pushed Saya up the sidewalk until the sound of a car horn parked on the side of the street took the wind out of her sails.

"Hey there!"

From the driver's side George's thick arm waved their way.

Saya walked timidly up to the side of George's car. Leaving a little bit of distance, Kaori followed Saya.

"Father, what are you doing here?"

"There is something I want to show you."

Saya had never seen his face look so serious. But it was only for a second. He then leaned forward to greet Kaori, and his expression went back to normal.

"Pardon me, Kaori-chan, but do you think Riku could come to your place for a little bit?"

"Riku-kun?"

"I know it's a lot to ask, but I need to talk with Saya, and I am afraid it's going to get late. I am hoping Riku can eat dinner at your place."

"No problem. My mom is always happy when Riku-kun comes to visit. Really, don't worry about it."

Saya sensed the subtle concern in Kaori's voice, and glanced at her consciously to give her a smile.

"Thanks for taking care of Riku, Kaori," said Saya. "I guess I gotta go."

George stopped the car at the side of a remote mountain road far from town.

The scenery hadn't changed since the last time he had been there.

George turned off the engine, pulled out the key, and got out to wait for Saya to exit from the passenger side. Together they started to climb the long stairway up the side of the green mountain. It was a worn and aged flight of stone steps.

During the long time sitting in the car Saya had hardly said a word. There were a bunch of things she wanted to ask, but she wasn't sure how to put them into questions.

Seeing the eyes of his daughter in pain made him grip the wheel tighter, and made his heart sink.

Not having a past meant it was hard to see your future. Even living in the present, the world must have seemed as hazy as the heat coming off the ground on a hot day.

This was Saya's burden. No one else could possibly understand what she was going through. Even her father, George.

George wished he could help his daughter by sharing her pain. But what he was about to do was give her the truth. That's all he could do.

The color of the sky began to give signs that night was approaching. The plants and trees also gave off the moist odor that signaled the end of the day was near.

At the top of the stairs the view opened up to a wide-open space. They stood with their backs to the dark blue hibiscus-tinted ocean, and faced a large and wide stone structure.

"A tomb. . . ?"

Thinking this was her first time here, that was Saya's assumption. She truly didn't have any recollections of that day.

She was mentally a newborn baby, so it wasn't surprising that she didn't.

Okinawa tombs had the unique and peculiar characteristic of looking like shallow sake cups turned upside down. Their size and dimensions weren't uniform, and the majority of tourists could probably look at one and not guess what it was.

"This is the final resting place for ancestors of the Miyagusuku family. My father and mother, as well as my wife and daughter who died are all here. Evidence of my life in Okinawa is here."

George was born in the U.S., but his parents were Japanese citizens from Okinawa. Despite his nationality, his blood was pure Japanese, and his roots were right here.

"Our relationship started here, as well."

"Started here?"

"Yes. As the daughter of George Miyagusuku. It begins again today. From tomorrow your true life begins."

"My life? Tomorrow?"

Saya looked up at George. Her eyes were shaking in anxiety.

"Am I . . . going away with David?"

"So you did hear us."

George wasn't too surprised. That's what he had assumed since that day at the clinic. He hadn't been careful and had let his attitude get the best of him. He'd ended up hurting Saya even more.

As David would say, he should have told Saya much sooner. His expression returned to that of a father.

It wasn't too late. David gave him time. Still, he was brimming with emotions.

"During the Vietnam War, I had a highly respected mentor. Just before he died, he entrusted you into my care. He asked me to take watch over you until . . . until Saya Otonashi woke up."

He told her everything he could.

That was why he'd brought her here. This is where it began.

"But I didn't know when you would wake up, or what to do when you did. Not knowing where to go, I settled down in Okinawa. A lot happened after that. I retired from the military, opened up the shop, and got married."

It was an ordinary day when his life was completely upended by that traffic accident.

"My wife and daughter died in an car wreck . . . And I even considered ending my own life to join them. It was then, after all that time, when I could hear your beating heart. . . and I understood it as you telling me, *keep living*."

This face of Saya, standing here listening attentively to George's story, was completely different from the face of that day.

Even more, the Saya of that day wasn't even in human form.

In this special place was a tomb with a six-tatami mat area inside. In that half underground open space was an enormous cocoon—that was Saya. He knew she was alive by the distant sound of her heartbeat in the dark.

The shell that surrounded her was in the shape of a woman's womb. For George, the beating of her heart was a sensation that couldn't be replaced. The spirits of his mother and father, and his wife and daughter, and even his ancestors had returned to this place to give new life to this soul. George honestly believed this.

"It was from that moment I decided to live life to the fullest. That's when I took in Kai and Riku, who had lost their parents in accidents. I did what I could to have a fulfilling life."

He had never felt any sense of self-importance as a rescuer of orphans, or treated them as objects rather than people. Every day was busy, frantic, and fulfilling.

Being a father to Kai and Riku gave George a reason to keep living.

"And then I got older, and Kai and Riku started growing into men. But you. You still stayed in that same state. You slept here the entire time . . . I should have had plenty of time to think about it, but I never knew exactly what to do."

He didn't know what to do when the thing in the cocoon awakened.

"But one year ago, when you finally opened your eyes, I made my decision."

When the finely spun white web broke open and a girl emerged on the floor of the tomb, groveling on her hands and knees, George didn't offer her food or a warm blanket. Instead he stuck the muzzle of a pistol in her face.

He knew how illegal it was for him to possess a semi-automatic pistol, and he didn't keep if because of any emotional attachment to his time in the military. It was strictly for his protection. Even though he personally wasn't an official member of the organization David was a part of, he still was allowed certain emergency provisions.

He'd pointed that gun at this girl's head due to nothing but unadulterated terror.

This wasn't a human.

He couldn't let it fend for itself, much less live among himself and his sons. At the time, that was his thinking.

However, the finger that George counted on to pull the trigger failed him.

From behind an amniotic fluid wall of dripping wet obsidian black hair came the soft and unsure, smiling face of a young girl.

It was the instinctive expression of a baby laying trusting eyes on a nearby face.

"It was at that moment that I swore to raise you as my own daughter."

A gust from the sea ruffled Saya's hair.

The first time he saw her, that hair was so long that it touched the ground, but now it was so short, even a light breeze could have its way with it.

The electric ring didn't fit with this naturally beautiful landscape, and, on top of that, signaled the end of this time together.

George pulled his phone out of his pocket and put it up to his ear.

"Hello."

"It's time."

"All right."

David's unsentimental phone call brought George back to the present, and he begrudgingly turned toward the stone steps.

What he wanted, more than anything, was to gaze upon his daughter's face.

His eyes were muddied with his feelings.

He wanted to pat her on the head and tell her, *It's fine, there's nothing to worry about, I'll always be at your side*.

But he couldn't.

The sun had set.

"Let's go home. The people that need you are waiting."

"So . . . now, what am I supposed to do?"

"I can't answer that question. That is for you to decide."

"What should I say to Kai and Riku?"

"I'll talk to them."

With Saya's back to him, George began the descent down the stone stairs.

✝

"Man, what are you doing taking apart your bike, all of a sudden?" asked Kato, standing in the shade of the gas station.

"Something's wrong with it, all right?" answered Kai as his hands never stopped moving on the repair.

Facing the highway, this self-service gas station was a perfect spot to fix a motorcycle. There were a fair amount of tools available for use, no staff working in the front, and from that spot in the parking lot no one would come and bother them.

Today was only a half-day at school, and since Kai and his friends had the freedom to go home when they pleased, they often enjoyed coming here after class and getting their hands greasy.

"I'm going to take Saya up to the north part of the island. That's why I gotta fix it."

"Saya's your little sister, right? Why go through all that?" asked Kakimoto as he kept himself occupied kicking an empty can.

"She's been kinda down lately, so I thought it might make her feel better. I just want to do something a good big brother would do."

"Hmph! This coming from the king of brawlers."

"Are you sure you didn't bang your head on something?"

The tossed-around Cheerio can flew in a high arc though the air and landed on the pavement with a high-pitched kiss.

The can sprung back and tumbled, bouncing off of Kai's bike.

Kai picked up the can and casually tossed it back at Kato, the one with the uncomfortably hot-looking, combed-down curly hair.

Kato's Timberland boot came down hard on the can, smashing it flat, and then Kai looked up hearing the sound of a car's quiet engine.

An old-looking compact car pulled into the gas station from the highway.

The curves in the body's shape would have seemed very cutting-edge forty years ago, but by today's standards it had a retro look.

However, looking at the driver who stepped out of the car with a cell phone at his ear, Kai guessed he didn't choose the car for the fashion statement it made.

He was probably in his late twenties or early thirties, certainly not yet middle-aged, yet his posture made him look fatigued and his expression was one of frustration. Yet, from his eyes Kai could tell this was the kind of guy who was rarely unprepared.

"Right. That's what I am saying. I keep digging and digging, but I can't find anything. This isn't normal. No matter how much we say the Status of Forces agreement is unfair, they still aren't returning the body. We've never seen this before, right?"

While talking on the phone, the man reached into his pocket with his left hand for some change, and ended up dropping a coin. The 100-yen coin rolled to where Kai was sitting and he grabbed it. Before the man picked the coin out of Kai's palm, he gestured a thank you with his left hand, and then dropped some money in the gas pump coin slot.

The press ID clipped to his vest pocket revealed that he was a newspaper reporter. The ID read "Akihiro Okamura."

"Now I am on my way to Teruya. Where? Obviously, it's where the Koza High teacher is from. Don't try and tell me not to go."

He seemed to be talking on the phone to a higher-up, but kept talking in a sharp, argumentative tone as he returned the nozzle to the pump, tore off his receipt, and got back in his little car.

"Must write for some rag. Those guys are all going crazy, too," loudly boasted Kato, after all traces of the 1970s had driven far enough away.

Since the incident, it was common to run into media-related people around the city.

With all these reporters and such causing a fuss and disturbing everyone, the locals couldn't help but be a little fed up.

On the other hand, would their efforts to dig up the truth end with this incident, or not?

Just as Kai was remembering that night, he was distracted by a figure shuffling down the sidewalk on the other side of the highway.

"Forest?"

Kai didn't know what he was thinking, wearing a thick hooded robe on such a hot day, but from his profile he easily recognized that face which he has seen sitting at the OMORO counter countless times.

"Forest? You mean that crybaby that used to be a regular at your dad's shop?" said Kato, returning his ever-present comb to his back pocket after making little progress in fixing the bird's nest on top of his head.

"Yup. Anytime something happened in the Marines, he'd complain about it to Dad," responded Kai, thumping a monkey wrench onto his sore shoulders.

"Yeah. I heard from the Amazoness GoGo bartender that he said he didn't fit in the military and was going back home. Guess he's still here, though."

After dropping the name of a GI nightclub, Kakimoto waved his hands in the air.

"Hey! Forest!"

From across the highway, which was blurred with moving waves of heat, the hooded figure's legs stopped moving, and his head turned to look in their direction. In the dark shadow all Kai could see was the figure's two glowing crimson eyes.

Kai's heart skipped a beat.

Exactly the same. The same as that monster from the other night.

Just as Kai collected himself to take another look, a long silver plate blocked his vision.

Leaving a trail of exhaust fumes, the freight truck passed between them on the highway, but after it did, Forest was nowhere to be seen.

"Huh? He disappeared!"

"You guys watch my bike, 'kay!"

Kai took off running before he could give the frantically shouting Kakimoto the chance to refuse.

He had a feeling something bad was about to happen.

Maybe it was just anxious fear, but there was no way he was going to let those eyes gaze upon Saya again.

On the entrance to OMORO hung a small wooden sign which read "Preparing for Business."

This time the door was ten times heavier than usual. The sound of the cowbell was jarring.

Saya had never once felt this way before when she had returned home.

It was gloomy. The walls behind the counter and the area around the sink were decorated with American southern-style and Japanese pub–style knick-knacks. It was just enough to rescue the shop interior from its dim lighting.

The shop wasn't open, but she could see the figure of a man sitting at the counter.

The expressionless face that turned and looked at her was none other than the face of David.

"You are late."

"I know."

David looked up at George's bitter scowl, and then returned his probing gaze back to Saya.

"I am a member of an organization called 'Red Shield.'"

"Red . . . Shield?"

"Red Shield was established and acts in the pursuit of a certain purpose. On that night at school you saw something. That monster."

A chill ran down Saya's spine.

*David knows about the grotesque beast.*

"We call it a Chiropteran."

"Chiropteran . . ."

"It is a monster that feeds on human blood."

That's right. She had heard the cello player say the same thing.

That giant creature killed people and then sucked out their blood . . . that was what it looked like it was doing to Mr. Inamine.

She didn't want to remember. Everything about that unbelievable event on an otherwise completely normal day couldn't be erased from her brain too soon.

But David wasn't going to let that happen.

"For a long time we have been gathering information and exterminating the Chiropterans. And so we need you, as our trump card."

"Me?"

If the person who had told her this had been anyone but David, she would have burst out laughing.

How could any of this possibly be true?

To think of asking a high-school student to help kill monsters— this wasn't some Hollywood action movie.

"To be more precise, it is your blood—you are the only person with the blood that can reliably kill Chiropterans."

"My . . . blood?"

Saya's gaze moved naturally to her upturned palms.

What could be so special about the blood that flowed through the veins under the surface of her skin?

And that otherworldly monster could be killed by something inside her body? This sudden self-awareness made her shoulders turn cold.

Right then the brass cowbell gave notice of someone opening the door.

"Sorry, but tonight we are . . ."

"George."

The voice sounded cracked and broken.

Wearing what looked like a tattered blanket over his head, it appeared that he entered to get shelter from a sudden squall, but there was no humid smell of rain coming off the asphalt.

"Could it be . . . Forest?"

George realized it was an old friend of his when he recognized this rather weak-looking man's face poking out from underneath the hood of his blanket. Saya also was able to recognize him, though he looked quite different from the handsome, well-bred man she remembered.

"Help . . . me . . ."

"Help you? What happened? Didn't you fly back home?"

His gestures were of someone who was completely exhausted. With great difficulty he hobbled over to the counter, his upper body barely keeping balanced, and somehow the young Marine made his way onto a stool.

As if he carried the weight of the world on his back, Forest laid his head down on the counter.

"Hey, you all right? Saya, water."

"Ye-yes."

Saya pulled a cup off the shelf and filled it from the drinking water tap, then placed it on the counter.

It looked as if he was trying to thank her. His pale face rose up, and their eyes met.

Saya then saw Forest's normally gentle eyes instantly muddy to a crimson red tone.

At the same time, his right hand reached for the cup. Suddenly cracks and fissures ran up his skin and pieces peeled off like old scabs. His human flesh dropped away, and she got a glance at the dark-brown dermis taking its place.

"Get back!"

She heard a thunderous crack, a sound she had only heard in movies, and at the same time she saw Forest's body careen sideways.

"Wh-why'd you shoot him?"

"It's a Chiropteran," answered David to the anxious George while still holding a giant pistol in both hands.

Saya wasn't sure, but she thought it might be a revolver.

"Get away. Hurry! Get outside!"

The completely dumbfounded Saya was grabbed by the wrist by George and pulled toward the doorway.

She could still see Forest slumped on the floor beyond David, who still held the pistol in front of him.

He must have been killed, right?

Wrong. He was still alive. The two arms laid out across the floor gradually pushed up his shoulders.

Again the sound of the pistol fire filled the air, one shot after another.

"Not even this will stop him," spat David in frustration as George and Saya ran out into the empty street outside the shop. She clung onto the fence which surrounded the basketball court in the park across from the shop, and turned around to see the door of the shop fly off its hinges.

The two men, wrapped in a violent embrace, followed right behind, tumbling into the street.

David's body crashed on the hard asphalt, and he rolled like a rag doll until his back stopped at a telephone pole.

Either from embarrassment or from being knocked out, David's head hung low and he stopped moving.

The pistol that should have been in David's hand was clamped between Forest's jaws. The teeth that carried the large lump of iron were long and pointed, like a shark's.

Saya also noticed that his arms were no longer the same as a human's. From his elongated arms and swollen fingers sprouted long, sharp claws which reminded her of a crane's bill.

"What's happened to you, Forest?"

There was no response.

His mouth opened wide, and the saliva-covered pistol fell to the ground.

As if he had received a signal, Forest bolted at them. He moved at an unbelievable speed.

The claw outstretched to grasp Saya's cowering figure didn't meet its intended target.

The brutal talons instead met the beautifully ornamented body of a cello case.

It was as if a giant raven had touched down from the moon.

Without making a sound, the young musician landed just before Saya's dumbfounded eyes.

With seemingly no effort, the tall man spun on one foot, sending his right heel into Forest's lower spine.

"Gwaa!"

His body bent at the middle, and Forest rolled head-over-heels past the fallen David and into the full plastic bags at a trash collection spot.

Saya looked up at the profile of the young man who had saved her life.

He suddenly placed the cello case on the ground, opened it up, and pulled out that same sword.

"Saya—fight."

Saya's shaking eyes focused on the large blade extended to her.

Fight? With this, again?

Like on that night. From the depths of her gut Saya felt a surge of violent emotion spread like a flame throughout her body.

As vegetable scraps and milk cartons fell to the side, Forest rose up off the ground.

Yet, Saya was unable to wrap her hand around the blade's grip.

"I . . . can't. I can't fight!"

A human blood-sucking monster? But until a few moments ago, he was a human, too.

Why was David able to fire a gun at him without any hesitation? If this is what it meant to fight, Saya was sure she couldn't follow suit.

Forest was coming straight at them, his beastly claws swinging madly.

A hand firmly grasped the scabbard of the sword from the young man's grip.

"Do you think I am going to allow Saya, my daughter, to be killed by that?"

Wrapping his fingers around the handle, George turned to face his transformed friend.

The unsheathed blade shone like a white sash slicing though the dark night air.

A hard blunt thud.

The blade stopped in the deformed right arm blocking Forest's face.

The counter blow to the superficial wound George caused was a grand swipe from Forest's long left arm. His left hand pounded through George, sending him sailing sideways into the air.

"Father!"

George's body crashed and twisted over the asphalt. Vivid red spots began appearing here and there around his abdomen. A hole was torn through his shirt and through the flesh below and blood periodically spurted out. Atop the black asphalt a puddle of thick-colored water began to spread.

As the pool of blood grew, in severe proportion, the bright red color of Forest's eyes began to disappear.

". . . George?"

"Simon . . ."

Calling him by his first name might have helped in bringing him back to reality.

"Uwa-uwaaa!"

Forest's still-deformed arms began to tremble, and he stepped backward away from George.

Whether he was reeling in terror from what he had done, or in terror of what he had become, it wasn't clear.

Saya took no notice of him as he stumbled down the road, his sobs mixed with shrieks echoing into the night.

She kneeled on the street and leaned over Goerge, calling out with all her strength.

She wasn't sure what the right thing to do was.

This was all her fault.

She pressed down on the wound in his abdomen with both hands, but waves of fresh blood flowed, soaking her palms.

"Dad!"

The rebuking tone of the voice blew through the desperate Saya.

The lights from the park revealed the figure of Kai, who must have run here from somewhere, as his shoulders heaved up and down frantically.

It didn't take more than a moment to realize that George's condition was extremely serious.

Julia's medical specialty was not trauma injuries, but she did know that deep lacerations into the abdomen led to extreme amounts of pain and shock, and that they were often fatal. The samurai that existed in this country years ago would avoid the pain of *seppuku* after committing an unforgivable mistake by employing an assistant to behead the warrior just as the short sword entered the shamed one's gullet.

More than any other time in history, we were blessed with anesthesia, precise tools and methods, and scientific knowledge uninfluenced by superstitions. And George was transported to Sogo Hospital's emergency room, which had the best facilities in the city.

After emergency surgery, George was taken to the ICU. At this point it was too early to say he was out of the woods, but his condition did appear to be stable.

But who really needed immediate care was, more than George, his daughter.

"What a rough day. But at least your father is doing better than he was, so why don't you get some rest. I will stay here with him."

"It's . . . it's all my fault . . ."

Saya was sitting on the bench on the other side of the glass from George, who laid face up, unmoving. Saya started at his every breath, the clear plastic mask over his nose and mouth clouded and then cleared again. She still wore the blood-stained clothes she had on when she came in.

"If it weren't for me . . ."

From her frozen complexion, Julia saw a hint of thawing around the edges of Saya's eyes. With reserved interest, Julia observed the young girl cry.

Mixed within those tears, how much built-up stress was being exhausted out of her body, as well? The human body was still full of mysteries. This was especially true with situations which involved the so-called "soul."

"I'll get something to drink," Julia said after settling Saya on the waiting area bench. Julia then walked again to the corridor.

Someone was waiting for her.

"I wish you had brought him to my clinic."

The steam from her 100-yen vending machine coffee curled around her nose.

"He needed emergency care. He wasn't sick."

With his back resting against the wall, the black business suit of this fit but obviously tense man was spattered here and there with mud, and had a few tears. A little fall wouldn't have done this much damage.

The organization had given this man the name "David" and he was now sneered at with a sideways laugh from "Julia."

"Business comes after personal feelings, I see. You haven't changed."

". . ."

She knew he was being pushed from above to hurry and get Saya prepared. However, David, the friend, had allowed George and Saya to be together until sunset today.

Julia knew that the monthly allowance given by headquarters to George for watching and protecting Saya was 50-thousand Japanese yen. She also knew that the envelope delivered to George by David usually held more like 70-thousand.

He pretended to be repelled by George's boisterous and genial nature, but in reality he was the closest friend he had, and David treated their relationship as something truly sacred. That's why George trusted him. He trusted him enough to give him Saya, the girl he considered his daughter for the last year. Men were constructed simply, but their actions were harder to grasp.

Julia's scornful chuckle was directed at his appearance, but also was like that of a mother laughing at a child on his tiptoes trying to grab something out of reach.

"As a member of the Red Shield medical team, I will do my best for him, but I can't guarantee that the events of this evening won't have an effect on her awakening."

"We have confirmed the worldly existence of Chiropterans. There is something in Okinawa connected with their extermination, so neither failure nor retreat is remotely acceptable."

"Is this search for the sake of your fallen comrades?"

". . . It is for the sake of my duty."

The bitter taste of the coffee in her mouth coupled with the sour look of David's hard profile gave Julia an odd sense of pleasure.

"And that is why we need Saya. But now she is in this mental state."

"The Marine named Forest—she had handled a Chiropteran before, but we weren't able to recognize any changes. However, she just killed a Chiropteran at her school the other night. So the question is—what was there at the school that wasn't there this time?"

Her blue eyes narrowed as she stared at the surface of the coffee she held in its paper cup.

"If you could figure that out, controlling Saya's performance will get a lot easier. It's not like this sort of weapon comes with a manual, though."

"The one that obeys Saya—Perhaps, he knows."

"Has 'he' reappeared?"

"Yes."

He hadn't been seen in thirty-three years. Julia knew what appeared in "Joel's Diary," but couldn't say any information about him beyond that.

She heard the distinct sound of sneakers squeaking across the polished white-chocolate-toned floor.

A young boy, twelve or thirteen years old, with chestnut brown hair came galloping in.

Without a doubt, he was George's youngest son. He looked a little like the high-school-aged son that had brought Saya to the clinic on his motorcycle. This boy had the same cheeky look in his eye, but he had more feminine, elegant features.

But at that moment this charming young lad looked so tense he was about to cry.

"Saya-neechan!" he yelled out at a volume usually not heard inside hospitals.

He ran past Julia and David to the waiting area, and his cries caused Saya to lift her head.

"Kai-niichan is . . ."

"Where is Kai?"

"He said he is going to kill Forest-san . . ."

Saya's face went pale.

It appeared this boy's older brother had a quick temper and made rash decisions. Julia frowned and exchanged glances with David as his cell phone rang.

"Louis? What happened?"

It must have been his glutton of a partner.

After letting the other end talk for a while, finally David opened his mouth.

"Idiot! Isn't it obvious doing that will only end up choking us?" The abuse wasn't directed at the person at the other end of the line. "What happened?" asked Julia.

"George's son took his father's gun and ran out of the shop. Louis, bring the car here."

Entering the alleyway from the main street, suddenly the night air felt very heavy. There were lights, but they weren't there to illuminate the road, instead the neon signs designed to grab the attention of passers covered the walls and attracted more insects than customers.

"In the basement down there," said Kato, the one with the cauliflower-shaped hairdo. Saya's eyes followed his finger to the place he was pointing at.

The door of the club located in the basement floor of a building full of small shops and pubs had a sign with blinking jellybean-shaped lights covering it. It read "Amazoness GoGo," and was apparently a nightclub which catered to American military men.

"This street isn't very safe at night . . ." leaked out Kakimoto. He seemed the most hesitant of the four of them, but Saya was relieved that he'd helped bring them here on their bikes.

She knew that these two were good friends with Kai. Saya felt lucky that she was able to catch them at the gas station where they all usually hung out. Unfortunately, she had already missed Kai, but the two of them knew where he was headed.

"We just told Kai, too. If you go to the shop where Reimi works, you should be able to find Forest. I heard they were going to get married and go back to America, but who really knows?"

She had heard this rumor countless times, but Kakimoto repeated it anyway.

These rough-looking loiterers used particularly cheery tones, probably in response to her downtrodden and obviously distressed expression.

"I wonder if Kai-niichan is okay . . ."

"Yeah . . ."

At that moment Saya slightly regretted not leaving Riku at the hospital. He was very intelligent, but he was still a kid. Yet, she understood painfully well his impatience and anxiety about his older brother. She couldn't just sit and wait, and had rushed out of the hospital when she heard what happened. It was probably her age, but she wasn't able to hesitate when it came to a family member.

"We have to hurry and find Kai and drag him home."

Saya, who had been trying to calm her little brother, was taken aback by this, and she stopped walking.

"What's wrong?"

Kakimoto's question flew in one ear and out the other.

Or more accurately, it was as if all sound traveling in the surrounding atmosphere had suddenly been banished from entering her ears. All but one.

It was either an extremely high or an extremely low frequency she felt. The narrow reverberation came straight to her from afar.

Saya's eyes searched around frantically.

In the space between two buildings she saw two eyes glowing in the darkness. No. It was just a stray dog.

Up in the window some people were looking at her . . . no, wait . . . those were just two typical lovebirds.

Where was it coming from—above?

Looking up, she immediately understood that the waves were coming from the night sky hidden in the shadows of the building. It rained down on her like ripples on still water.

The cry of a monster.

That sound was one she would never be able to erase from her memory as long as she lived. It was the same sound as the cry of the monster which had broken the school's windows that night.

"Hey, you listening?"

The spastic shaking of Saya's arm by Kakimoto drove the sound away, and brought Saya back to reality.

"Ah . . . eh? What?"

"No 'whats' . . . I said, 'Are you okay?'"

"Yes. I'm sorry."

Trying to hide her embarrassment, Saya sped the pace of her gait.

"I wonder what that voice was," Riku muttered from behind her.

"Voice? I didn't hear anything," replied Kato, looking down at Riku suspiciously.

Which meant that only Saya and Riku heard the voice?

Maybe the stress of trying to find Kai made their hearing super-sensitive. Regardless, hearing the voice of the beast at such a relatively close distance caused Saya to feel a bad premonition in her chest.

As Saya gripped the metal banister to walk down the stairs to the club's entrance, at the same time another young girl came up the stairs. Saya reflexively moved to let her pass before they bumped into each other.

"Mao!" cried Kakimoto.

"What are you doing here, at a place like this?" asked Kato.

The two boys' voices were jumbled as they came over to the rather tall young girl.

"I should be asking you the same thing."

The words were directed at the two boys, but Saya sensed some hostility as the girl glanced at her. Saya knew about Mao Jahana. She was a year older than Kai, yet she saw them together quite a bit.

"We are helping these two look for Kai, right?"

"Me too. He called me a little while ago asking me to look up any info I could on some Marine named Forest—"

"Where is Kai?"

Time was of the essence. Saya interrupted Mao's story only to receive another fishy glance.

"He already left. Wasn't your name Saya? Why are you trying to find Kai?"

"Kai . . . left our house with a gun . . . I heard."

"What a jackass! What is he planning to do?!"

Insulting the one young man who wasn't there, Mao proceeded to hit the CALL button on her cell phone, as she agilely slid her long hair behind her ear.

"Yes, Daddy? Yeah, it's me. Let's see, I am trying to track down a woman named Reimi who works at a shop called Amazoness GoGo . . . huh? I know! I am not doing anything you need to worry about. A friend is in a little trouble . . ."

It appeared the person she had called was her father. As she talked she slowly walked closer to the street.

"Yes. Right. I know. Bye. I love you, Daddy."

From out of the driver's door of the large black foreign car parked in front of the shop stepped a man in a peony-patterned aloha shirt. He opened the rear passenger door and wordlessly gestured an invitation to Mao.

Mao was from a well-off family, and her father was involved in some special business, at least according to what Saya had heard. On top of that, she seemed to get whatever she wanted from her doting father. Saya had no idea what Mao thought of her father's work. One time she did see Mao almost strangle Kai after he carelessly referred to "Jahana Industries" as the "Jahana Syndicate."

Putting her cell phone back into her Louis Vuitton purse, Mao turned and looked over at them.

". . . Aren't you getting in?"

"Huh?"

"You want to find Kai, right?"

Saya gave a hesitant look, but in her heart she wanted nothing more than to thank Mao for her help.

Riku hurriedly piled into the car behind Saya. Mao stuck a hand out the window and waved to Kato and Kakimoto, still standing on the curb.

"You guys can go home now."

"You gotta be kidding! Leaving us in this crappy neighborhood . . ."

Kakimoto's protest withered away as the grizzly faced driver placed his baseball glove–sized hand onto his shoulder.

Mao turned toward the driver's seat and closed the car door. The heavy thud of the door made Saya assume that they were probably bullet-proofed in case of a Mafia attack. The conspicuously large and gloomy looking driver didn't help matters, either. He must have been a bodyguard.

"Let's go."

With no discernable feeling of acceleration, the car began to move.

Sitting on the sofa-like seat next to Riku, Saya passed the time during the ride in the car by staring at the night view passing by the window.

Every second seemed longer than the last. It didn't happen when she was walking around looking, but now that her body wasn't moving, her impatience came in the form of a heavy pressure in her stomach.

Saya barely heard the constant monotone beeping of the keys on Mao's cell phone and the brief phone conversation she had with someone.

"Is your dad okay?" asked Mao, still facing forward. She was looking at the screen on her phone.

Riku's round eyes grew even wider.

"Huh? How did you know about that?"

"A big incident like that? How could I not know? So Forest is the one who did it?"

"Well, I wasn't there, so I can't say for sure . . . but . . ."

"But, that's what Kai thinks, right?"

"Yeah . . ."

"That's so like him. He can't calmly talk things through with someone. Once he gets his mind set, it doesn't matter, he'll attack an American Army officer or a policeman . . . especially for his family. If someone messes with you or with your dad, he can't let it go."

Mao leaned forward onto the back of the driver's seat and peeked over at Riku.

"That has its good points and its bad points . . ."

The bitter smile on Mao's face stayed there as she faced forward again and put her phone up to her ear.

"It's been a while. How are you? I know this is out of the blue, but you haven't seen Kai?"

Her voice was cheery but the reflection of her eyes in the rearview mirror couldn't have been more serious.

It was then that Saya understood that Mao was truly a good person, and that she was also very worried about Kai.


Location. Location. Location.

That was a common business expression. Whether it was trading barbs with the heads of the Rostrum at Oxford, or mixing chemicals with the medical researchers at The Tokyo University of Science, it was paramount to have first-hand experience in a variety of fields. Valid, marketable goods and strong business plans could be undermined by the loss of insight into a raw, undiluted market.

Be that as it may, the location inspection Van was going to today was purely to feed his curiosity and satisfy his interest.

At the very least, that's what the other men in the truck thought of Van's presence.

"You still can't find him?"

"We still don't have confirmation."

The response from the man sitting next to him was gruff. He didn't stop tapping on the keys of his computer which was relaying detection data.

"I came all the way out here thinking I would see the samurai man who cut down a 'mouse' . . ."

The folding chair Van sat on squeaked in agreement with his disappointment.

The squeal of the chair was grating on the military officers' ears.

"Please, keep it down, Mr. Argeno. We are in the middle of a military operation."

"Yes, yes. I'll be quiet, *monsieur*."

Regardless of the rank and post of his Army comrade, he wasn't a particularly sociable individual. With sarcasm and ridicule dancing off the tip of his tongue, Van raised both palms above his shoulders in deference to the cowboy.

". . . How'd we get stuck with this guy?"

"Orders from the top."

Van heard every word the Americans said. It was likely out of an attempt at politeness that they dropped their voices ever so slightly, but there was no doubt that they intended for him to hear every word.

From long ago, those with French-accented English and those with American-accented English have had difficulties with compatibility. Americans didn't realize that French children see all the Hollywood movies, and then they turn around and speak ill of the ambiguous subtleties of Godard. There weren't such problems when France gave them the Statue of Liberty.

Popping the piece of candy he had been playing with into his mouth, Van moved aside the curtain covering the windows from the inside of the truck and peeked outside.

"I wonder if the second 'mouse' won't reveal itself soon."

It had been so long, the sun had already set.

They had found traces of the "mouse" at a café-restaurant in the city called OMORO. It had attacked the owner there, but by the time they'd gotten this vehicle on the road, the "mouse" had dropped off the radar, and the police had already blocked off the area.

Since there was no body of a "mouse" recovered, it was safe to assume that it had escaped the scene. After that faint signals were received, but no precise location could be determined. It meant nothing other than the rat wasn't making a peep.

Radar had the ability to pick up frequencies beyond those of human hearing. If the mouse were to "squeak" then, in theory, the radar should be able to catch it, but it wasn't a system without flaws. If the target had returned to human form, then there was little that could be done.

"Switching back and forth and back and forth from monster to human, he sure is busy. Reminds me of this country's businessmen."

Seeing the disapproving scowl of the man in the driver's seat, Van shrugged his shoulders.

"Staring at me isn't going to help us catch the 'mouse.'"

The call on the wireless radio broke the tension inside the truck, and all three of them breathed a little easier.

"Yes. He's right here."

The man who had taken the call held out the wireless headphones to Van. Van took the wireless, and in exchange placed a piece of hard candy in the man's palm as a tip.

"Must be the commander . . ." he said into the headphone's mic, and then covered it with his hand and leaned over to the man's ear.

"It's *ume* flavor," he whispered, as if it was of monumental importance.

This variety of Japanese candy was an exquisite treat to savor. The *ume* plum flavor had an acidity similar to wine coupled with a raspberry sweetness. In addition it elicited a minty cooling sensation. A truly unique delight.

"Yes, OMORO? Oh, yes, where our incident took place . . . the victim is alive? That is splendid news. We'll need to bring him in. I hope you can help, as you always do."

It was a one-sided request, but the commander didn't turn him down.

Surely he knew that refusal wasn't an option from his end. It was those below him who didn't know that . . . namely, these two dunderhead soldiers barely masquerading as covert agents.

Van pretended to ignore the uncomfortable glance shot his way as he returned the wireless. He hung the wireless headphones on his index finger until the man snatched them back.

The information he learned from the commander turned Van's expression into a bullyish sneer before he went back to his business strategist look.

The "mouse" was the monster. The chances of a human surviving an attack from one were rather low. They must have transported him to the hospital right after the attack. It must have been the family members there.

But beyond that, there must have been someone there that scared the "mouse" off. There were also reports of small arms fire.

Would our samurai have put down the sword and picked up a gun?

"So, it appears there is someone besides us up and moving . . ."


Despite having just repaired his motorbike, Kai had no hesitation exposing it to the salty sea air. It takes months for the corrosive particles to seep into the tiniest fissures or loosen the paint. Kai had spent an about an hour getting his bike back running.

"Where is he?"

Kai was at the warehouse and rental storage strip on the reclaimed land near the bay. During the day it was a busy area with forklifts moving containers onto trailers, but at night, with no one around, it was like a ghost town.

After leaving Amazoness GoGo, Kai had observed Reimi buying fast food and men's underwear at a convenience store before taking a taxi here. Kai had carefully followed the taxi, realizing that Forest was concealed somewhere among these warehouses.

"This sucks . . ." spat Kai as he ran along the row of warehouses.

To make sure he wasn't spotted, when the taxi pulled over he stopped his bike in a place the driver couldn't see him. Unfortunately, the result of that was he didn't see where Reimi ran off to.

It would have been better to have asked Reimi directly where Forest was. Kai wasn't one to raise a hand to a girl, nor did he want to, but if she had seen what he was carrying, then Reimi probably would have told him everything she knew.

As Kai stopped and let his eyes adjust to the dark he rolled up the hem of his T-shirt. From the small of his back, he drew his father's pistol.

"Maybe over there?"

The ground in front of the warehouse next door seemed to be scratched up. Looking more closely, the shutter-style door looked as if it had been punched in by a speeding car, and the illumination from the interior factory lights leaked under the bent door.

"KYAAA . . . !"

It sounded like fingernails running down a chalkboard, but it took no time to realize that it was someone screaming. Kai's body was immediately in motion.

He ran to the side of the suspicious shutter and rushed to what must have been the employee entrance.

It didn't move. It was locked.

Instead of trying to break off the locked doorknob, Kai carefully smashed through the window next to the door, and reached his arm in to unlock the door from the inside. He flew through the doorway, and then stood for a moment to view the surroundings.

Inside the bare warehouse, he saw Reimi.

She looked as if all her strength had been drained from her, and she had laid down to rest.  No, she was being lifted up. Floating in the air.

She was being carried by the neck between a set of uneven fangs. A single light illuminated the lonely and deformed shape of Forest as the figure holding her.

His face still possessed the basic qualities of the sensitive Marine. But it was the body below his neck that confused Kai. It was a darker-skinned tone and in an elongated, beastly shape. It looked as if a monster was using Forest's face as a mask.

". . . Forest!!"

The demon's shoulders furled tight and it let out a bloody roar. It was then that his pure crimson eyes glowed. This monster that responded to the name "Forest" opened its jaws with a grin.

The desanguinated pale body of Reimi fell to the blood-stained floor. Nothing about her condition indicated that she might still be alive.

The monster roared.

Kai's eyes grew wide, and his lower body squatted in anticipation. Kai released the safety on the pistol.


"Stop the car!"

"Saya-neechan?"

Ignoring the shocked Riku, Saya jumped from her seat.

"Please, stop!"

"Stop here," said Mao, which caused the driver to put on the brakes.

Probably in order to not further upset his already obviously tense passengers, he smoothly decelerated and safely pulled the car to the side of the road.

"What was that all about?" asked Mao, her eyebrows squeezed together dubiously.

Instead of trying to answer her, Saya chose to throw open the rear door and take off down the sidewalk.

She had heard it.

No mistake. It was the same roar. And it wasn't far. But if she didn't hurry . . .

Not stopped at a signal, the large foreign car started receiving honks from the line of cars stuck behind it.

On top of that the cars going the opposite direction were experiencing a similar problem caused by a single vehicle. Tires screeched on the asphalt, and the other car forced itself to the side of the highway and came to a stop.

"Saya!"

She heard the sounds of car doors opening and closing and the sound of David's voice calling from behind her.

Without looking back, Saya barreled down the walkway. She couldn't let that growl get away. She ran in its direction. Every second counted. Faster.

Scraping the rubber soles of her shoes, Saya turned at the corner of a building.

Right then she stopped.

In the darkness stood a tall young man. Over his right shoulder she could see a cello case. It was the same young man as before.

"You can hear the voice, can't you?"

She nodded up and down slightly.

"Tell me. Kai might be there!"

Without even realizing it, Saya had grabbed both of the man's wrists and dug her nails into his sleeves.

"I want to help Kai. I don't want anyone else to get hurt. So I am begging you to tell me what to do."

She glared straight into his eyes, waiting for an answer.

Saya didn't want to fight. She simply wanted to help her family. If that meant she had to fight, then she wanted to know who she was up against. And now.

"..."

Without saying a word, the young man started to unwind the bandage that wrapped his right hand. The exposed limb had the dark and shiny finish of a polished piece of woodwork. He pressed the blade of a short dagger against the fantastic-looking hand, and cut a thin red line along the palm.

At no point did the long face of the young man show any sign of pain.

He then held the oversized and blood-soaked hand to Saya.


"Wait! Come back!"

"I'm sorry. Thank you for the ride," said Riku as politely as he could turning back toward Mao but chasing after his older sister at the same time down the sidewalk.

He saw Saya turn the corner at a nearby building.

Riku had a feeling he knew where Saya was running to. He was sure it was toward the direction of that sound.

Even though he was in the nightclub district, his ears were filled with . . . what was that voice? He had never heard an animal cry out like that. And it was strange that other people didn't seem to react to it.

Sliding around the corner, Riku took one step into the alley and was relieved to see his older sister's backside.

"Why did you leave me behi—?"

Riku's sharp tongue suddenly got very heavy inside his mouth.

He had seen the young man standing in front of Saya somewhere before.

That's right! This was the cello player that played on Park Avenue, sending housewives on their way home from shopping.

Saya noticed his gaze, and looked over her shoulder to meet Riku's.

Her eyes were the same red color as her mouth. Her hand moved over it, but Riku knew what was spread across her lips. It was blood.

"Saya-nee . . . chan . . ."

The words tumbled out of Riku's mouth, and he wasn't even sure that he had said them.

His spinal column felt as if it had been struck by ice.

Until now he had never seen Saya look so mean.

And her eyes—they looked like two moons dipped in blood.

With absolutely no sign of emotion or even recognition, she turned back away from Riku.

As if he was waiting for this, the young man lifted Saya into his arms and bent his knees. He then jumped straight up and their silhouette looked like an owl before they were swallowed up by the darkness far above Riku's head.

The breeze left behind ruffled Riku's bangs.

Riku heard footsteps behind him, but he didn't turn around. He wasn't sure when he did it, but he found himself seated on the ground. He felt tepid beads of sweat form on his back.

"Was that Saya and . . ." said David to himself looking into the sky. He stopped when he got to Riku's side.

"Are you all right?"

"It's growling."

"What?"

". . . What is this? It sounds like a lion . . . What is it? What?!"

Riku grasped his ears as he looked up at David desperately.

The moaning of what sounded like one long breath being exhaled had become more focused, and was rattling his brain.

It was the sound of something on the attack.

✝

The iron was torn through like cardboard.

From inside a container with a shipping company's name and number on the side came an abnormal noise. Kai rolled out of the way to avoid swinging claws.

He rose up just in time to dive under the gigantic arm again, kicking off the ground, and slipped into a gap between some barrels lining the wall.

"Goddamn you, freak . . . !"

He knew better, but he couldn't help but release a little contempt.

Kai didn't think that Forest retained enough sense to understand the insult but—the beast seemed to swing his right arm in response.

The barrels were empty, but still too heavy for a person to lift. Despite that, they were now flying in every direction like popping popcorn, and crashing on the floor with jarringly loud bangs.

The jagged tears in the barrels that had smashed onto the ground reminded Kai of the jaws of insect-eating plants.

Looking for a clear shot, Kai raised the pistol and chose a spot on the monster's chest to aim for.

"Eat this!"

Blasts of gunfire! The recoil from the discharge pushed Kai's arms up and sent him backward.

Bullets didn't land in the chest as planned, but Kai noticed blood streaming from the beast's left shoulder as it stumbled a few steps back.

Kai had correctly predicted that using the gun wouldn't be as easy as they made it look in the cop movies. With his first shots he didn't inflict any damage. He hit concrete and polymer boards that shattered like glass windows, so a bullet into the actual target could be considered a step toward success.

Yet even with that small victory, the enemy was not finished.

Several small silver specks of metal were pushed out of the shoulder wound and landed on the tire skids on the floor. It was the crushed remains of the bullet.

Kai knew when a hollow point shell entered a person's body that it broke apart, causing massive damage to the flesh and organs, but in the case of the body of a monster like this, the results were obviously different.

There were no traces that the monster had taken a bullet in the shoulder moments before.

The claws of the beast tore through the last barrel from the bottom up. There was nothing left to shield Kai from the creature. Kai tried to escape to his side, but a giant container blocked his path. He was cornered.

"Shit."

There was no need to escape. Even if he was thickskulled, a shot to the head should do it.

Kai steadied the pistol and pulled the trigger, but what came out were only words of frustration from Kai's mouth.

Nothing happened.

Did it jam? No. Out of bullets.

". . . You gotta be kidding."

If fate had appeared in human form at that moment, Kai would have never grown tired of punching it in the face.

The angry and shaking Kai's field of vision was filled with the red eyes and white fangs of the huge creature.

Haa . . . The monster let out a long breath, smothering Kai with the stink of blood.

So this is how it would end.

This was how Kai would die.

Without knowing if his dad pulled through or not.

Five very real claws drew closer to Kai.

Kai clenched his teeth and closed his eyes.

In the next moment his throat would be sliced open.

But that moment never came.

Frozen with fear, it took all of his power to open his glued down eyelids.

The monster was still there. Its pointed claws were just in front of Kai's nose.

Yet it wasn't looking at Kai. Its chin pointed upward as the monster stared toward the ceiling.

Suddenly a gust of wind blew through the giant open space.

Between the monster's flanks and long arms, Kai saw what looked like bat wings expand outward. The monster raised the wings up above its body.

After several flaps the monster flew up toward the high store-house ceiling. It was hard to see in the darkness, but it seemed to tear a hole in the roof and disappear.

Pieces of tile and scrap fell from above, and Kai squatted down to protect himself. Feeling confident that the building itself wasn't about to collapse, Kai stretched out a knee.

"What the hell is going on?" muttered Kai. His question received a response in the form of a thunderous boom.

It sounded as if someone had swung a giant hammer into the metal shutter covering the entrance.

Something was going on outside. Kai's eyes stopped on Reimi's pale dead body. After a few moments of hesitation, he ran for the entrance.

Kai opened the door, and when he looked to the left, he saw something move quickly in the corner of his eye.

It was the monster.

Extracting its body from the shutter, it rushed forward.

It was headed toward the figure of a defenseless man. The cello player.

"Look out!"

As was expected, the man didn't react to Kai's warning. He had already been informed by the figure of his sister in her school uniform, standing behind the young man.

As it turned out, he should have been warning the monster.

The young man deflected the striking claws with the cello case, and then spun the giant figure like a tornado. Kicked in the leg hard enough to break bones, the beast fell to one knee. Aiming for the side of the monster's head, the young man rotated once, swinging the cello case into its target.

The giant body tumbled through the air like a discarded piece of trash. It slammed into the metal shutter, again, and was wrapped up in the mangled door.

The monster wasn't going to put up with this humiliation time and time again.

With a menacing howl, the beast shook off the metal scrap of the shutter and like a four-legged beast leapt up and began to climb the outside wall. Klak klak klak—the beast made it close to the roof, high in the ocean breeze, and then kicked the wall with tremendous strength.

From the end of the fingers of his right hand, Kai barely saw the silvery glint as the young man casually flicked his wrist. The cross-shaped dagger flashed in front of the numbers on the front of the building, heading straight for its target. But the target jumped toward the ground, and the dagger missed by a hair.

It looked like a pterodactyl as it spread its wings in the night air. It arched up, and then came back around, picking up speed.

"Saya!"

Saya half closed her eyes, and didn't move.

Just as the beast, swooping at a steep angle, was about to snatch its trophy, a snack of pulverized flesh and bone, it was the young man, again, who got in its way. The single-minded beast was on a straight course for the defenseless Saya, when the tall man bounded in with a series of jumps from the side. The demon swung a giant arm at the intruder, and the young man caught the swing in his hand with relative ease. Using the angle of the beast's attack against it, the young man squatted down slightly and pushed up and forward against the blow, causing a considerably painful counter to the temporal attack.

With no chance to bellow its pain, the demon's own momentum was used to spin it to the ground with a thud. He rolled past Saya like a crashing airplane.

Landing smoothly, with only his cuffs and long hair disturbed, the young man wasn't even breathing hard.

"Wow . . ."

Kai couldn't help but respond out loud.

They were moving so fast, it was difficult for Kai to see everything that was happening. What's more, he couldn't believe humans could move like this.

He had caught the monster's swing, crushed its elbow, smashed it in the head and sent it rolling all at the same time. No extravagance, all moves done efficiently. He had an ingenious approach at weaponless combat.

But what was even more impressive was that he was using these moves against a monster.

Kreeee! . . . The hair-raising sound echoed throughout the abandoned warehouse street.

Ten claws scraped across the concrete, and it stopped its ugly glide with force. The monster wriggled its dorsal muscles oddly, and then stood up.

"Not a scratch on it . . ."

To be more clear, it would get scratched, but within moments the cut or injury was gone.

The same was true when Kai shot it with the pistol. The areas cut up from the friction on the roadway were at this very moment bulging out flesh, and the bent-backward right elbow was fixing itself.

It was either in anticipation of the regeneration of its body, or maybe it was more pain than the demon could endure, but it was kicking the ground with both feet.

With none of the elegance of a large bird, the flying goblin took to the air and came around to attempt a swooping attack on Saya's backside.

"Saya!"

This girl, who had been facing the ground looking as if she was taking a nap, suddenly lifted her head up.

Her wide-open eyes were painted a rich ruby color.

With her right hand she pulled the grip of the large sword from the scabbard she held in her left.

She cut her thumb at the base of the blade and her blood flowed down the blade as if it had arteries.

The blade cut through the air with a pointed exhalation.

From the hilt to the point was dyed a rich, red fire.

Following Saya's motion, the arc of her blade matched that of the moon, and, for a moment, a red glaze hung in the air bisecting the heavens.

Accompanied by a gust of wind, a giant shadow fell over Saya's head.

The exhausted and shaking Saya corrected her posture and returned the sword to its sheath.

PACHIN—the unmistakable sound of a blade.

It was a sign of death.

The giant bird-like form which had swooped down like a paper airplane spewed a fountain of blood from its mouth.

The beast was sliced open from its right shoulder through its abdomen, and its flesh and insides were spilling out.

Starting from the wound, the nearly bisected demon began to transform, and by the time it hit on the concrete, nearly its entire body had crystallized.

The crash broke the lifeless monster into thousands of pieces which slid across the ground.

Kai took a deep gulp.

At that same moment Saya fell to her knees. She was hugging her sword with her shoulders hunched over. She was crying.

He searched his heart for comforting words to say to his sister, but nothing came.


The situation was far from ideal, but they did collect some valuable physical evidence.

One of these was in a watertight bag that Louis placed in the back of the van—the remains of the Chiropteran. They also collected the remains of a female victim named Reimi. Julia would surely be excited to get a sample from this body.

The last piece of evidence stood bathed in the van's break lights. It was a chance meeting with the young man.

The decades-old, faded photo with the man dressed as a servant overlapped exactly with the cool features of the young man standing right before David's eyes.

"Are you the one that follows Saya's orders?"

No response.

He only gripped the strap in his cello case and gazed at Saya, sitting quietly on the bare ground in the empty night. From her profile David saw a wise but melancholy expression, and she was shaking. The thin cotton blanket wrapped around her shoulder did little to help. Battle must be horrifying for her.

". . . Has she completely awakened?"

"Not yet."

David was discouraged by the young man's mumble of an answer.

Red Shield would not yet be able to play its trump card, and Saya would still suffer in this incomplete state. On the other hand, having made contact with him was real progress.

"Kai-niichan."

It was George's youngest son, Riku, calling out to his older brother.

The older brother didn't look at him.

". . . I couldn't do anything this time, either."

He was a wild kid who didn't know the meaning of self-control or consequences, yet his answer to his brother seemed rather thoughtful.

The demons were not simple opponents for those too attached to their emotions. Twice he had encountered Chiropterans, and twice he had lived. There was more than a little luck involved there.

David's train of thought was interrupted by the ring of his cell phone.

"It's me. What's wrong?"

From the other end of the line, Julia gave David some unexpected information.

George Miyagusuku had been transported from the ICU at Sogo Hospital. Naturally, it wasn't by her request. All of his family was there with David.

"What is going on?"

"I don't know. But I did see the convoy transport him to Kadena Air Base."

"The Army?"

"Their investigation into the Koza Commercial High School incident the other night must have led them to him . . ."

David clenched his teeth.

He shouldn't have admitted George into a regular hospital. Julia's clinic didn't have the proper equipment, and at that moment he was concerned with getting George out of danger, but if he had taken into consideration how insidious the Army's intelligence network had become recently, this never would have happened.

"Understood. Let's put a plan together when we meet."

After David hung up the phone, he gave a summary of what had happened to Kai and Riku.

They were George's family. They deserved to know.

"Father?"

Saya, who had been in a daze up until that moment, woke up like she had been slapped in the face.

"What happened? Why Father . . . ?"

"We don't know. Julia just saw it happen."

"She just watched them take Dad away without saying anything?!"

The son, Kai, lurched forward trying to grab David by his collar, but David deftly grabbed his hands first and returned them to Kai's hips.

"If they catch on to what we are doing, they'll be glued to us like stink on shit."

Information on the attack at OMORO must have made its way from the prefectural police to the U.S. Army. If David did anything to bring attention to himself, the results would be equivalent to self-strangulation.

More important than finding the source of the Chiropterans was keeping his Army friends away and keeping the present state of Red Shield a secret.

"So what're you going to do to help Dad?"

"The very best I can."

Releasing his fingers from Kai's wrists, David's gaze turned to Saya.

"If my guess is right, there is a Chiropteran where they have taken George. We are going to need you."

"Me . . . ?"

"Yes. Come with us."

Like an unsure child, Saya pulled the blanket tighter around her shoulders.

Saya looked over to her older brother for help with constructing an answer.

But Kai didn't say a word. His eyes wandered everywhere but Saya's face.

"All right."

The now calm Saya almost seemed to laugh as she answered. It was in the way someone who had given up responded to bad news.

"David," called Louis quietly after shutting the van's rear doors. Apparently everything had been stowed away.

Without having to say a word, Saya started walking toward the vehicle.

The young man with the cello case on his back followed behind her as if it was his duty.

David turned to look at George's sons.

"You two as well. If the police pick you up and our cover is blown, it will cause serious repercussions."

"Niichan . . ."

"I know."

Giving his little brother the shortest response he could, Kai turned and walked toward his motorcycle.

Riku quickly followed him, but then turned back.

Like it was the most natural thing to do, the young attendant stopped and peered over toward the young boys.

"Um . . . Thank you. I mean, you protected Saya-neechan, right?"

". . . No."

David heard it not as a counter to Riku's question, but as a humble, self-effacing reply.

Riku turned and jumped on the bike behind his waiting brother.

## 03

IN THE IRRESOLUTE summer of the southern part of the country, the sky in October was dyed the same color as the sky in July.

"Even the heat and cold wait for the equinoxes . . ."

Pulling down the zipper to open his vest, Akihiro Okamura turned from the parking lot toward the main entrance of Naha University.

The majority of a newspaper reporter's work time was dedicated to follow-up research on stories, but this was nothing less than a fishing expedition for a lead. The police cited the Status of Forces Agreement for their inability to cooperate. That's one issue, but not the only one.

To avoid backlash from the Japanese public it was very normal for the American Army to allow a "cooling-off" period before turning over a suspect to the Japanese authorities. Even more crucial than that, the attention span of the mainland media was shorter than the tempers of the local citizens, and it wasn't long before they were focused on the next big scoop.

Though they claim it is in the interest of public safety, the general opinion is that the police bow down to the inferior intelligence of the American military much too easily. This has been deemed wrong by the TV media reporters in the press office. The supra-legal tactics by the American government and military are then sold back to the Japanese public as brave and noble.

That might work for maintaining diplomacy. America guarantees Japan's honor is maintained, and Japan can't resist. Regardless, the American military is only held to the American law, and in the present state of Japanese thinking this is acceptable, as Japan depends on America's military strength to maintain security in the region.

It always follows the same script like a theatrical performance.

People who were born and live in Okinawa don't trust Japan, as they were practically given to America. Of course, they love Japan, but they don't feel loved by Japan. Cut off and tossed away after the war, it's like they were a burden on Japan's back, sacrificed to benefit the entire country. That's the sense of the people of Okinawa.

Yet Okinawa-born Okamura found this most recent incident especially bizarre.

It wasn't only that the Army was protecting their accused suspect, but they had taken the victim's body, and continuously rejected requests for its return by the bereaved family.

"What am I doing here?"

He had gotten frustrated, but there was no need for him to swim against the feelings of Okinawa's citizens.

Commanded by his editor, Takeda, to get this story, Okamura had driven around so much the last few days there was probably a noticeable increase in global warming. Finally, as a last hope, he had made his way back here.

"Hello, it's Okamura."

He had walked through the door not waiting for a response to his knock.

The research lab was just as cluttered as it always was.

Avoiding a tower of books stacked up from the floor, he made his way to the rear of the room. On the shelves of specimens there was a supposedly three-million-yen detailed model of the human body, plastinated internal organs and some perfectly preserved slices of a human brain.

"You again. What do you want today?" asked the middle-aged professor sitting at the desk by the window surround by chaos. He adjusted his glasses as he looked up at Okamura.

"C'mon, Professor, don't be like that. Let's have a little chat. It's about that recent mysterious case . . ."

Although it was covered with carefully arranged reports, Okamura sat down on the room's sole sofa.

"You know, the one where the victim's throat was cut and the body was drained of all its blood. You did the autopsy, right, Professor?"

"And what if I did?"

This old man was more than just a well-known authority on human anatomy, but he also performed a lot of autopsies as a forensic pathologist. As a crime reporter, Okamura often asked him for his opinions, and for better or for worse, the two had become acquaintances.

"I was just thinking how people would react if I were to print that the soldier the Army captured at Koza High was actually a vampire . . ."

"Indeed, I was called in by the police to perform an autopsy investigation. But the Army barged in during the autopsy and took the body. I wasn't able to complete an investigation."

"And the body of the victim has been kept at the base ever since."

"Yes. I was so angry, I did take photos of those who took the body."

Like an old tree, the professor's fist slammed hard down onto a pile of documents on his desk.

Okamura noticed a few pictures tucked between the pages. It appeared they were taken secretly with the camera used to record autopsies. A pretty bold move for the old man.

"Oh, I'd love to see them."

"You can't expect me to show them to an outsider."

After a few moments of silence the professor rose from his chair. He turned his back to Okamura, and headed toward the hot water pot near the window.

"Coffee fine with you?"

"Oh, uh . . . please," answered Okamura as he stood up and hopped over to the professor's desk. "Don't you think they have gotten a little big for their britches lately?"

"Our voices can't make it to the inside of the fence. Nothing has changed from the past. That's the reality of Okinawa."

The professor did not turn back toward Okamura. He took his time preparing the cups of coffee.

Okamura took advantage of his "kindness." He opened up the notebook on the professor's desk and pulled out the photos.

As a photographer himself, Okamura initially noticed that the pictures weren't quite in focus, and that the subject of the shots was sometimes cut off by the edge of the photo, but what was captured was still quite fascinating.

The photos depicted men in full body bacterial protection getups.

The metal containers they were transporting had biohazard seals on them.

If they were just transporting the remains of a corpse, this was really overdoing it.

"And this isn't the only body the Army has taken in these phantom attack cases."

This was turning into a truly extraordinary story.


Stepping out onto the rooftop, the sky shone an incredible cobalt blue.

For some reason it was easier to relax out here than it was inside.

Three days was a really long time.

When doing a high jump, you focus on seeing yourself as high in the air as possible in order to make it over the bar. Timing your breathing, you dash as fast as you possibly can and then push off the ground with your legs to get into the air.

It is at that moment, when Saya imagines she has wings and is floating as time slows down . . . that sensation and her present comprehension of the importance of time and of cohesion couldn't feel more separate.

She hadn't heard any new information about George.

David hadn't allowed her to go home or to go to school. She had been staying at Julia's clinic, and all she could do was wait for some good news.

"Things are never going to be the same again . . ."

Everything she had known up until now would be different.

So what would life be like from now on?

She didn't like getting mixed up in conflicts. But if there was something she could do to help George, she wouldn't hesitate one second.

She walked toward the young man—whom she eventually had learned was named Hagi—standing in the shadow of the building's water tower.

"Are you going to help me?"

"If that is what you wish," he answered curtly, without any change in expression. She felt his lack of emotion was very sincere.

"Thank you."

At this point she still didn't know what kind of person he was, or why he was willing to help her. All she knew was that he knew more about her than she did. The confidence she felt in her ability to trust him began to grow.

The door leading back inside the clinic opened up.

David's leather shoes stepped out onto the sun-bleached concrete.

She could see Julia as well. She wore the bland white doctor's garb like an Emilo Pucci summer coat, accentuating her curves.

"We know where George is located."

"Father?"

She was hoping to hear something positive, but David's expression kept her from getting her hopes up.

"He is at the Yanbaru Nature Conservation Center."

"It is a research institution created to protect and study the unique flora and fauna of Yanbaru's ecology. It's a U.S. Army facility, but civilians are also able to study there," explained Julia.

"But why there . . . ?"

"It must be a front. They tout the facility as an environmental protection institution, but we have found that they are bringing in a lot of DNA sequencing equipment. That doesn't seem so natural."

"Louis was able to determine, just like in our phantom attacker case, the Army has secured the bodies of other victims and taken them to Yanbaru. The only facility in that area where the Army is seen coming and going is the nature conservatory. We can presume that George is there, as well."

Which meant the monsters called Chiropterans were there, too.

David's extra cool composure was probably to suppress his anxiety. Saya thought she would probably need to adopt this attitude as well, even if it was out of harmony with the Okinanwan way.

"We'll leave tonight. The mission will require me, you, Hagi, and then Loius. Got it?"

"Yes," said Saya as she nodded her head stiffly. She then heard the angry shout of her older brother.

"Just wait a minute!"

Kai came to get into David's face.

"Are you just planning on going off with out us?"

"Kai-niichan, cut it out! David-san is going to go help Dad," pleaded Riku, following a few steps behind his brother."

"That's what I am saying! He's our father. Did I agree to just sit around and wait?"

Kai brushed away Riku's hands that were tugging at his sleeve and glared into David's cold eyes.

"You are taking us with you."

"You'll only get in the way."

"No! We won't!"

"You need to learn your place."

"Won't you please teach me then?!"

What Kai did next showed a real lack of manners.

He leaned on his right leg, turned his upper torso, and swung a fist at David.

The perfectly aimed shot coming from a lower diagonal straight at David's chin was stopped short by David's hand.

When Kai pulled back he received a painful punch to his flank, and then his legs were kicked out from underneath him, sending him straight to the concrete.

"Kai!"

"Niichan!"

Both Saya and Riku tried to run over to Kai, but their legs stopped moving when he shouted back at them.

". . . Keep your mouths shut."

Rubbing his side he lifted himself and looked over at Saya and Riku. He gave them a cramped smile.

"You were going to teach me right? My place?"

"With pleasure."

David removed his jacket and loosened the buttons at his cuffs to roll up his sleeves. Julia held his jacket, yet had a look of resignation.

"You are serious?" she asked.

"If I am not serious he won't learn anything."

Even though the educator was dedicated to his lesson, the student didn't seem to have any concern for his own safety.

David couldn't blame Kai for suddenly striking out at him again.

He simply moved his head out of the way, allowing Kai to hit nothing but air. The following barrage was a strategic chess game of David moving away in counter-rhythm to Kai's punches. Not one of Kai's strikes came close to landing on David's face.

It was just like that time before.

In Saya's mind she overlapped the spectacle of these two going back and forth with the scene at the beach. Attacking

Hagi in a frenzy, Kai ended up looking like a child. It was the same this time, with Kai lunging at David. Nothing is accomplished, and he just ends up looking silly. Besides his tussles with Dad, Kai had always boasted how he had never lost a fight, even with adults.

Saya got it. David, Kai, and Hagi had all done the unimaginable. They had battled with Chiropterans and survived.

David had allowed the young boy to expend his energy on fruitless attacks long enough. Now it was his turn to go on the offensive.

It took just one punch.

The blow to Kai's gut caused him to vomit air as he fell to his knees.

As Kai groaned, facing the ground on all fours, David shot a sobering look at the back of his head.

"You think this is over?"

Suddenly Kai's body darted quickly.

Keeping his left hand planted on the ground, he used it as an axis to sweep his right foot around just over the surface of the concrete.

He missed his target's leg by a hair's breadth, and as a result, David remained standing. On the contrary, David's foot, which had risen up to avoid the strike, came back down.

Kai crossed both arms in the air, and the heel of the shoe landed on his shoulder.

"Ooof!"

Kick after kick came to the spot where Kai was kneeling. His arms couldn't block the barrage. From the corner of his eye he saw the sole of a shoe coming toward his head, and the next moment Kai went flying sideways.

If the wire screen hadn't been there, he likely would have fallen off the roof of the clinic.

With the loud crash into the mesh, Kai didn't stand up. He'd had enough.

"This is the world we live in. It's not a place for delinquents and gangsters who fight in the streets."

"..."

"Saya, let's go."

As David faced the doorway and slipped his arms into the jacket Julia held out for him, Saya didn't answer.

"...Saya..."

The moan from Kai kept Saya from moving.

Without turning around, she could see him. She could see her older brother trying to pull himself out of the wire mesh screen that had saved his life.

"Stay here," she told him as she continued to face forward.

Her own voice sounded like it came from far away. It was someone else telling him.

"Stay here and wait with Riku."

"Wha-what are you saying?"

"You'll just be in the way. It's like David said, there's nothing you can do, Kai."

No.

She wanted him to be next to her. That was the truth.

But the family shouldn't be wrapped into this any more than it already was. Kai and Riku . . . and George.

Without a doubt, she was bringing Father home.

"So wait here."

Saya walked through the darkened doorway.

Following the lead that Hagi and the others had just made, Saya entered the building and made her way down the stairs.

She didn't look back at her brothers sitting in the white sun, but the glares on her back were truly painful.

At night, the forest gets denser. The shine from the moon and stars cannot break through the thick layer of foliage covering the living world above the earth.

On this Yanbaru night, the syrupy darkness was interrupted by an unnatural illumination.

Birds and insects weren't expecting the headlights of the car which pulled to a stop on the dirt road. The driver, David, got out of the car and walked over to another vehicle stopped on the side of the road.

Saya stepped out of the car to get a whiff of the forest air, and noticed where David was going.

"You brought the weapons?"

"Right here," answered the overweight black man who was wearing sunglasses, even though it was night, as he opened the rear of his car.

His name was Louis, and he was a member of Red Shield. There was little doubt he was a fan of French fries as a late-night snack.

His trunk was arranged like the produce section of a supermarket.

But what were on display weren't fruits or vegetables, but matte black and in a variety of shapes and sizes.

David picked up a long gun that looked like what the SWAT teams used in American movies when they storm a location.

"This will do."

Saya was pretty sure it was called a "shotgun."

"Is that all? That won't kill a Chiropteran."

"I won't be the one hunting Chiropterans."

"Are you sure you guys are okay?"

"We have no other choice."

Saya sensed the gaze of the two men, and turned away.

Right then Hagi opened the trunk of the car they had been riding in and removed his cello case.

Even though they were about to begin a dangerous assignment, this tall man moved as if nothing was at all out of the ordinary. He was still wearing his tailored suit.

Now that she thought about it, David was still wearing his suit, and Saya was still in her school uniform. Maybe she should have put on her track wear, but being stuck at Julia's clinic for so many days, she really didn't have anything to change into.

Suddenly Hagi put out his left hand.

"Huh? What is this?"

"A package for you."

It was a wrapped ball, about the size of a cantaloupe. Saya hadn't seen this before.

Saya picked up the ball and pulled away the wrapping. What she uncovered was a giant-sized rice-ball.

"Is this . . . from you, Hagi?"

"No."

Of course it wasn't. For some reason she couldn't imagine Hagi cooking. Least of which, creating a melon-sized *onigiri*.

Inside the wrapping was a note on a piece of scrap paper.

*Do your best.*

That's all it said. But those three little words caused Saya to sniffle.

"Kai . . . Riku . . ."

Saya wanted to get home as soon as she could to thank them.

All she could do at that moment to show her appreciation was to eat the unusually large rice ball.

"Thank you."

Eating was one thing she knew she could do.

And when you eat, the food becomes energy for your body.

As David discussed his request with Louis, Louis stared stunned at the young lass consuming the giant *onigiri* at a break-neck speed. With the corners of her mouth speckled with grains of white rice, Saya gave the young man an order.

"Hagi, my katana."

Reflexively, as if he had done this countless times before, Hagi opened the cello case and held out to Saya the sword she requested.

She grasped the scabbard. The heavy iron weight was reassuring.

She was about to fight.

The energy she received from Kai and Riku would make her that much stronger.

"It's not like I am being difficult."

As he sat on the sofa with his legs crossed, Van compared the two high-ranking American Army officers in his mind.

It was amusing watching their respective mimetic muscles convulse and tighten.

"Dust always settles after a strike, if that dust isn't cleaned up, it will get back at you, correct?"

"You are the ones that created 'Delta 67.'"

He was correct about that.

The yet-to-be-released Delta 67 was indeed manufactured by Van's company, Cinq Flèche Pharmaceuticals. However, its practical use here, in Okinawa, was by the U.S. Army, and them alone.

Van figured that "personal responsibility" was not a term that appeared in any American dictionary.

"'When using this product, please pay strict attention to the warnings listed.' I am almost positive it says this on the label."

"You wouldn't dare . . ."

The stereotypically well-built American colonel conspicuously grinded his teeth.

Recently the atmosphere in the Kadena Base control room was tense due to the inquiry and discipline meetings, 80 percent of which were thanks to him.

"Instead of getting upset, how about a piece of candy?"

" . . ."

Van extended his right hand holding the wrapped piece of Juntsuyu brand hard candy he had been fiddling with until that point, but the only response he got was the Colonel's rolled eyes. To Van, he looked like a drunk when he did that.

Despite its simple presentation, this was one refined piece of candy. Thinking about it, the black tea flavor candy he plucked from the variety pack would probably be wasted on a typical American palette.

"This all happened because you let a 'mouse' escape from Yanbaru."

From Van's perspective, Delta 67 was still in the developmental stage, and should have still been considered a hazardous substance. Well, it would be more accurate to call it "specimen grade" material.

That's why he was brought in to act as a monitor. Up until now the U.S. Army was its own monitor, and that's why mistakes like this happened.

"So, naturally, I am here as an advisor and I also have expertise in 'cleanup' operations. It would be a waste to have come this far and ended up with negative results . . . you must agree."

The nature conservatory was now infested with "mice."

The "mice" had escaped.

The recent release of two "mice" into the general populace had indeed been forgiven, as the whole situation made for fascinating research for Van, but he hadn't forgotten the tiniest mistake could bring the entire empire down in the blink of an eye.

Van had no choice but to place a question mark on the American Army's crisis management abilities, as they didn't seem to learn well from their own mistakes.

They should be worried about one of the two "mice" that had escaped which was tracked to a warehouse area near the harbor, but which had disappeared.

At a warehouse and on the street outside they'd discovered bullets, bullet holes, and a small amount of a crystallized mineral. There was little doubt that the samurai man who had sliced open the first mouse had also done the same to the second one.

After that, with no mention of the "mouse" from any media outlet, Van was able to conclude that the parties responsible for the death and removal of the "mouse" must be a clandestine organization working outside the scope of the Army.

Van was not one to believe in fate, but it was very possible that the breakdown situation at Yanbaru Nature Conservatory Center was divine intervention.

It would be best to be done with the whole place.

"I will repeat my humble request for your assistance. Commander, how about putting Option D into effect?"

"Leaving Yanbaru a crater?" asked the base commander in a stony voice. Quiet through most of the conversation, the base commander had listened as his head rested on his hand with his elbow on the desk.

"No, think of it as returning it to the jungle."

It was written in the Bible—dust to dust.

"Impossible. The uproar that would cause is unimaginable."

"This way the damage is limited to the Center. If not, Okinawa could be infested with 'mice.'"

"But . . ."

"Commander, this isn't a decision that we can wait on," offered the Colonel, giving the defeated-looking man responsible his support.

". . . All right, then."

"The world's police, doing their job. This superb decision will bring order to the chaos."

The commander glared at Van bitterly. Van popped a cylindrical-shaped candy into his mouth.

"If there was any way possible, I don't want to use it, Monsieur Argeno. This will put a strain on our relations with Japan."

"That's what the Status of Forces Agreement is for. The real issues are the 'mice' and Delta 67. If we don't get them in order, your president will likely be forced to give up his office."

The commander didn't immediately respond to Van's remarks. He was no longer in the mood for cynicism. The commander stood up from his seat and faced the colonel standing at the edge of his desk. He handed him a laminated card.

"Brickman, Richard. Today's code is Tango. Alpha. Echo. Zero three zero four. Option D approved. Order to execute."

"Yes, sir. Immediately."

With a muscular salute, the colonel turned from the commander. He and Van watched the colonel speed out of the room.

"The preparations should take about two hours."

"I see. But it's too bad. It looks like I won't have time for the fireworks display. I have orders from headquarters to fly to the next location."

As the hard candy rolled around in his mouth, Van stood up from the sofa.

It was time to leave this Far East country.

It was a short stay, but very valuable.

It was just dumb luck that he was able to acquire a sample from a dead "mouse." The Delta 67 research team should be inspired by that.

On top of that, he was surprised by the variety and quality of Japanese candy. It was hard to admit, but the candy available on the market in Japan exceeded those of the French sweets. If Cinq Flèche Corporation ever entered this field in the future, the Japanese market would be a tough one to crack.

On the downside, Okinawa is too influenced by America. And for that reason, Okinawa rubbed Van the wrong way.

This representative of America in front of him snorted in dissatisfaction.

"Leaving before it's all over?"

"I believe in you. We are partners, aren't we?"

Van extended a hand to wish farewell, but it was only met with the commander's sharp glare. Nothing more.

Hunching his shoulders, Van retracted the lonely hand.

"I wish you nothing but the best of luck. *Au revoir, Commandant*."

It seemed like the hands of the clock had barely moved.

Surely it had been at least three hours since Saya and David left, but looking at the clock hanging on the wall in the waiting room, it had really only been about an hour.

As he sat on the sofa Kai unconsciously tried to speed time up by breathing out his nose and smacking his lips repeatedly.

"I wonder if Saya-neechan found Dad yet . . ."

"Who knows?" answered Kai bluntly to Riku's question. Riku sat on the sofa next to Kai, and had also been staring at the clock the entire time. This must have been the fifth time they had had this exchange.

"When Dad gets back, we'll be able to go back to the same old lifestyle we had, won't we?"

Kai didn't answer.

But Riku was a smart kid. He found an answer in the silence.

"I need to return a game I borrowed to Atsushi, and I didn't tell the Kinjou family where I was going when I left . . ."

"Things will go back to normal."

That was all he could say. Kai hoped it would come true, too.

"I promise. It will all go back to normal."

"I wonder why all this had to happen . . ."

"I don't know. Ever since those Chiropteran monsters showed up, everything's been all screwed up."

Even recalling those episodes in his head, they still didn't feel real to Kai.

He had seen the not-human-but-not-animal—whatever they were—two times now. When they were standing right in front of him he was scared out of his mind, but now thinking about it, he really couldn't believe they existed and were walking around in this world.

Open any animal book and you'll find creatures much stranger. Look at the animals that live under high pressure at the bottom of the ocean, or at the bizarre creatures crawling around under the fallen leaves in the dense jungles. They still seemed more real to Kai than the Chiropterans.

It might have been because they had some resemblance to humans that he found them so frightening.

"What did you say?!"

It was Julia's voice.

Kai hadn't realized that she spoke Japanese fluently.

From the dim waiting room, it was easy for Kai to spot her through the crack in the doorway of the brightly lit examination room.

Until now Kai had only heard her smooth-as-glass calm voice, so hearing her shriek threw Kai for a loop. Something was seriously wrong.

Opening the door to the examination room, Kai saw the beautiful doctor frozen in place, holding her cell phone at her side.

"What's wrong?" asked Riku.

"They have initiated Option D . . ."

"Option D?" asked Kai.

Julia may have been only partially conscious when she answered Riku's question, yet after Kai opened his mouth her gaze slowly turned toward them.

The white color of her face at that moment was as pale as Kai had ever seen a Caucasian.

"The U.S. Army is planning an air strike on Yanbaru in three hours."

Air strike?

Kai was struck speechless for a few moments.

It wasn't like the USA was dependant on Okinawa, a part of Japan, as an economic resource. Would Okinawa be blown apart like the set of a war movie?

"Wait . . . Did you tell the group that went to Yanbaru?"

Her thin limbs that wouldn't look out of place in a Paris fashion show loosened like a doll's, and she fell back into her chair.

"All transmissions into that area are being jammed. We have no way of getting a hold of them. Route 58 is the fastest way there, but it is so jammed at this hour, we'll never make it in time."

"So, then . . ."

Riku looked up at the two older people in the room for reassurance, until Kai interrupted him.

"My motorcycle is parked out back, right?"

Julia immediately figured out what Kai was thinking.

"You can't . . ."

"On a bike you can't get stuck in traffic."

"Stop! It's too dangerous. And if you didn't make it in time . . ."

"I'll make it in time," Kai declared with a strong assertion, but an impatient undertone. "That is something I can do . . . It's all I can do."

This Okinawa conflict seemed to have struck Julia quite hard.

The fact that there was no time to argue or discuss it was one thing she and Kai could both agree on.

"Oh, all right. Please, hurry."

"And please watch Riku. Riku, I am not coming home without Dad and Saya, got it?"

"Un-huh."

Kai heard his brother's response after he had already turned to go. His body flew through the hallway toward the rear exit.

The elevator stopped moving and the door split in half to the left and right.

At the same moment, Saya lifted her head in surprise, holding her breath for a moment.

"Wha—?"

A man was lying on the floor.

He must have been a researcher. He wore a white robe, but she could see that his back was wet with a dark red stain. Something the color of meat peeked through under the lab coat.

"It's all right. He's dead," said David after checking the body. David lifted his pistol and proceeded down the corridor from the elevator.

"It's safe. Let's hurry."

"O-okay."

Saya had felt weak in the knees since getting off the elevator. She gripped her katana with both hands and moved to get as far away from that corpse as she could.

To the left appeared to be a security station. One wall entirely made of glass. Another was covered with monitors, but they all must have been broken as the screens showed nothing but gray.

The ambiance down here was very different from the atmosphere above ground.

All places called nature conservation centers were basically small-scale museums. There are carefully tended tropical plants and stuffed versions of endangered birds and wildcats. These displays are arranged in an attractive and efficient way throughout the building.

Naturally they had entered after hours. The lights were out and the staff had all gone home.

They discovered a gigantic freight elevator, and when they got out in the basement, it looked like the inside of a completely different building.

As if white lights banished any dirt or germs away, the sterile corridor felt like being inside a white rectangle.

David's gait slowed. He must have been committing the layout to memory.

"Isn't it kind of strange that the man was dead?"

"I know what happened."

With no change of expression, David moved toward a door facing the corridor.

Next to the door was a keypad. Apparently the intention was for visitors to enter a pass code to go through the door, but David had received an ID card from Louis.

As David quickly glanced through the door after it opened outward obediently, Saya was struck dumb.

The floor and fixtures of this locker room were all drenched the same color red.

The blood came from all the human bodies scattered around the room.

Maybe the person that had almost made it to the elevator had had better luck. He didn't have to see all his coworkers being slaughtered and he'd lived a few moments longer, perhaps.

"Horrible . . ."

It was stating the obvious, but she hadn't grown accustomed to seeing human death.

Turning away from the vicious scene, Saya's shoulders hit something hard, and whatever it was grasped her softly.

She looked up to see Hagi's face looking around the room. His hands held her shoulders. He had no emotional reaction whatsoever. The blood which covered the room might as well have been water. His calm composure reassured Saya.

David didn't show one iota of change, either.

As if they were bales of hay, David walked between the corpses and stopped at a long desk to start typing at the laptop computer sitting on it. The screen lit up, the only bright spot in the room.

Saya noticed that the room was almost completely lined up with rows of tall-standing locker-like metal boxes, but something was different.

These weren't lockers like she was used to. They housed computer equipment. It was nothing a high-school student would be too familiar with, but Saya guessed that these were all servers of some kind.

"Where is Father?"

"That's what I am looking up right now."

With his gun propped on the desk, David's eyes darted across the computer screen as his fingers hammered the keyboard. Suddenly his brow wrinkled.

He pulled a RAM card from his cell phone and inserted it into the proper slot on the side of the laptop.

"Did you learn something?"

David's answer wasn't what she was expecting.

"It seems the American Army has been artificially manufacturing Chiropterans here."

"Manufacture? Those monsters?"

So the Chiropteran at the school and Chiropteran Forest were born here?

From embryonic stem cells, they had made clones of sheep and cows.

She had heard on the news that the use of this technology ventures into murky ethical water, but she didn't think that was true when it came to the creation of Chiropterans.

"But why would they do that?"

"According to our records, up until the Vietnam War, incidents involving Chiropterans were relatively few. Across the world there was maybe one incident every few years. But since the war, the incidence rate has skyrocketed."

Saya was more concerned about George, but didn't have the nerve to say anything.

She still didn't know what species of animal the Chiropterans were. What she did know was that somehow she was connected to them.

"If you look at the locations of the incidents, all of them took place where an international conflict was occurring. Incidents where the American military was involved."

English writing scrolled down the computer screen.

"There's one more thing—in places where the Chiropterans were reported, the U.S. military was present, and they always used their Far East base as a jumping-off point to go to areas of conflict."

"You don't mean—"

"Right. Here in Okinawa. We came here to find out what was happening in Okinawa."

Then this research facility was the main target of David's group's mission. So knowing that Chiropterans were connected with the American military brought Red Shield that much closer to their goal of complete Chiropteran annihilation. But this still didn't explain Saya's involvement with the Chiropterans, and Red Shield still wouldn't be able to shed light on that point.

To hunt the wolf, the hunter must sleep in the same forest as the wolf. The mud and the weeds and the fog must become his allies. Perhaps it is in order to get closer to the Chiropteran that the agents of Red Shield mingled closer to the dark side of society.

". . . D67?" spoke David sharply, his eyes glued to the screen.

Something he'd found in the data made him speak that unfamiliar phrase out loud.

"There can't be Delta 67 here . . ."

"Delta . . . sixty . . . seven?"

As Saya repeated the words to herself, a thin white vertical line entered her field of vision.

The line as thin as a spider's web extended from the ceiling and touched down wet on the computer's keyboard. Saya already knew what it was.

As soon as David looked up to see where it came from, a loud crunch of metal came from the ceiling. It fell down with the bent covers from the ducts above the ceiling.

A large, dark, partially human-shaped figure came crashing down onto one of the server boxes before jumping to the floor.

"Saya! Fight!" shouted David as he picked up the shotgun and pushed the stock down and back again. He then pulled the RAM card out of the computer and put it in his breast pocket.

The sound of the empty shell casings hitting the floor rung in Saya's ears like an alarm clock, and she saw the giant beast fly into an innocent row of the tall, rectangular metal boxes. The monster didn't stay down for long.

It was a Chiropteran.

Its frame was the same as the other ones she had seen, but its look was somewhat different, like the difference between a lion and a tiger. Its teeth and claws designed to tear flesh and smash bones were still there, and a baby could see how dangerous this living beast was.

"Saya!"

She heard the second calling of her name, but Saya couldn't move.

It felt like her right hand was glued to the scabbard of the sword.

Fight . . . Yes . . . She must fight. Clearing her head, right when she was about to unsheathe her katana, the behemoth was just before her.

The swing of its claws cut nothing but air as Saya was pushed to the ground.

"Stay down."

The straightforward whisper was so close it tickled her ear.

Hagi immediately sprung up behind Saya's back, and she looked over her shoulder to see him block the Chiropteran's blow using his tightly flexed left arm.

The dimwitted beast was confused by what was happening.

But only for a moment.

As Saya squatted on the floor, a flash glittered from Hagi's right hand.

The Chiropteran waved its free hand through the air, but it was too slow. Before the steely claws of the monster could tear into Hagi's face, Hagi drove the similar-looking nails of his transformed right hand through the creature's throat.

The hoarse squeal of the beast put a crack in the laptop's monitor and the monster threw its head back.

From behind the Chiropteran came gunfire which blew apart the monster's thick legs, sending it reeling onto the ground.

"Retreat!"

It was David. Even if Chiropterans were immortal, without knees, they had difficulty moving. It was a good technique for buying time.

Even though it no longer had legs, it still had arms. The Chiropteran turned toward David, who was trying to run past the creature to get to the entrance. The monster swung its arms madly at him.

"Oof!"

"David-san!"

"Run!"

David fired a quick series of slugs into the creature's head, rendering it unrecognizable. Saya quickly began running toward the corridor also.

David left a trail of red droplets on the floor behind him. Saya could see the side of his dark suit was clearly wet.

They made it out through the entrance, but the flight of the three was cut short.

They hit a dead-end. This corridor should have continued to the rear of the facility, but apparently emergency systems had been engaged, and a solid barrier wall blocked the trio from continuing on. Could it be that the workers here didn't know what was happening until the last moment when the lockdown had happened?

There were no other doors around.

If they went back the way they'd come, they would run into that Chiropteran again.

Saya turned to see the mirror image of the Chiropteran from a few moments earlier walk out the entrance to the data processing room they were just in.

Looking like a hairless rabid dog, its head turned toward them.

"Guns aren't enough . . ." grumbled David out of the side of his mouth, yet he still lifted the shotgun to hip level in preparation.

The sound of the gunshots and the start of the Chiropteran's dash toward them happened at almost the exact same moment.

David's aim was dead-on, but the Chiropteran's flesh was so resilient, the metal slugs had little effect. At first the beast staggered a bit from the impact, but then the holes in its shoulder gurgled a slimy juice and closed up, allowing the Chiropteran to lean into another sprint. It was like it wanted them to see the regeneration as a taunt.

They had no escape.

Saya's eyes frantically examined the panel by the door. Maybe if they hit a button the emergency barrier wall would rise back up.

"Unn"

"Wait!"

David's words of restraint came after Saya had already stretched out her scabbard to hit the buttons on the panel.

". . . Huh?"

As Saya thought, that was a barrier wall switch.

As a warning alarm sounded, a thick iron slab began to descend from an opening in the ceiling, blocking the passageway. That wasn't the switch to open the barrier in front of them, but to insert a barrier behind them.

The Chiropteran's head came under the half-closed barrier, and Hagi pounded its face with his leather boots until it retreated.

With hardly a sound, the barrier wall politely finished closing off the corridor. The lack of a final thud, ironically, startled Saya.

After a few seconds of silence, the new barrier rattled with a gigantic knock, which startled Saya again. The mannerless monster must have been throwing its body at the thick wall.

"Our way out is now blocked."

"I'm—I'm sorry. It's all my—"

"It's kill or be killed. In war you and your enemy put your lives on the line. When standing on the battlefield, the first thought should be of survival."

David removed his jacket and opened up a small first-aid kid. As he skillfully tended to his wound, in no way did his facial expression harbor any blame or discontent, but Saya still felt it was her fault.

*If only I had fought, no one would have gotten hurt.*

She squeezed the scabbard of her sword with both hands as these words repeated through her head.

Saya realized the obvious—an emergency barrier wall basically can't be opened from the interior.

If you could, the whole purpose of isolating that section would be lost.

So at this point in time, Saya's action brought down another barrier wall, which had placed the trio in an airtight cube. Either they could wait here, or reopen the barrier wall that they had just come through. But it didn't appear they had any control on the other wall they were trying to get through.

"There are more of them then, aren't there?" muttered David as he checked the time on his cell phone. Saya, who was also sitting on the floor, raised her head up.

The metal and ceramic resin barrier door had countless numbers of inward divots. The poundings from the other side had not only not subsided, they had grown in frequency. It couldn't have been the work of just one Chiropteran.

The idea that George was safe somewhere within this facility was slipping further into fantasy.

*Come to think of it, the worst case scenario . . .*

This thought popped into Saya's head. Chiropterans see any non-Chiropterans, especially humans, as food. If the conscious researchers and staff couldn't get out alive, what expectation was there that her unconscious father would have made it?

"Father . . ."

Still sitting on the floor, she laid her head on her knees, trying to hold back her tears.

*How can I ever look Kai and Riku in the face?*

But that probably didn't matter. Saya was losing faith she would ever see the light of day again.

David suddenly stood up.

"Lift the barrier wall."

"But . . . !"

"A position is held because reinforcements are expected. In our case, we do not have that expectation."

When there was no sense that the situation was going to get better, it was time to change the situation. Saya understood this much.

"All right? First I'll go out. You take this and run for the elevator."

"I don't know if . . ."

David showed her his cell phone. In it was the RAM card with the downloaded information from the laptop.

He grasped her hand with one hand, and placed the cell phone in her palm with the other.

His hands were unusually hot, and she sensed a quiet power in them.

"Many of my colleagues died trying to get what's in here. You need to get it home."

He talked about the delivery of the information like he wasn't going to be there, too.

Saya's confusion turned to dread, and she looked David in the eyes.

"But, David-san . . ."

"Here we go."

David let go of Saya's hand, made a fist, and punched the panel to open the door.

The barrier door began to lift off the ground.

Even though it wasn't clear if it was safe, David ducked his head down and went through the opening while the thick door was still rising up.

Saya could see the Chiropteran waiting just on the other side of the door as it bent over backward, powdered with gunfire.

But her eyes quickly caught the three other similar-looking beasts waiting just beyond.

"Saya! Hurry!"

"Watch out!"

The Chiropterans that hung from the pipes above fell to the ground like monkeys in the corners where David couldn't immediately see them.

Hagi held on to Saya's back, guiding her with him as a single unit.

There was no time for hesitation.

Saya unsheathed her sword. She slid her thumb across the ridge above the hilt. The hot pain told her that her blood was flowing through the body of her blade.

She gripped the sword with both hands, as if she was in a trance.

The blade rattled, meeting resistance as she penetrated flesh.

Too shallow. The tip of her blade barely made it into the fatty tissue beneath the beast's thick skin.

The Chiropteran getting poked in the shoulder roared out in anger. It set its sights on a new target. The heads of all the beasts turned from the adult-sized man with the gun to the tender-fleshed little girl—an easier enemy to handle.

Krkk—the fang-flashing monster's head suddenly snapped sideways.

A man who had bounded out a doorway to the left continued to beat the Chiropteran with his fists. With drool flying, the beast fell to the side. If this had been any normal animal, the position the neck was contorted in would have meant death.

But this was a creature that could stand up after having its cranium blown into tiny pieces. A broken spine was the same as a stubbed toe. With a crackle, the head of the monster found its way back into place. Then it searched for the source of the surprise attack.

"Gurrr!"

The man that had started this melee with the now-standing Chiropteran came at the creature again, pounding it with both fists. The incessant barrage of punches drove the much-larger monster into the wall. Saya could not tear her eyes off the back of the figure beating the man-eating monster with his bare hands.

"Father?!"

"Do it! Now!"

Her father's voice pulled Saya back into reality, and her body was immediately set into motion.

The tip of her sword slipped into the skin of the beast her father was beating.

"Unnh . . ."

Saya pressed the blade further, sensing the blade meeting resistance from the monster's powerful muscle tissue. Saya gritted her teeth and Hagi wrapped his hand around the hilt of the sword. Suddenly the blade fell straight into the monster like tofu, meeting no resistance whatsoever.

From the point of penetration in the Chiropteran's chest, the transformation process began almost instantly. Its blood began to crystallize and as the monster turned to stone from the inside out, it gave out a dying shriek before its throat hardened up. George stepped away from the statue-like inorganic body of the monster and slumped with his back resting against the opposite wall.

"That's what happens when you mess with my daughter."

George's shoulders heaved up and down as he grumbled. His facial expression from three days earlier hadn't changed one bit. It really was George!

The light-colored smock he wore looked like a hospital gown.

"Father . . ."

"Hey! How have you been?" said George, using his regular greeting. Then the smile fell from his face.

"One more of them went over there."

"Oi!"

The Chiropteran avoided David's gunfire, but as it quickly crept closer it couldn't avoid George's massive arms. He nabbed the beast by both shoulders and swung it the other direction into the air.

At that moment there was no question about his military experience. He wasn't afraid of the Chiropterans. On the contrary, George was on the attack with out any concern for his own safety.

The Chiropteran was headed in Hagi's direction.

Saya panicked, but the young man remained completely composed.

He calmly turned his body to the side and kicked the Chiropteran in midair.

"No time to enjoy our little reunion, huh?"

"George! Over here!"

Without hesitation, George followed David. He trusted him.

Hagi and Saya ran after him.

In the chaos as other Chiropterans began to arrive, it was their only chance for escape.

As they ran down the hallway, David gave George a summary of what had taken place.

"I see. So you left Kai and Riku behind."

"Yes, but more importantly, what happened to your wound?"

"See for yourself."

George shouldn't have even been able to stand at this point, but there was no trace that he was ever hurt.

"When I woke up, I was completely healed. They gave me some pretty powerful medicine."

David picked something up off the ground.

It was a used I.V. pack. Saya was behind David, and couldn't see his reaction, but she could hear him swear under his breath.

"Delta 67 . . . You know about this?"

"They used you and the others in their research. In any case, we need to get out of here, now."

"Right . . ."

Delta six seven—David had said those words when they were in the data processing room.

That must be the name of some sort of medicine. Saya should have felt happy that it healed her father, but something about it didn't seem right.

She couldn't figure out what about it was bothering her.

They did strange experiments here, and made Chiropterans. That repulsive thought may have been what was bugging her.

Saya wanted nothing more than to get away from this place.

The path to the elevator was clear, and they didn't run into any other trouble.

Laying eyes on the closed elevator door, Saya felt a little bit relieved.

They would go in and get above ground. It was a dreadful journey, but they'd found George safely and David had gotten the information he was looking for. Mission accomplished.

But Saya's self-congratulations came a little too soon.

David was looking dubiously at the control panel indicator showing the elevator's location after pushing the button.

"On the first floor?"

"Maybe someone upstairs called the elevator?"

"Not possible."

David quickly negated George's idea.

There shouldn't be anyone in the building.

David didn't waste time explaining his reasoning. No reasonable person alive would still be in the building.

David's gun pointed back toward the dark hallway behind them.

Saya was swept with a wave of dizziness, and she lightly brought her hand to her forehead. George looked at her.

"What's wrong?"

It was possible she had not fully recovered and had overextended herself.

"Chiropterans. Have they caught up with us?"

Saya could hear the threatening growl, and turned around to look.

Down the dark hallway tinged with the red emergency lights the color of the summer sky at dusk, Saya could see the reflections of a countless number of crimson eyes looking her way.

Hagi took a half step forward to protect her. Looking at his profile, she thought that any emotions he had were deeply repressed.

Eventually he used up all the remaining shells he had for the Frachi SPAS.

He had blasted the closest targets, but once the shotgun had run out, without wavering, he used the shotgun-turned-metal-rod into a weapon and swung it at the next monster.

Crawling over a fallen Chiropteran with half a head and half a pile of meat sauce, another beast made its way even closer, and David put two .500 Magnum shells into its forehead at point-blank range.

"C'mon . . ."

The elevator was taking its time in making it down to the basement floor.

Outlook was not good.

Hagi was indispensable. It was easy to see he was an incredible warrior. He'd left the cello case, which could have been used as a blunt weapon, in the car, and with his bare hands had stopped a great number of beasts from getting any closer. Words could not describe David's awe in Hagi's martial artistry.

And George. He was swinging away like the old Marine that he was. With no regard for his own safety, he and Hagi made a pretty balanced duo—well, despite George's healthy and robust military build and fearless assault on inhuman goblins, he still didn't have the power to fully overwhelm them.

Hagi was the only one with strength remotely close to that of the Chiropterans. But George was fighting with incredible resolve. And the reason was obvious. Delta 67. It deviates from normal physiology and gives humans a paranormal strength.

But any cynicism or complaint about George's super-strength would be nothing but ironic at this moment.

Still, the powerful duo combined with David's pistol was only enough to delay the inevitable.

It was a war of attrition, and sooner or later—

"Saya! What are you doing?!"

"Ri-right!"

Saya pulled her sword from its cover.

With a grimace, she slid her thumb across the back of the blade, feeding it her blood. It was this blood and this blood only that could take down a Chiropteran.

But she didn't have the fighting spirit. Her sword was serving no purpose.

"Yaa!"

She swung the naked blade downward at a Chiropteran who had made its way close to her. The beast easily avoided her slash.

This was not representative of the sword-wielding he was expecting. David had heard her fighting in Vietnam described as that of a "Diablo."

"Father! Look out!"

Saya's cry was mixed in with a shrill, piercing echo.

The tempered glass from the security office shattered into a million pieces and a never-before-seen type of monster leapt unexpectedly through the hole at George.

George dove out of the way just before the creature crashed on top of him.

The creature landed with one knee on the floor, and Saya sent the white blade into its thick leg.

Saya's strike was too shallow for crystallization to happen.

The daughter glared at the Chiropteran culprit.

"Kyaa!"

Saya pulled the blade out, sending her backward to the floor.

Five sharp claws sliced through the air toward Saya's throat.

"Saya!"

The sound of flesh being torn.

The floor was splattered with blood.

"Fa . . . ther . . . ?"

George had come between her and the monster as she lifted her sword.

The five razor-sharp claws had buried themselves in George's chest.

"Damn you, beast . . ."

George's vicious growl was cut short from hemorrhaging in his lungs.

"Keep away from . . . my daughter!" George shouted, gurgling blood as his thick body went into motion.

With both hands he grabbed the creature by the elbow and pulled it around. He spun the stumbling beast one full rotation and sent it flying, back first, into the wall.

A red arc of blood floated in the air as the Chiropteran's claws were pulled from George's chest. Saya drove the point of her sword straight into the center of the monster's chest.

With its back still against the wall, the monster almost immediately went cold from death. Its color changed as life escaped its body.

However, George's life was also escaping out of his wound.

Seeing that Saya was safe, a smile appeared on George's sweaty face. For a moment he was able to forget about the pain in his chest. Losing his balance he fell onto the floor on all fours.

"Father!"

Saya leaned down and helped George lie on his back, resting his head on her knees.

"Just relax . . . Father . . . No! We just found you!"

". . ."

*Don't lose focus on the battle*—These words reflexively passed through David's mind.

He dumped the spent casings and using a speed-loader put five new shells into his pistol. He fired off a few rounds at the remaining Chiropterans.

There were three left. Already injured, it appeared it would take them a little time before they would be on the attack again. The powerful Hagi was there to protect Saya, and for the time being it looked as if the handgun would be enough to keep the remaining beasts at bay. This battle appeared to be over.

A cool tone told David that the elevator had arrived.

From behind the giant dividing metal doors spilled out a young boy.

It was Kai. He was the one who'd called the elevator to the ground floor.

"We got trouble! They're going to air-strike this place! Something 'Option D'—"

"Air strike?!"

Kai didn't answer David's question.

As if he was walking through a fog, the boy took careful steps, peering over his sister's shoulder. His eyes were focused on the blood-soaked figure of his father lying on the ground.

"This is a joke, right . . . ?"

"Is that Kai?"

"Dad . . ."

George's voice was surprisingly calm, yet the hopeful look melted from Kai's face.

Saya held her breath. David did as well.

Suddenly the blood stopped gushing out of George's chest.

Through the tear in the hospital gown they could see the edges of his wound reforming tissue, morphing and shrinking the hole.

". . . This is strange, isn't it?"

With a bitter smile George held up his right arm. It was already not his.

His skin was almost black and he had metal-looking claws for fingers. George's arm was transforming into something like Forest's.

"David, is this Delta 67 . . . ?"

George seemed relaxed. It was possible the pain had stopped.

"I'm afraid so. Your body is gradually going to mutate into a Chiropteran."

Delta 67. The godforsaken chemical compound that robs humans of their souls and turns them into simpleminded gremlins.

The beasts must have known George was one of them, and that's why they didn't eat him while he slept when the compound went on lockdown.

"Don't say that . . ."

Saya wept as she slipped her hand into George's left hand.

Her father's palms were big. He wrapped his right arm around Saya's body. The monster-like feature on her father made her back stiffen.

"Left like this, I will end up like Forest. Since I began to heal, I can feel my consciousness slipping."

"Father . . ."

"Saya, please let me die while I am still your father."

There is only one person in the world who can slay a Chiropteran.

Saya's weeping face contorted into hopelessness.

"What? Isn't there something we can do?" cried Kai critically.

David only turned his head slightly to the left and right in response.

"Goddammit!"

"Kai, you have heard me say this before, right? A man is tested in the eleventh hour. If you are a man, then act like a man, and let your father go."

A critical tongue-lashing would have fallen on dead ears, but his father's words combined with his smile were too much for the young boy's heart to ignore.

Kai hadn't completely given up, but conceding to his father's wish was as painful as his own guts being torn out.

"Saya, please."

Kai made no attempt to hide his tears as he gazed upon his younger sister.

He was doing what he could to help her. That's why he looked in the eyes, instead of at the floor. Leaving the act of killing their father to his sister was more than anyone should ever have to ask. His only regret was that he wasn't able to take the responsibility from her.

As their father would have said, David could see the determination of a man inside this boy.

It was something a man could understand.

But what about the young girl, Saya? She writhed in the same anguish as her elder brother, yet the heart-breaking duty fell into her hands. Like a prisoner gazing at the brightest star in the night sky, Saya looked up at Hagi.

"It is all up to you."

No one could force her to do this. What they didn't have was a lot of time for her to decide.

The injured Chiropterans further down the corridor were regenerating and were beginning to get restless.

From Hagi, Saya's gaze moved to David. He couldn't muster any stern commands.

"You can either let George die a man, or wait a few minutes and kill the demon that he turns into. Those are the only two choices."

It seemed as though Saya forgot how to speak.

She slowly rose up and pulled her sword from the stone Chiropteran up against the wall.

She held the palm of her left hand against the blade. She slid her hand across the blade, and blood trickled down her wrist.

She kneeled down next to her father again and held out her hand over his chest.

George silently gave his consent. It was in recognition of her bravery.

Saya's expression contorted drastically. She squeezed her five fingers into her palm so tightly, it seemed she might cut her skin further. Matching the tears flowing down her face, deep red drops began to hang at the bottom of her trembling fist.

One drop fell, then another—

Like red raindrops, the blood hit the writhing wound, and soon penetrated into George's bloodstream.

". . . Urghh!"

George had quietly gazed as his blood intertwined with his daughter's blood, but suddenly he arched his back up.

It wasn't only his face or his chest and head, but his entire body appeared as if there were earthworms crawling just beneath the surface of his skin. His blood had begun to mutate. He probably didn't crystallize immediately because his body wasn't yet completely that of a Chiropteran's.

Both Saya and Kai moved in closer to their father.

"Father!"

"Dad!" shouted Kai raising his hands into the air, his face stained with tears and snot.

"Silly boy. There's no need to cry."

Kai couldn't respond to his father. He was too young to be able to say goodbye with a smile on his face. But he did suppress his need to cry out, and clenched his teeth to try and stop weeping in front of his father.

Seeing this, George's lips tightened.

Despite the incredible pain, George surely felt proud to see his son turning into a man.

As the life in George's eyes began to fade, he turned to his daughter.

"Saya . . . No matter what happens, follow the path you believe in . . . Accept your past . . ."

The young girl nodded faintly.

"When things are hard. Remember *Nankurunaisa*. Live today for the sake of tomorrow . . . and don't forget to smile."

"I will."

But she couldn't at that moment.

Seeing Saya's contorted crying face made George grin.

"What a beautiful smile."

George's breath was getting shallow. He then took a deep breath and let it out slowly into the atmosphere.

With the smile still on his face, George's lips stopped moving.

"Father—"

Just as Saya's final cry faded into the darkness, David was startled by a metallic sound.

As David lifted his pistol, a metal grate came crashing down from above. Along with it followed a Chiropteran.

BLAM! BLAM!

David fired two shots from his pistol, scattering pieces of skull and tissue into the air, and sending the beast crashing to the ground. But that was not the end of the fight.

"There are a lot this time . . ."

One after another, more enemies dropped from the hole in the ceiling. David only had so many bullets.

From down the corridor he could also hear the growls and movement of a number of large creatures. To make matters

worse, the three beasts that they had fought earlier had completely recovered and had joined the ranks of the other Chiropterans closing in. By David's estimation there were at least ten monsters.

"Get to the elevator!"

When David was just above the shoulders of the seated boy, one petulant creature flew in close. From its large open jaws dripped strings of sticky saliva.

It made a swooshing sound in the air.

The bounding beast with arms outstretched flew just over Kai's head, and tumbled onto the ground like a doll.

Sprays of blood followed the trajectory of the beast, and red droplets fell on David's head.

Looking at the fallen creature, there was nothing above the lower jaw. The rest of its head was gone.

The upper half of its head was stuck to the floor near Saya.

Lowering the sword she held in her right hand, Saya dropped one foot onto the chunk of head, smashing it into pieces.

Even through there was no wind, Saya's silver-tinged hair was rustling.

She glared at the swarm of goblins and her eyes swirled into two red-hot spheres.

"She hasn't lost control, has she?"

"No. She has simply remembered what she must do."

Hagi's answer was devoid of any emotional intonation, but as he watched his master run into battle David noticed a sentimental expression on his face.

"To protect what is important to her. That's why Saya fights."

Saya stepped in to challenge three Chiropterans that had surrounded her.

A moment later her blade danced through the air like a bird in flight.

Then the blade froze in midair. Saya's body stood rigid with her sword extended upward diagonally, an extension of her right arm.

The three Chiropterans split apart into several large pieces. Heads, limbs, torsos, all fell to the ground as lumps of meat.

Without watching the slabs of flesh transform into stone, Saya's body was in motion again.

She used the same technique on two more Chiropterans who approached, attracted to the smell of blood. Like a fish, she wriggled between them.

The strong arms of the monsters swung into nothingness.

With her blade still in the air, she continued forward to a single target directly ahead of her.

Their quick meeting resulted in spilled Chiropteran blood. This one was cut from his below its arm and laterally through its chest. It was easy to see when the top half of its body separated from the bottom half.

It was a diagonal downward strike and the creature slowly fell to the ground. David could just see Saya's face through the fountains of blood shooting out of its body.

The vision of a goddess at war.

"Let's go!"

It was not a request, but a demand.

"Ye-yes."

Coiled in a storm of blood, Saya responded to David's clear instruction after cutting down enemy after enemy. She might actually have been a little afraid of him.

After lifting Kai by the arm, they all rushed into the elevator.

Suddenly Kai, who had been watching over his sister attentively, cried out.

"Watch out!"

The warning to Saya wasn't necessary.

She had already taken a step to the side to avoid the chunk of crystallized beast corpse that had been sent flying at her. The giant rock just grazed the hem of her skirt.

As the stone broke into pieces upon impact on the floor Saya gracefully spun like a ballerina and jumped forward.

In a moment she was in front of the Chiropteran tossing his brothers' body parts. She leapt again, using both hands to drive her long sword up into the beast, forcing it to stand up straight.

The cut curved up from its nether regions through its head, leaving a red line marking its path.

It was already crystallizing before the bisected body of the beast split and fell either way onto the floor.

Probably waiting for an opportunity to strike, another Chiropteran came at Saya's back while her sword was down. The monster swung both of its giant hands at her sides in an attempt to grapple her.

In front of Saya was a wall.

The Chiropteran attempted to grasp the slender girl in a bone-crushing bear hug, but ended up wrapping its giant arms around nothing but air.

Just before its claws had come together, Saya had kicked off the wall and sent herself soaring over the monster's head.

Without fully registering what had happened, the monster found a Koza Commercial High School official uniform leather shoe planted on each of its shoulders.

Before it even had a chance to look up, Saya drove the tip of her blade like an arrow into the top of the beast's skull, through its windpipe and deep into its chest.

As it stood there the Chiropteran turned from living thing to stone statue. As if it had been shot by a sharpshooter's rifle, the head of the stone creature exploded magnificently. Saya, who had been standing there moments before, was nowhere to be seen.

A similar-looking Chiropteran fingered the pieces of its brethren's head with a talon-like claw.

It was at that point that David saw Saya up so high her uniform grazed the ceiling. She twisted in the air like a cat and came down at an angle, landing inside the opening of the elevator.

BOOM—the giant metal box resonated from her arrival.

Neither David nor Kai knew how to respond. They were like two sticks blown horizontally by a sudden gust of wind.

In order to slow her slide across the elevator floor Saya stuck out one shoe, planting it into the rear wall of the oversized elevator.

The friction caused the soles of her shoes to smell like burnt rubber.

"Close the door."

"Ri-right."

David quickly pushed the button with his finger.

The doors began to close.

The remaining Chiropteran knocked down the headless stone sibling that stood in the corridor, and bayed up to the ceiling.

By all appearances, that was the last remaining Chiropteran.

Although the actual need to fight had disappeared, the monster that remained hadn't satisfied its savage needs.

The yell which shook the walls seemed to be self-empowering, as the Chiropteran then rushed the elevator.

Clicking his tongue, David lifted his pistol, not about to allow this monster any reward for its efforts.

Through the closing gap in the doors, the beast's gaping mouth was pierced through with the blade of a sword.

The brawny body of the Chiropteran froze in place.

From deep down the monster's throat came the crackling sound of death.

As expected, Saya pulled back her sword, which was followed by a shower of blood from the gaping jaws. Still, the crystallization process had already begun.

Saya swung her blood-drenched blade back into the elevator, and fell down into the fetal position at the moment the elevator doors shut, closing the curtain on the bloody massacre she'd just committed.

It was also her last farewell to George.

"Father . . ."

She turned and pressed her forehead on the elevator door.

Resting her brow on that cold metal, what could be going through her head?

Was it her hatred for Chiropterans? No. It must have been for the loss of her father.

At this moment she was just was acting not like a killer, but like a typical young girl.

The elevator began to move upward.


Running out of the nature conservatory with the others, Saya's heart was burning.

Standing in front of the van, Louis was diligently on lookout with a machine gun in his hands.

He must have recognized the group as he quickly pointed the muzzle of his weapon at the ground.

"What happened? Both the wireless and cell phones are useless out here. And then a little bit ago that Kai kid all of a sudden—."

"No time to explain now. Hurry."

Despite the amazing revelation that his partner didn't have a mouthful of food, David didn't act surprised, and pulled out his car keys.

"I told you, didn't I? The Army is gonna bomb this place."

It wasn't Kai's snide tone but the content of the message that got Louis's large body in motion.

"An air strike . . . They are really going through with Option D."

"Do you think I am kidding?" asked Kai without laughing. Kai stood straddling his bike.

Louis squeezed his large build into the driver's seat of the van without another word, and Saya and Hagi crawled into the back seat of David's car.

As the back door closed, David pressed down on the gas.

Inside the speeding car Saya turned to face the window.

Above black shadows of the tropical forest she could see the night sky.

George lay resting among all those machines.

She wasn't sure how many minutes they had sped down this gravel road, but suddenly a giant boom split the air.

Two planes flying at low altitude passed overhead, demonstrating their speed by the time lag of the sound.

"They've arrived. Get ready for a shock."

Saya wasn't able to hear David's warning.

She had scooted as close to the door as possible, and her face was up against the car window.

From the other side of the forest she could see the first break of dawn.

No. That wasn't the rising sun. It was a manmade fireball rising up from the surface.

It made no sound.

The sky turned completely red and a gigantic cloud of smoke rose into the air. It formed into the shape of a mushroom.

It was then that the atmosphere began to rumble.

A thunder-like shock rattled the car windows, and the tremors running through the ground could be felt from inside the moving car.

"Waah . . ."

The window clouded from Saya's yelp.

Here father had been reduced to ash.

But she would never forget him. How could Saya Otonashi forget she was the proud daughter of George Miyagusuku?

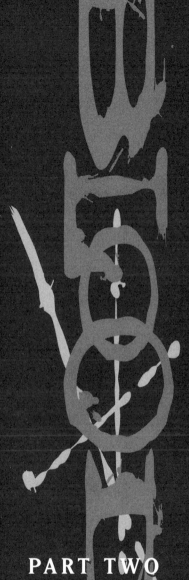

PART TWO

IT WAS DARK.

But it wasn't darkness from night. Inaccessible to the outside world, this place was never lit up by natural sunlight.

Holding her breath, Saya was running down a worn stone corridor. She was sprinting as if her life depended on it to catch up with the person just barely in sight running ahead of her.

Her footsteps echoed like splashes against the dark walls and ceiling.

"Father!"

George didn't turn around and didn't stop.

"Wait!"

No matter how fast she ran, she couldn't catch up to him.

Her foot fell into a puddle on the stone floor.

There was a door ahead.

It was an old, but solid-looking wood door with inlaid iron fixtures.

Saya had remembered seeing this place before.

Behind the door was something awful. It shouldn't be opened.

Mocking her, it creaked.

The door opened.

With no hesitation the figure of George went through the dark doorway.

The door began to close, blocking her view of George's back.

"Father!"

Pressing her body against the door, Saya peeked through the crack, scanning the darkness for a sign of her father.

It was him.

He was lying on the floor, and his eyes were closed.

Kneeling at his side was an elegant-looking girl.

Her long flowing black hair was the same color as the darkness, and she was tearing open her white dress.

Saya had the feeling she was looking in a mirror.

It was her own face grinning back at her.

There was a wet crimson smear across her lips.

Her face was drenched in the blue reflection of the winter moon.

"Father!"

She jumped and sat up. It took her a full three seconds to realize that she had fallen asleep in her school uniform.

She pulled away the blanket that was covering her body.

"He's dead."

There was a metal needle sticking out of her right arm. It was taped down in place and connected by a tube to an IV drip.

There was a small circular window next to the bed.

She peeked out the window, and saw an expanse of blue water.

"The ocean?"

From her narrow field of vision she could also see a harbor. She must have been on a docked ship.

She had fallen asleep as they drove away from the nature conservatory. She wasn't sure if this had something to do with her lost memory, but it seemed to happen every once in a while, so she wasn't particularly concerned. But why was she here, and not at Julia's clinic?

She knew she wasn't dreaming when she heard the knocking sound coming from the walls of the spooky room.

It was coming from the other side of the door.

"Hey, Riku! Open up!"

"Riku, I have some tasty soup for you."

It was the voices of Kai and Louis.

Saya pulled out the needle, opened the door, and peeked out into the hallway. There she saw the two standing a few doors down.

"C'mon, Riku. You have to eat something."

"That's right. If you don't eat, you can't grow big."

In the overly-big black man's hands were cute bunny oven mitts holding a big bowl.

"Riku!"

Kai's tone was a little stronger, and he pounded on the door, only to then notice his sister.

"Saya."

"Umm . . . Where . . ."

"Did you get a good sleep?"

"Ye-yes."

Saya felt a certain comfort in Riku's unchanging gruffness.

Immediately after such a tragedy, he was already back to normal.

"You know, you slept for two full days."

"Wha—?"

Saya's eyes got big hearing what Louis had said. It wasn't so immediately after, after all.

"What's wrong with Riku?"

"Ever since he heard about Dad . . ."

Seeing Kai's expression darken wearily as he turned his gaze to the metal door caused Saya's heart to feel heavy. Naturally, he hadn't had enough time to come to terms with Father's death.

But after a second Kai lifted his head up, and his mouth formed a grin.

"Well, it's something his big brother can help him get through. Make sure you get enough rest."

"Listen to what Kai says. Even warriors need to rest."

Louis placed one bunny-covered hand on Saya's shoulder.

She hadn't talked to him much before, but he seemed like a very pure-hearted man. He seemed much too cheerful to be David's partner.

"But first, Saya, you must be hungry."

It was strange that the same thing always happened when that topic came up.

Before she could answer with her voice, her stomach replied first.

Louis's belly jiggled as he laughed in response.

"Okay, I'll get some delicious soup ready for Saya, too. Come with me to the mess hall."

Saya covered her stomach with two hands and her cheeks went flushed as she followed Louis down the corridor.

When they walked out onto the ship's deck, Saya squinted from the bright sunlight.

On the deck of this large freighter ship was a gigantic opening. Through this hole Saya saw shipping containers that had been loaded.


The soup truly was delicious.

Louis, who loved nothing more than the topic of eating, was a chef with some extraordinary talent.

However, eating alone in the ship's cafeteria was a little lonely for Saya, who was used to bustling and busy mealtimes.

There was always Kai, Riku, and George, then usually Kaori or some other friend over.

Now, no one was there.

Saya was able to distinguish the difference between "hunger" and "appetite" as she laid her spoon down on the edge of the bowl.

A soft vibration flowed through the air.

Something from outside, a solemn melody—it was Bach, being played on the cello without accompaniment. It felt like it was calling directly to her.

Saya stood up from her seat and walked out to the corridor.

She went into the salty air and saw the outline of the young man sitting on the deck.

He used a handrail to sit on, and looked aristocratic and wise as he communicated the music through the classical instrument.

He looked like a man from another time, another place.

That was certainly the history of Hagi's past. He came out in his music. His past was tightly intertwined with her past.

"I want you to tell me."

"Tell you what?"

The music stopped, but the song seemed to continue through his words.

"About my past."

"What do you plan to do if I tell you?"

"I want to know. I want to know where I came from."

She had asked him this before. It had been on the beach during sunset.

She was so upset at that time, she'd just wanted to grasp anything about herself. She'd wanted to talk to anyone who knew the slightest thing about her past. She'd needed it to affirm her existence at that moment.

Hagi had hesitated in telling her then, saying she would "lose the now" if he did.

But things were different now.

George's words had given her direction.

*No matter what happens, follow the path you believe in. Accept your past.*

It was no longer to accept who she was now, but to prepare her for the future.

"Please."

She didn't raise her voice, but stared intently at Hagi.

Hagi didn't answer in the negative, or in the positive.

He laid the cello case down, undid the clasp inside the lid, and removed the stowed katana.

Gripping the handle with his bandage-wrapped right hand, he freed the white blade from its sheathe.

"Hagi?"

*Watch*—was the command she received, but not from his words, but from how he moved. And she did.

Hagi left Saya where she stood, and held the long sword with both hands. He swept the blade diagonally.

The edge sliced up through the air.

The blade flashed brighter than Saya expected.

The next move brought the sharp edge over and downward, turning and cutting the emptiness in front of him. His feet slid rather than stepped, giving his movements a seamless flow, as if he was dancing.

He lifted the katana to his shoulder, then struck the weapon straight down in a sweeping gesture before turning his body adroitly out of the way of an nonexistent enemy.

Hagi dropped his foot in an earth-splitting stomp, and again swept the blade from his upper-body down.

Just as she thought that was the next move, the katana moved up and twisted, like a feather in the wind. As if eliminating a number of enemies, the sword fluttered to the left and right, flashing brightly as it descended toward the ground.

Saya understood this to be the end of the demonstration.

She let out a deep sigh.

She realized she had been holding her breath.

It was less like a fencing *kata*, and more like a beautiful dance.

"This is what I know of your sword-fighting technique."

The sound of the hilt meeting metal resounded as he returned the sword to the scabbard.

"This is your art, and I can teach you. It will lead you down the path to your past."

"That's not what I mean. I want to know more clearly."

"If you do that, you will lose the now."

"That's what you said before . . . but, why?"

"You are not ready to accept your past yet."

There was still something missing inside her. She was still weak. Saya assumed that's what he meant.

Hagi—Who was the Saya Otonashi that he knew?

"I want my past back. I want to know where I am from and what it is I must do. Father told me I need to accept my past. So tell me, how do I do it? How do I learn my past?"

Hagi raised his right hand to Saya's eye level.

He thrust the large covered blade toward her.

"Fight the Chiropterans. That's where you will find your answer."

"That's what Father told me. He said I needed to be strong."

Saya extended her hand and accepted the sword.

"I have no choice but to fight."

She didn't want Kai and Riku to feel any more pain.

The pain George's death had brought could not be repeated.

Dad wasn't coming back.

When Kai had said that, the color drained from his surroundings.

It couldn't be.

Riku cried out, but Kai didn't say anything. It was only when Kai held his brother and whispered *I'm sorry* in his ear that Riku began to believe that it was true.

In the two days that had passed since then, Riku wouldn't see anyone. He didn't want to talk about it. About anything.

Things would go back to normal. That's what Kai had told him . . . but those ordinary days would never come back again. And neither would George.

It was dark inside his cabin.

With the lights turned off, it was like he was in a hazy, gloomy iron cube.

Without moving, Riku sat on one corner of the bed hugging his knees.

Kai was talking from the other side of the door.

"Say, Riku. Do you remember that one time? It was about a year ago when we went with Dad and Saya to the beach. Just like now, you locked yourself into the car."

He hadn't forgotten.

"Saya had torn up some book that you really liked."

It was *Fabre's Book of Insects*. That's what Riku had been so mad about.

It wasn't the kind of anger where he would scream and shout and make a big fuss. From long ago, and even now, Riku didn't like letting his emotions boil above the surface.

If you got upset and out of control, the other person could feel hurt. Riku didn't like the thought of that. The last thing Riku wanted to do was be the cause of friction or negative feelings. It was more important to spend time laughing with the people around you. But, naturally, everyone has moments when they get angry. Like when Saya had wrecked his book.

That time was back when Saya first came into the Miyagusuku family, and she was completely clueless. She was as ignorant as a baby. She talked like a little kid, and if something caught her attention, she wouldn't stop until she got her hands on it. Left alone she would eat things like soap and erasers, and Riku remembered that trip was a difficult one for George and Kai.

Riku had locked himself into the car, because he knew that if he had gone outside and seen Saya's face, he wouldn't have been able to help but yell at her. He didn't want to complicate the problem.

Riku just wanted everyone to be happy.

But what was wrong with having a favorite book you always read and kept close by? Why did she have to choose that book to tear up and toss around?

Of course, Saya hadn't done it to be mean.

Even a child could understand that much. It really wasn't her fault. But the same could have been said for Riku.

Even though he hadn't done anything wrong to her, why should he accept the destruction of something important to him?

If she hadn't messed with his book then he wouldn't have gotten upset, and he wouldn't have felt like kicking Saya out of the family.

Something that shouldn't have broken did. Not knowing how to deal with such an irrational incident, Riku had placed a wall between himself and the rest of the world.

"Do you remember what Dad did then? He was sitting on the beach, and I wondered what he was up to when I saw he was using the rice from our *bento* to paste the pages of your book back together."

Kai laughed recalling the memory.

Riku paused a moment. He hadn't thought about that day in a while, yet he didn't allow himself to lose his composure.

"I'll never forget what Dad said after that. 'Anything with a form will someday break. But the Miyagusuku family add a little caveat to that expression,' he said."

Riku remembered it well.

He had used mashed white rice to paste the spine back to the pages, and reinforced it with cellophane tape. He'd chuckled as he held up his handiwork for Riku to see.

"If you don't give up, and do your best, you can fix anything back to how it was. Look, Riku. Can't you see your book is back to normal?"

From the outside it looked a bit misshapen, but Riku didn't mind.

"It's just like us, you know," George had said optimistically. "We aren't blood relatives. By all rights, we shouldn't even know each other. But just like this book, if we work at it, together we can be a family. If somehow we get torn apart, I'll stick us back together with mashed rice."

It was after that day Saya seemed to become a real member of the Miyagusuku clan, and they were able to live and function as a family. It was then Riku was able to look up to Saya as his big sister.

Kai continued from the other side of the door.

"That was about the time I busted my elbow and quit the baseball team, and I was running around all night instead of coming home. Somehow Dad's words really hit me . . . and now he's gone. But, you've got me and Saya. We're your family."

After that Kai's tone was less cheerful.

"And the one that is hurting the most is Saya, the one that had to help him die."

That hadn't occurred to Riku.

She'd had to use her hand to kill Dad. What could that have felt like?

Of course, it wasn't something she had wanted to do. The only person who could have freed George from the agony of turning into what Forest turned into was Saya.

"Yaaah!"

A guttural yell resonated from somewhere.

It was a scream. No. More of a battle cry.

Riku lifted his head and looked over at the window. He lifted up the blind covering it and looked out.

He couldn't see much, but he did see Saya standing on the ship's deck.

Not far from Saya was Hagi.

Stepping in with her right foot, she swung the sword she held down. As she looked up into the sky, her lips moved.

"I will do my best . . . so that everyone can look forward to tomorrow with a smile."

"Tomorrow . . . with a smile . . ."

Riku repeated Saya's words and looked out across the ocean feeling more hopeful.

The bright sunset set the horizon aflame with a carpet of crimson.

The four members of the family all had seen it together before.

"Something about the sunset is kinda sad. It's like the sun is separating from us."

"Is that what you think?"

Riku had responded affirmatively.

"How about you, Saya? Do you think it is sad?"

"Um . . . Yes. It's scary. It will . . . get dark again."

George had stroked Saya's short hair as she gave her answer in stilted Japanese.

"You know, even when the sun sinks at night, it rises again the next day smiling in the eastern sky. Then everything brightens up again. If something bad happens, you can meet the new day with a smile, too."

Saya was probably remembering that day now, too.

Riku slipped down off the bed.

He put on his sneakers and walked over to the door.

He grabbed the handle and turned it.

Kai, who had been sitting on the floor leaning on the wall, lifted his back up and turned to his brother.

"Riku."

"Did Dad say something?"

"Eh?"

"At the end. Did he say something?"

"Oh. Yes. He said don't forget to smile."

He had guessed right. Riku grinned.

"That's sounds like something Dad would say."

"Yeah. He died for us, you know. But now we are going to have to try even harder."

"Un-huh."

As Riku repeated Kai's last words to himself to solidify them, Saya swung her sword. For the sake of the family.

Riku had the same feeling.


Considering the size of Yanbaru's forest, the damage was about the same as a pinprick.

But to Okamura's eyes it looked like a crater from an asteroid had fallen from space.

"They say this was caused by the crash of a plane carrying a bomb?" Okamura asked himself as he examined the exposed surface of the earth and a gigantic bowl-shaped hole that was roped off with yellow tape.

The twisted earth had made a small embankment surrounding the crater. The trees had either been knocked down or blackened, skeletons of their former selves. A little way from there an Army spokesman was explaining in Japanese the unfortunate accident at the Yanbaru Nature Conservation Center to Okamura's press corps colleagues.

"There's no way it could have happened like they said."

It was a perfectly aimed shot that had eliminated the facility completely, but no more and no less. Coupled with the recent attack, the U.S. Army's activities smelled suspiciously of a cover-up.

"Okamura-sempai!"

He turned around to see a smart-looking young man with his suit jacket tucked under his arm.

"Oh! Sorimachi!"

He was a younger student from Okamura's college days. Last he had heard, Sorimachi was at the Tokinichi newspaper's Osaka bureau.

"Hey, it has been a long time. I was just going to grab a bite . . ."

"Is it already that time?"

It didn't seem as if he was going to find anything at the crater, and the Army spokesman gave nothing but canned answers to questions. Being there was a waste of time.

Okamura and Sorimachi walked into a roadside shop.

It was a rustic little place which catered to travelers and campers. Along with the typical souvenirs they also sold a few cheap snacks and some fresh food.

They sat down at the single table in the shop and each ordered a bowl of *soba* noodles.

"Sempai, not *sooki* rib *soba* for you?"

"Is it strange to order *tempura soba*?"

"You're an Okinawan now, aren't you?"

"Listen here. Do Osaka natives only eat *takoyaki*? Do Tokyoites eat *sushi* every day? Or do people in Nagoya only eat . . . um . . . *uirou*?"

"Well, that's true, but . . ."

"But you haven't told me yet what you are doing here. I bet it's for the rugby team alumni championships. Or did you get demoted from the Osaka office and sent here?"

"Let's just call it a change of locale to advance my career. But the mainstream media has really taken over down here. Just a giant burnt hole in the ground doesn't make for much of a story."

"It was a facility also used freely by civilians, but it gets leveled by a plane doing a test flight?"

"But nobody was in the building. Nobody died, right?"

After bringing his bowl to his mouth and taking a slurp, Sorimachi continued.

"It's only been two days, and they are already giving guided tours. National papers like ours aren't going to want to run any articles."

On the day of the accident, newspapers, TV news, and every other media outlet made their reports, but were already on the lookout for the next story elsewhere. Considering no one had died, and that it was a U.S. military–owned, rather than public, facility, the mass media quickly lost interest in the story.

Naturally, the U.S. military along with the Japanese politicians they had in their pockets received much criticism from local officials and media, but the only ones sucked into continuing the coverage were the left-wing newspaper journalists.

"Hey-hey! How are things?"

An obvious regular walked into the shop.

He was dressed like a hiker, and directed his greetings to the shopkeeper sitting behind the register.

"Going bug hunting again, huh?"

"It's long-armed scarab beetle season, you know."

Sorimachi seemed bored by what he was overhearing.

"Lucky guy. Gets to spend his time bug collecting."

"He's a poacher. The Yanbaru long-armed beetle is a protected species," responded Okamura quietly, scoffing at his junior's lack of preparedness. He leaned over to pick up the conversation between the customer and the shopkeeper.

"You mean they said it was an American plane that crashed into the nature conservatory?"

"Yeah, it was carrying a bomb when it crashed. Made a real ruckus."

"That doesn't make sense. I was in the mountains that night, and I heard the sound of the explosion, but the sounds of planes continued afterward. I didn't hear the one going down."

"Your ears were probably playing tricks on you."

"Use your head. Since doing this work my hearing has gotten even more sensitive," snorted the poacher unexpectedly. "And that's not all. I had seen guys in yellow space suits going in and out at that place before. Aliens must have taken it over, and that's why the U.S. Army blew it up."

"Ha ha! Those are biohazard suits. That's what Yasujiro, the Nago garbage man, said."

Okamura's chopsticks stopped moving.

American military in biohazard suits? That sounded like what he'd seen in the photos at the university.

So the bodies recovered from the mysterious murder cases by the biohazard suit–wearing U.S. Army were taken to the Yanbaru Nature Conservation Center.

This might turn out to be a very important clue.

"What's the matter?"

"Sorimachi, go home."

"Excuse me? We're in the middle of the forest. Um . . . Sempai?"

He was trying to take a bite of noodles and get his colleague's attention at the same time. Ignoring the floundering Sorimachi, Okamura stood up from his chair.

Switched into work mode, Okamura put on a fake smile and walked over to the poacher and shopkeeper.

"Pardon me for barging in, but could you tell me a little more about what you saw?"

+

Splitting off with Sorimachi, Okamura went from Yanbaru to the city of Nago. With the address he received from the shop-keeper in hand, he drove his car to an industrial waste disposal station.

The U.S. Army employs their services, but much to Okamura's surprise, there was no security, and it was just a typical small-time enterprise.

The owner, Yasujiro, was operating a backhoe, when Okamura arrived, and he stopped what he was doing to greet him. He had been pushing waste dumped from a huge truck into one of many giant piles of garbage.

"Sure. I saw 'em. The haz-mat suits, yeah."

For a reporter, the owner was a dream, happy to give information from the operator's seat of the backhoe.

"Yes, I am sure we picked them up from the nature conservation center in Yanbaru."

"What kind of work was going on there?"

"How should I know? We were just there to pick up medical garbage. Around here, we're the only outfit that will deal with hospital waste."

It made sense. Looking at the mountains of garbage, Okamura spotted many items that would fit that description.

Used needles, test tubes, prescription bottles, empty medical wrappers, and chloride packaging . . . empty I.V. drip packs with D67 written on them. That must be the name of some kind of medicine.

". . . What's that?"

Okamura's eyes rested on something that didn't fit in with the medical waste.

Empty wine bottles.

A closer look revealed it wasn't the cheap stuff, either. The label read Chateau Duel, 1967.

"What are these?"

"I don't know. It was part of the garbage they asked us to haul away from the conservatory."

"Would it be okay if I took one?"

"Fine with me, but they are all empty."

"That's perfectly okay."

Okamura had a new location to check out.

The name of the company which brought the wine from overseas to the Yanbaru Nature Conservation Center was printed on the boxes holding the empty bottles. Contact with them should lead to the source of the wine.

Okamura got a hold of his editorial department with the information he had, and had them look up a list of importers in the area. Five minutes later he got the name and location of the most likely company sent to him by text message.

The trading company had an office set up in a building housing various businesses in Naha City.

Okamura didn't have to wait long for the man in charge to come around the sofas facing each other used for talking with clients.

"I wanted to ask you about this wine . . ."

"Right. I don't remember the brand name, but we did bring in a bunch of wine once. Why do you ask?"

"The empty bottles were mixed in with garbage from a U.S. military facility in Yanbaru. If our taxes are going to buy their alcohol . . . I mean, that's pretty underhanded."

Of course, that was a cover.

He didn't like having to do that, but there was a chance this could be the clue to link the incidents in Koza with the destruction of the Yanbaru Nature Conservation Center.

"You reporters have a tough job. Let's see, we received an order to import some French wine from a distributor in Vietnam."

"Vietnam? What kind of company was it?"

"Uhh . . . Give me a minute."

The man got up from the sofa and came back a few moments later with a blue-colored file already opened up.

"Lycee du Cinq Flèche. It's not a trading company, but an incorporated school."

"A school?"

"Yes. It's an all-girls boarding school. Apparently it's a pretty famous school catering to rich girls. The trading business must be a side project."

That wasn't the answer Okamura was expecting.

It would be a real hassle to import French wine through Vietnam to Japan, and through a school, no less. It was making less sense by the minute.

"Vietnam, huh?" mumbled Okamura as he rubbed his unshaven face with the tips of his fingers.

The muscles from her shoulders along down her arms were as hard as stone.

Saya became intimately aware of how draining on the body it was to swing the still unfamiliar heavy sword again and again.

"This is what I'll use to cut them down."

In order to pluck the life from the demon Chiropterans, something this heavy was necessary. The blade would become a natural extension of her arms. The time at the school, then at the warehouse row, and finally at the nature conservatory . . . every time she struck down a Chiropteran it didn't feel like it was her, but like a completely different person had borrowed her body. Even at track practice, she felt the amount of power in her body was different when she fought the monsters.

Saya made a decision to correct this. She needed to be able to reach her goals on her own.

As she wiped the sweat from her chin, she was interrupted again by the blond man.

Like a teacher of few words, Hagi glanced over Saya's shoulder, and then quietly headed toward the cabins.

Saya turned around to see David walking toward her.

"Saya, there is something I want you to do."

"Me?"

"It may be a tough job, but you are the only one who can do it."

"Okay."

Biting her lip, Saya nodded her head.

"I want to put you undercover as a student at an all-girls boarding school."

"A school? Where?"

"Vietnam."

"Vietnam? . . . All by myself?"

This was not the location she'd been expecting in his answer.

If he had said someplace like Tokyo or Sapporo, then she would have easily accepted the assignment.

To go to a foreign country and enroll in a school as a spy might be easy for people like David who were used to that kind of thing, but how would Saya fare in that sort of situation?

"Julia analyzed the data we got from the Army's Nature Conservation Center, and she found they imported something that had nothing to do with their work there. They imported wine."

"Wine? You mean, alcohol?"

"Yes. For some reason Bordeaux wine was brought through a private company to Yanbaru. It came through order of the U.S. military, so it's not like it was smuggled in."

So at the same place where they were doing research into making man-made Chiropterans they also were secretly importing wine?

"But what does wine have to do with it . . . ?"

"That we don't know. But we do know that the wine didn't come from a typical exporter, but from a well-known school for girls in Vietnam called Lycee du Cinq Flèche. In the past there have been several incidents of students turning up missing or killed."

"You mean by Chiropterans?"

"That's what you are going to find out. I am not going to ask if you are up to it. You must do this."

"I see."

Saya squeezed the cold, sweat-soaked hilt of her sword tighter.

"How nice for you to get a paid vacation and get to go out of the country . . ."

From the living room he could hear the slightest sarcasm in his mother's voice.

"Are you all packed? Do you have your passport?"

"Just relax. I am not a kid, you know."

As he spurned his mother's questions, Akihiro Okamura did a U-turn back into his bedroom and opened his desk drawer. As he dug through his business card holder and signature stamp and important documents, from the back of the drawer popped up his dark–red–covered passport. He quickly put it in his pocket and returned back to the shop.

There was no one in the store. Having never been concerned with the latest fads, since opening the place had never been remodeled or redecorated.

To say Okamura Photo Studio had a long history might be somewhat of an exaggeration, but they had been providing reliable service in the community for many years. However, since his father had passed away, business had almost completely dried up.

"Always scrambling to the last second. You are just like your father."

"Give it a rest. It's always 'Dad this' and 'Dad that.'"

Okamura put his bag up on the shop's counter and threw in several rolls of film and a portable tripod.

"A-kun. You aren't going to miss your plane, are you?"

"I got it. I got it."

Having not changed in thirty years, the nickname she used for him would have been embarrassing to any man who had already participated in the coming-of-age celebrations at age twenty.

Despite his tireless efforts to rise as an ace journalistic photographer, for all he depended on from his parents over the years, Okamura couldn't deny that he was still "A-kun."

But things were going to change, and he sensed something big happening on the horizon.

Discovering the wine bottles the day before, and then uncovering they had been imported from a boarding school in Vietnam, Okamura had made his decision on the spot. He had to go to the source for his investigation to continue.

Obviously he wasn't sure he could make a connection with this and the incidents involving the U.S. Army at Koza.

But he had a feeling. It was a photographer's sixth sense passed down from his father to him, and he could feel it smoldering deep in his thirty-something-year-old body.

But for whatever reason, the newspaper wasn't being as helpful as he had hoped with what they considered a wild goose chase. He had to secure his own funds to continue the information gathering. That's also why he had to use his paid vacation days.

"Vietnam, huh?"

Finishing his preparations, Okamura was about to put his bag over his shoulder when something on the shelf behind the register caught his attention.

It was his father's single-lens reflex camera, and it was arranged on the shelf like a monument to him.

He lifted the camera off the old box-like stand it rested on and moved the box to the counter.

Inside the box was a stack of photos. His father was actually a well-known battlefield photographer, and had been in Vietnam taking pictures during the war.

He casually flipped through the pictures until he got to a certain one.

It was a girl. No, it was a young woman, taken from behind.

She held some kind of stick in her right hand, pointing to the ground. It looked like a Japanese katana, a long-bladed weapon.

The scorched earth appeared to be covered with bodies. They must have been dead. And there wasn't just one or two of them.

The young woman was looking at a huge black form hanging over her—and it was not that of a jungle-dwelling tiger. That part of the photo was out of the focal range, but it looked like the blurry outline of a giant-sized person.

Flipping the photo over, Okamura found the date written on the back.

*December 26, 1972—outskirts of Laos. The day after Christmas.*

"Was it fate that a local reporter like me has to go to Vietnam, the same as Dad did years ago? Is this in our blood, too?"

Smiling sourly, he put the photos back in the box and shut the lid.

"Now, A-kun, you aren't forgetting anything are you?"

"I know. I know."

He had given up on getting her to call him by his name a long time ago. For a second time, Okamura reached out for his bag, but his eyes rested again in the Leica M4 model camera still sitting on the counter. After a moment of hesitation, he picked it up and put it in his pocket.

"Okay. I'm off."

"Have a safe trip."

At some point she had popped her head in from the behind the curtain to the living room and gave a light wave. Okamura walked out of his home.

BOOK TWO: VIETNAM

## 01

EVEN INSIDE THE airport terminal, the humidity overpowered the air conditioners.

Walking from the arrival terminal to the main lobby, Van Argeno pushed up his glasses, which has slipped down his nose due to perspiration.

"It is so humid here. That's why I will never like this country."

The main lobby of Hanoi's Noi Bai International Airport was congested with people. The inside of the building felt more like a backwoods shopping mall, and the space wasn't large enough for the amount of traffic.

To add to that, the ride by car to downtown Hanoi would take over an hour, compounding Van's bad mood.

"I feel terrible forcing you to come to a place like this."

"No, really . . ."

The young Caucasian man pushing the suitcase resting on a cart had come with Van from Okinawa. He was actually one member of the U.S. military research team from the Yanbaru Nature Conservation Center who had happened to live through the ordeal. As bothersome as it was to have to conduct an on-site "mouse" observation, having a young and capable lad drop his Army duties to assist him was a perk. With permission from the home office, he was able to reimburse double the normal compensation from Cinq Flèche to pluck him from his duties.

"Monsieur Argeno."

The voice sounded like it was reading from a script.

It came from out of the blue, with no hints or footsteps preceding it.

Van turned around and saw a younger man standing there. Van's thin eyebrows trembled as he looked him over.

"Let's see. I know you."

"Karl Fei-Ong. I am from Cinq Flèche Pharmaceuticals' Vietnam branch."

His facial features made him look quite young. His long black hair flowed past his shoulders, and the hair in the back of his head was knotted up in a traditional style. It was partially the fault of the long traditional garb he wore, but he had a certain air of female elegance.

"Oh, it's been a long time."

Van extended a hand to him, and Karl stared at it intently.

His eyes got big and radiant like those of a nocturnal bird of prey, and were somehow rather gloomy.

It was when the man's leather-gloved right hand didn't come to meet his, hanging bare from his suit's cuff, that he realized his mistake.

"Oh, that's right! You can't do handshakes. Pardon my rudeness. At least take this as a token of our meeting again."

And his hand moved to his breast pocket—but there wasn't one, so Van dropped a piece of candy into the collar of his traditional dress, and then turned to exit out the glass doors.

"Well, shall we be on our way? There's much I want to ask about your Delta 67 production."

From between the curtains the sunshine poured into the room, bright on his eyelids.

"Morning . . . ?"

Taking in a whiff of the clean pillow, Kai rolled over on the bed and spied the other bed in the room.

Lying on the bed on the other side of the room was Riku, with his girlish-looking face, still sound asleep.

Kai's head felt heavy.

The air inside the room was different than the air in Japan. The high humidity wasn't so different from Okinawa, but if felt hotter here. Since they had come by ship, the time change shouldn't have had much affect. Maybe it was breathing foreign air for the first time that had tapped his energy.

So this was Vietnam.

Taking a deep breath of the hot and sticky air 20 degrees south from where he was accustomed, Kai pulled away the sheets and stood up from the bed. He stepped to the window and from between the curtains, looked down on the harbor below.

The freighter which had carried them from Naha was being unloaded by crane.

It seems that David's group—was it "Red Shield"—was a bit more subdued than he had imagined. His vision was more of MI5 and James Bond, a worldwide organization of country-hopping spies hatching schemes on a global scale, but in reality there weren't any nuclear missiles, jet planes, or laser guns, and they traveled by smuggling themselves on freighter ships.

But still, he needed to be thankful for them bringing them this far. David didn't have to bring Kai and Riku with them, but did so out of compassion.

Perspiration soaked through the back of the T-shirt he'd worn to bed. Kai turned to go to the bathroom, but something on the round table caught his eye.

"Passports?"

A black credit card was there, and a white envelope.

Kai had no recollection. Hadn't he and Riku left their passports at home?

Considering the other items on the table, David must have put them there. Having counterfeit passports arranged was probably no problem for him.

Inside the envelope was a note written in child-like Japanese.

*With this credit card, we could buy even a tank?*

The number at the bottom of the note must have been the PIN number.

"He didn't!"

Kai hurried out the door to the hallway.

At the same time, a hotel employee, a middle-aged woman wearing a uniform, appeared from out of the room next door.

She tossed the bed sheets she was holding into the big laundry basket on a cart resting in the hallway.

He peeked into the room, but there was no one there.

This was definitely the room that David and Louis had stayed in the night before.

"Excuse me. Where are the two men that were in this room last night?"

She had the darker-toned skin of a Southeast Asian, and she looked at Kai suspiciously.

She said a few words in the local tongue, and pushed the cart down the hall. Since he couldn't understand her, Kai guessed she was telling him to ask at the front desk.

Kai hurried to the lobby and asked the same question there. Using his poor English, what he gathered was that the only guests in the hotel at that time traveling from Japan were Kai and Riku.

David, Louis, Hagi, Julia, and of course, Saya.

Their five traveling partners had checked out a long time ago.

Kai and Riku were left behind!

Kai cursed himself for thinking nice thoughts about David a few minutes earlier.

"Hey, Riku! Wake up!"

"What's wrong? We don't have to go to school, you know, Brother."

"School is the least of our worries right now."

After pulling Riku from the bed, Kai changed his clothes and they made an early morning trip to Hyphong Port.

The freighter they'd come in on was still being unloaded. A forklift carrying some of the containers made its way toward a warehouse.

A hard hat–wearing sailor walked down the ship's gangplank.

"Hey, you know where David is?"

"Who the hell you talkin' about?"

Interrogated by Kai out of the blue, the sailor seemed dubious about Kai's intentions.

"He was a passenger on this ship. There was also a girl named Saya."

"Hell if I know."

"What are you talking about?! We rode on this ship from Japan!"

"Look at it. It's a freighter. It ain't no passenger ship."

"But he's telling you the truth. We rode this . . ." protested Riku, but his voice got weak as the sailor grimaced.

Kai, Riku, and the others had had cabins separate from the sailors, and they'd used the mess hall at different times, but they'd still shared the same closed space. During the passage on the ship they'd traded glances countless times.

There was no mistake. This was the ship they'd come on.

"Let me see the inside of the ship."

"You're getting to be a pain in the ass. Maybe I should just call the cops."

As Kai attempted to make his way up the gangway, the thick-skinned hands of the sailor grabbed him by the arms.

Hearing the exchange, another sailor popped his head over the handrail from on the ship.

"Anything wrong?"

"Just these punk kids . . ."

"What the—? What're they doing back?"

"You dipshit."

The sailor on the ground grabbed his own face to suppress his frustration.

Realizing his gaffe, the above sailor's expression shifted to embarrassment.

"I knew it. You know who the hell we are. Why don't you tell us what's going on?"

"What can I say?"

He rubbed his tanned brow and blew out a cigarette-stained sigh.

"The main guy and those people you left with yesterday? They ain't been back."

"And Saya, too? Where did they go?"

"You got me. Even though we was told not to say anything if you showed up, we really didn't know anything in the first place. We move stuff from one place to another. Containers, people, it's all the same."

The sailor gave Kai a cold pat on the back and then turned the other way.

He didn't act like someone who was hiding anything more. There was no point in pushing the sailor further. And if he really did keep his promise of calling the local police, well, that would just cause more problems.

Kai watched the man walk toward the containers for several seconds, and then ran his fingers through his red-tinted hair.

"We got played."

Riku nervously tugged at the hem of his shirt as he looked up at Kai helplessly.

"They left us here, didn't they?"

"Pretty much."

"So . . . now what do we do?"

". . ."

If this were the Sea of Japan in winter, the sea breeze would have chilled their bones.

Unfortunately they were in the sub-tropics of Southeast Asia. A seagull landed on a nearby dock pole, and looked up at the sky with contempt.

Just like in Japan, transfer students in Vietnam start classes on their first day of school.

Once a French colony, the school system was modeled after the French style, and one class lasted ninety minutes, which felt like a very long time for Saya.

It was still morning, but the temperature was already pretty high. It reminded her a little of summer in Okinawa.

The limestone-colored passageways reminded her of a Greek or Italian villa facing the Mediterranean Sea, and being in the shade, they were surprisingly cool.

Also, the school uniform was designed for the climate, and helped keep her from getting too hot. The traditional dress for Vietnamese women was called an *ao dai*. This was the school uniform at the all-girls boarding school Lycee du Cinq Flèche, and was what Saya was wearing as she started school there.

Draped in the long *ao dai* tunic, Saya entered the restroom.

After closing the stall door, Saya pressed the DIAL button on her cell phone.

"It's Saya."

"What's wrong? Don't forget our scheduled call time."

"I'm sorry. I am just not used to all this."

"Okay. It's all right."

She didn't get the impression he was actually angry.

"How is the inside of the school?"

"Umm ... It's a very nice place. It seems more European than Southeast Asian. The flowers in the central garden are very beautiful."

"That's not what I am asking . . . I mean the Chiropterans."

"Oh, yes, of course. Well, nothing yet."

"Saya, stay focused. There is a possibility of Chiropterans in Lycee."

"Yes."

"We'll pursue the Delta 67 trail. If you discover a Chiropteran, don't hesitate to kill it."

"I know."

That was the whole reason she was here.

Saya hung up the phone and checked her hair in the restroom mirror. She then sped off to the hallway, but suddenly her legs stopped moving.

A figure as thin as a nail was waiting for her.

It was a dignified middle-aged woman. She had the expressionless look of someone who valued order above all, and Saya found it quite intimidating.

The *ao dai* the teacher wore looked more like a military uniform.

The dormitory's head-mistress, Ms. Lee, spoke to her without any emotional inflection.

"Aside from faculty, the use of phones in school is strictly prohibited."

"I am very sorry . . ."

"That includes the possession of portable telephones."

Saya averted her glance from the woman's gray-colored eyes and swung her hand holding the cell phone behind her back.

Ever since she'd met this woman who'd given her a tour of the campus and dormitory, Saya felt a cold chill when she looked her in the eye.

"I'll let it go. This time. Being that you are a mid-semester transfer student."

The smile that remained on her face wasn't nearly as generous as her words. At the same time, Saya could hear footsteps coming up behind her as the teacher walked away.

The already flustered Saya's tension level rose again.

"What happened?"

She turned to see the twinkling eyes behind the glasses of a younger-looking girl.

It was her new classmate, Min. They were also roommates in the dormitory. Min had already been a big help, as Saya didn't speak Vietnamese.

"Oh, I see. Your phone. Did Ms. Lee see it?"

"Yeah."

"Is that phone from Japan? You don't have any *purikura* stickers on it? We have it here, too, you know. Japanese TV shows and *anime* are really popular here. Do you know the band SMAP?"

"Oh . . . yeah."

"Have you ever met them?"

"No, but . . ."

As Min slipped her arm under hers, Saya felt a little perplexed by this girl's proactive affection.

Introduced as a transfer student, Saya hadn't known her classmate for even half of a day, yet Min treated her as if she was a member of her family.

"After you left the classroom you took so long in coming back, I figured you got lost. For a second, I worried the Phantom might have taken you away."

"The Phantom?"

"The Phantom likes girls with black hair."

Min squeezed Saya's arm as they walked back down the hallway.

As they came to a corner which turned at the garden in the center of the school, Min stopped and raised her arm up diagonally.

She pointed to a tall Christian-looking bell tower that must have been used to signal certain times of the day.

"In that tower. That's where the Phantom appears. Once every few years."

". . ."

"They say he fell in love with the most beautiful girl in the school. But the Phantom wanted the girl to make a vow of eternal love to him. He could never be betrayed. If he was . . . then certain death."

Min's eyes glared over her glasses at Saya.

An out-of-place cold chill ran down Saya's spine.

Min's expression suddenly changed.

"At least that is how the rumor goes. I'm sorry. Do these kinds of stories bother you?"

"No . . . no."

Even though she replied with an awkward laugh, Saya was a little anxious.

Yet, this talk of a Phantom seemed little more than typical high-school folklore.

At Koza Commercial High there were similar tales. Like the one about the portrait of Mozart with moving eyes in the music room, or the one about the blackened ghost of the girl who died in a fire showing up in the teacher's bathroom after school. Kaori used to talk about that stuff a lot.

Suddenly faced with the story of the Phantom, it was difficult for Saya to just write it off.

The main reason was because there was a Chiropteran in this school.

"Do you know what the Phantom looks like?"

"No one has really seen him clearly. But I think he must look like him."

Min was looking at the central garden, and her cheeks were flushed.

Saya heard the sound of iron scraping.

She turned her head to find out what Min was so absorbed by, and could hardly believe what she saw.

There were a couple of gardeners pruning a tree under the bright sunlight.

One was an old man, and the other one was—

It was the soul-snatching good looks of a handsome young man. Hagi.

Dressed as an unsophisticated groundskeeper, his movements and posture couldn't hide his natural grace and elegance. Held in those hands, even a rose or lily would be hard-pressed to find complaint in his delicate treatment with the pruning shears.

"You really shouldn't be snipping those."

". . ."

Hagi remained expressionless as the older gardener poked him in the chest as he spread the petals of the rose he had just picked. It was almost like he was meditating.

It wasn't as if this garden was completely pristine.

"Don't you think he is totally cool? They just hired him. And ever since he got here . . . well, see for yourself."

Saya stared at the out-of-place young man in mute amazement. Noticing Min looking at Saya's confused expression, Saya turned away feeling incredibly uncomfortable with the whole scene.

From the corridors surrounding the garden, students started traveling back and forth and milling about. It was a break between classes.

Girls were resting their backs on the pillars chatting about class preparations, or walking in pairs through the passageways toward the garden, but Saya noticed that every single girl was stealing long glances at the young gardener as he worked.

They gazed at him as if they were the fair maidens and he was the prince who had ridden in on his white horse ready to whisk them away.

Naturally, Min was no exception. She held her hands together in front of her chest and was looking up as if she were wishing upon a star.

"If he was the Phantom, I would easily profess my undying love!"

"Hee hee . . . Ah ha ha"

Saya couldn't hold back her laughter.

"Don't laugh. It's a romantic story."

"So-sorry."

Despite Min's cross expression, Saya couldn't stop herself from giggling.

Seeing Hagi dressed in the gardener outfit was funny enough on its own, but then to have all these girls drooling over him made it even more hilarious.

"Stop laughing!"


Maybe it had been from laughing too hard, but she sat through the following class without really listening.

She couldn't really carry on a regular conversation in Vietnamese, and her mastery of reading and writing left a lot to be desired. She had a pretty good idea what was going on in math class when they were talking about numerical formulas, but when it was Vietnamese language or history classes, Saya was completely lost. If it wasn't for Min's explanations Saya wouldn't have understood anything taught in those classes.

But there was one positive discovery.

Saya was good at French.

French was Vietnam's second official language. As they traveled on the ship from Okinawa, Julia taught Saya some phrases in French, and Saya picked them up very quickly with surprisingly little struggle. It wasn't like she was learning it, but just refreshing her memory.

"Memory is like a sword. When it becomes rusty, all you need to do is polish it for it to become sharp again," teased Julia.

That's all that Julia taught her, but Saya was able to conclude that at some point in her past she'd lived in a French-speaking environment.

At any rate, Saya would have to continue to try and overcome her struggles in the classroom, at least until lunchtime.

The cafeteria looked more like a western-style ballroom, only the air was filled with the smell of *nuoc mam* fish sauce.

It was the equivalent of soy sauce or *miso* in Japanese cooking. For the people of this country, the smell of rotting fish was apparently a staple in their cooking.

"A lot of non-Vietnamese don't really like this smell."

"Really?"

"But, it doesn't bother you, Saya."

Min watched in wonder as the mountain of food set in front of Saya disappeared at an alarming rate.

Saya's chopsticks and mouth never took a rest. Not being picky eaters was a forte the entire Miyagusuku family shared.

"You must have been hungry."

"Well, this is normal for me."

"No way. And you don't get fat? And I am on a diet, too."

Min's comment caused Saya's chopsticks to stop moving for the first time.

"What is it?"

"Nothing . . . I had a friend who said the same thing to me . . ."

That had been the day before the big track meet.

But Saya wasn't able to participate in the meet. That night she'd had had her first confrontation with a Chiropteran, and her entire life had changed. It was possible that she would never get so speak with Kaori again.

The sounds of surrounding conversations and spoons clanking on dishes returned to Saya's ears.

". . . You and me, we're friends, right?"

Min seemed angry as she leaned into her question, but then smiled, and couldn't help but laugh.

"Here, take mine."

"Thanks!"

Proving her friendship, Saya picked up the *bo bia* spring roll her classmate slid to her and took a big bite.

"So, what are Japanese schools like?"

"What are they like? . . . Just normal, I guess," Saya answered as she chewed.

Thinking about it, Koza Commercial High School was the only other school she had any other knowledge of. She really had no idea what other Japanese schools were like.

"So you lived in a dormitory?"

"No, I commuted from home. I was always running late, and Kai would give me a ride on his motorcycle . . ."

"Kai?"

"My older brother."

"You have an older brother?"

Planting both elbows on the table, Min leaned into the conversation.

Her curiosity was clear through the speed and intensity with which she asked the question, along with the sparkle in her eye.

Saya realized that it wasn't that Min was on a diet as much as Min preferred conversation over eating.

"Yeah. A younger brother, too."

"Did they come with you to Vietnam?"

"Yeah . . ."

The long Vietnamese chopsticks Saya held paused in the air, and her gaze lowered.

She wondered where Kai and Riku were, and what they were doing.

It had been a week since they had separated at the harbor. They had come together that far, but it was too dangerous for Kai and Riku to be a part of the hunt for Chiropterans. That was the only reason they were separated. Saya assumed David had already made their arrangements to get back to Japan.

"Are they going to school in Vietnam?"

"Yeah . . ."

Saya's tongue felt heavy. She didn't want to have to lie to someone she had just met. Min had already called her a friend . . .

"Then introduce me!"

"Huh?"

Saya was surprised to look up and see Min's eyes almost touching hers. If crawling up onto the table like Min had was really against the rules, surely someone would have warned her by now.

"I am sure your older brother and I will get along great."

"Bu-but, I thought you liked the gardener . . ."

"I like him, too, but in the meantime I want a boyfriend. The only people in our class who haven't kissed a boy yet are me and Anna-Marie."

"Wai-wait. No, no!"

Saya shook her hands in the air, waiving off the implications of Min's statement.

"Then maybe she can give me a little advice?"

The pointed words hit Min's back like a snowstorm. She pulled her head back, and from behind her Saya could see a tall girl standing behind Min's chair.

She was an amazingly beautiful young woman. The girls that had walked up with her looked mostly Southeast Asian and Chinese, but the one who had spoken was a Caucasian girl with pale skin that looked as smooth as silk.

"Spreading rumors about someone isn't only a sign of a person with poor character, but will also cause their friends to lose trust in them."

She stood in front of her cohorts, and even though her words came out calmly, her cheeks had turned red and her eyes showed nothing but contempt.

Saya had heard that Anna-Marie was the student with the highest honors in their grade. She initially came across as a striking figure, and the way the other girls seemed to hang on her every word showed Saya that this girl was the queen of the campus.

"Let's not worry about them, Anna-Marie."

"That's right. There's no point in wasting your time on that blabbermouth, Min."

Taking her minions' advice, Anna-Marie turned her back and walked away from their table, as Min visibly bit her lip.

"She's Ms. Lee's pet. If she tattles on you, you might get sent to the detention room. Saya, you should be careful around her."

Anna-Marie must have been within earshot, as she spun around and came back to the table.

"Did you say 'tattle'? Do you really think I would stoop that low?"

Her voice had no emotion, but she had come in so close, her nose was almost touching Min's as she glared into her eyes. Anna-Marie's face was rock hard, but her ears had turned red. Her pristine, mannered, rich-girl exterior was beginning to show signs of cracking. The intimidated Min reeled back stiffly and gave an ingratiating smile.

"Aah . . . I-I'm so sorry. You are right, I went too far. Say, are you hungry? Here, take this."

From her plate Min picked up what looked like a spring roll and placed it in Anna-Marie's palm.

"Why, thank you."

Without missing a beat, Anna-Marie clenched her hand into a fist, squishing the roll. Peanut sauce oozed out like blood from both sides of her hand. Shocked by the display, Saya's face went pale.

Saya was afraid it would escalate beyond this, but, thankfully, that's where it ended.

It seemed the school princess didn't like to resort to using force. Min and Anna-Marie's followers had all stopped breathing as they waited to see her turn, once again, from the table.

After squeezing out the entire contents of Min's roll onto the floor, Anna-Marie walked away with a practiced catwalk-like gait. The students in her path quickly moved out of her way to let her pass.

Min waited until Anna-Marie was completely out of sight before she let out a deep breath, as if she had just risen up from the bottom of the ocean.

"Uwaa—that was scary . . ."

"Yeah . . ."

Min wasn't completely fault-free, but what Saya understood as the balance of power, and it didn't have anything to do with home countries, was very fragile and volatile. Saya knew from her school in Japan that there were honor students and trendy, fashion-conscious students and introverted students, and they did fine on their own. However, when individuals from one interacted with individuals from another, then friction could happen.

The relationship problems of high school students might seem trivial to adults, but the politics of these relationships completely dominated young people's everyday lives.

Saya only had memories of the last year, so she had no experience of dealing with long-term issues. She was more familiar with the isolation of being the new girl. It was still a foreign concept to her, but her first sense of feeling like part of a group had been when Kaori invited her to join the track and field team.

That thought felt like so far in the past, like an old faded photograph, as Saya observed Min and Anna-Marie's volatile relationship with envy. They fight with each other and complain about each other, and this is their high school day-to-day life.

Saya would likely never be able to return to the life of a normal high school student. Besides studying and club activities and shopping on weekends, Saya had something else important she had to do.

"Can you tell me a little more about the Phantom?"

"I get it. You got a thing for the new gardener, too."

"No, that's not it . . ."

"Doesn't he look just perfect holding a rose in his hand?"

"A rose?"

"The Phantom gives a rose to the girl he loves. A blue rose."

"Blue rose . . ."

There were roses in Okinawa, but Saya only remember seeing white and red varieties.

This might need to be investigated further.

After classes were over a majority of the students returned to the dormitories. Since the dorms and the school were in the same place, Saya felt like no matter which she was in, it seemed like the same place, and most of the students didn't chat and relax, but went to their rooms to study. A lot of the girls enrolled in this school were daughters of foreign diplomats, Vietnamese government officials, and company heads. They were much more focused than typical Japanese public high school students.

It was also better being out of the public eye.

It was a late afternoon hour when Saya and Hagi were the only two in the central garden.

From inside the pagoda in the center of the gravel path, Saya could her the twitter of tiny birds taking a rest on the roof.

"Roses really have a unique smell."

"Yes."

The beautiful gardener gave a brief response as he kneeled to check under the green leaves of the roses for signs of insects.

"Hagi, have you heard of blue roses?"

"There is no breed of rose which will bloom a blue flower. It's not a necessary color."

"They say the Phantom gives girls blue roses."

"Phantom."

"It's a mysterious person that appears on this campus. I think it might be a Chiropteran."

Saya looked up at the bell tower. It cast a long shadow over the garden.

"I heard girls who betray the Phantom are murdered up there. I think I am going to go take a look."

To enter the bell tower, one needed to go through the cathedral. Saya started walking that direction.

"Here."

Saya turned to see what Hagi was saying.

In his left hand he held out a silver cross to her. No, it was a bare dagger.

"For your protection."

"Thank you."

Of course, she wasn't able to walk around school with her long sword.

"Does David-san and the others know you are here?"

"No."

"I see. Well, it makes me feel better having you close, Hagi."

Saya took the dagger from Hagi's palm and turned once again to enter the cathedral.

They walked under the Romanesque archway and into the building.

The interior of the cathedral was cool and dark.

To get to the entry of the bell tower they walked up a flight of stairs which led to a balcony inside the cathedral. They made their way to the tower door.

In front of it was a velvet rope, like the ones at a museum.

Just as she was about the step over the rope, Hagi looked down into the interior of the cathedral.

"Just what do you think you are doing?"

Saya recognized the voice, but it wasn't usually this uncomfortable sounding.

Lit by the colored rays of the afternoon sun through the stained-glass windows, Saya could see the creases on Ms. Lee's forehead were more than usually profound.

"That area is off-limits to students."

"Oh . . . I am so sorry."

"You again? Most new transfer students aren't quite this careless about the rules."

Saya hurriedly stood up straight, hiding the dagger behind her back.

Ms. Lee's voice and expression sent a message of true irritation.

"Is there some sort of problem?"

From the partially sunken sanctuary area in the back of the cathedral on the same ground floor came the voice of a young man.

"No, sir, Chairman."

Suddenly Saya had the impression that Ms. Lee was not so upset at Saya because she broken the rules, but was more worried that this man would notice it. As he walked in front of the left-hand transept, exiting the inner sanctuary, Saya was able to see the figure of the man who spoke between the gaps in the stone pillars as he walked down the aisle.

She'd called him Chairman, so he must been in charge of this campus, which would put him in the upper echelons of society here. However, he looked incredibly young.

In the thin darkness he flapped his long garb like the wings of a hawk.

"And you are?"

"I-I am very very sorry. It won't happen again."

For Ms. Lee's sake, and for her own sake, she didn't want to make matters any worse. Saya stood stiff and bowed so low her head almost hit her knees. And without waiting for a response she turned the other way.

Saya grabbed Hagi by the wrist and bolted down the stairs, careful not to bump into Ms. Lee, and went through the front entrance.

They split up again at the central garden.

"That outfit looks good on you."

". . . Yours on you, too."

As far as compliments go, they couldn't have been less heartfelt.

Saya giggled as she pulled up the long hem of her *ao dai* and fluttered it like a butterfly as she skipped out of the garden.

Something caught her eye and she turned to see the door to the cathedral slowly closing. From the shrinking gap in the door she could see the young man called the Chairman walking back to the transept.

She couldn't see his face clearly, but she had the distinct sense that he was looking at her the entire time.


"Anna-Marie is pretty angry."

These were the first words out of Min's mouth as Saya walked through the door of their dorm room.

"Huh?"

"She heard that you and that handsome gardener were talking alone."

"Oh that . . . Well . . ."

Saya stuttered as she tried to come up with an excuse.

Rumors in a school like this could surely take a life of their own, so there was no point in trying to hide what was already known. Saya wondered who had seen her, and from where. In a closed system where all the students live together, apparently everyone knows what everyone else is up to. Saya would have to be careful from now on.

"I just wanted to take a walk on my own, and happened to bump into him."

Already changed into her sleepwear chemise, Min's laugh almost sounded accusing.

Saya grabbed her sleepwear, and felt extremely uncomfortable as she entered the bathroom.

Seemingly unaware of Saya's discomfort, Min crawled from her bed on all fours toward Saya.

"So what did you two talk about? What's his name?"

"No, I don't know . . . I mean, I just asked him about blue roses."

Saya pushed back Min's barrage of questions with both hands.

Min was back on her bed, sitting on her sheets, hugging her pillow. The corners of her lips were turned down in disappointment.

"C'mon, that's all? Really, what did he say?"

"Well, he said that blue roses didn't exist."

"Really? But, like, this school is sponsored by a drug company, and they can make new kinds of roses now."

"That reminds me, I saw the school's chairman earlier."

"He must be getting ready for the annual ball."

"Annual ball?"

This phrase was completely out of Saya's realm of comprehension, and she surely didn't hide the confusion in the volume of her voice well.

According to Min, at Lycee du Cinq Flèche they have a large-scale organized social event.

Nothing like she described would ever happen at a Japanese high school. It was a dance social combined with a culture festival that was attended by parents, guardians, and sponsors, as well as consulate staff from many different countries and was held every year.

"If I could meet a cute boy there, that would be perfect . . ."

"Oh, yeah . . ."

Saya forced a smile as she opened the door to the bathroom.

Even when it was time for lights out, Min continued the conversation in the dark.

"I was in a room by myself for so long, I am really happy you came here, Saya."

Min giggled to herself bashfully, but then soon became quiet, telling Saya that she had fallen asleep. Saya carefully slipped off her bed, making sure not to make any noise.

She stepped out of her room, and into the empty hallway. Looking down onto the central garden from a hallway window, the moon burned brightly on the tall spire.

". . . Phantom."

She gripped the dagger she'd received from Hagi tightly, and her palm was slick with nervous sweat.

Although it was believed that the southern Asian countries live in eternal summer weather, at night the temperature took a significant dip. Saya wore a robe over her chemise dress as she tiptoed toward her destination.

It was when Saya was about to step over the velvet rope to the bell tower that she noticed it.

The double doors leading to the stairway up were open a crack. Saya took it to be a provocative grin.

Saya pushed on the big wooden doors, and they spread open effortlessly.

A faint orange glow danced off of the stone walls. It wasn't an electric or gas light. It must have been candlelight. And it was coming from above the stairs.

Taking extreme caution, Saya slowly started to climb the stairs. The winding staircase hugged the four walls of the bell tower, and reminded Saya of a slithering snake. Finally, she reached the top of the staircase to find a large bell surrounded by a narrow balcony.

The thick golden bell reflected the moonlight off its surface. This school's chimes were not electronically reproduced, but done by hand with this gigantic copper bell which hung from an enormous beam in the tower's ceiling.

There didn't appear to be anyone else up there.

"..."

The tension in Saya's shoulders waned, but then she noticed something else bizarre.

The top of this tower wasn't in the dark.

The source of light was a candlestick resting on the windowsill.

However the flame writhed in agony, fighting to stay alive, but anticipating certain death.

The fact that there was a lit candlestick meant that—

The carbonized wick of the candle was no longer insulated by the melted wax, and the flame went out.

Darkness took reign over the top of the bell tower, and Saya became very aware of the movement of the night air. She turned around.

Right in front of her face Saya saw what looked like a man-sized bat spreading its wings.

The wings wrapped themselves around Saya's body.

A moment later Saya threw herself backward away from the dark enclosure.

"Phantom?!"

Had this school's ghoul actually revealed itself?

The moonlight flowing through the window illuminated the upper half of the figure assaulting Saya.

It was framed like the stage entrance of a play's demon or vampire. He was wearing a sinister-looking disguise made up of a long black cloak and a mask. It was such a stereotypical look that if it had been daytime, Saya might have burst out laughing.

However, alone in the middle of the night, Saya was not in a joking mood.

Saya noticed something else about him.

The eye staring at her from behind the mask that covered the top half of his face glared at her feverishly.

Then he moved.

He become one with the shadow on the wall and moved at an unimaginable speed, closing in on Saya.

"Oof!"

As Saya moved sideways to avoid being struck, she thrust the dagger as hard as she could.

Blood sprayed into the air as the man fluttered his cloak and turned around at the window. His lips parted slightly, revealing his white teeth.

"Unh . . ."

Saya followed the banister, staring at the man, but also putting as much distance as possible between them.

The handle of the dagger buried deeply through his cloak and into his abdomen moved slightly. The man's flesh was pushing the dagger out from the inside.

Saya heard a refreshing plop, then the sound of the dagger hitting the floor.

The red cut that was visible through the tear in the fabric closed up and disappeared amazingly quickly.

This power could mean only one thing.

". . . Chiropteran."

His wide grin affirmed Saya's guess. As if he was dancing, he threw out his arms spreading his cloak wide, and took a step toward her.

He then suddenly jumped, not at Saya, but to his side.

It was to avoid the silent strike from an enemy who had attacked him from his rear.

Tearing only through the cloak and sticking out of the floor was a cross-shaped dagger similar to the one Saya had held only moments before.

"Hagi!"

He must have jumped up from the roof of the cathedral. He flew into the belfry like an owl, and he spun his right hand around as his feet slid across the ground. The cello case was positioned as a battering ram, and he aimed it at the man's abdomen.

"Ha ha ha."

His jubilant laugh echoed throughout the bell tower.

He twisted his body around gracefully, and held out his cloak like a matador taunting a bull. He jumped up and spun off the balcony handrail and swung at Hagi's cheek with the back of his gloved right hand.

The vision of blood smeared across Hagi's face sent a chill through Saya's body.

However, Hagi had pulled back, and the gloved fist missed its target. Hagi continued the motion coming back around with another swing of the cello case. It was an overhand swing, and despite the weight of the case, his enemy was able to fend it off with only his right arm.

Even if he was a Chiropteran, how was he able to fend off Hagi's attacks? His hand and skull should have been crushed.

The impact sounded like something hard hitting something hard.

Countless shreds of cloth from the man's sleeve fell through the air.

But his naked arm showed no signs of injury. "Naked" maybe wasn't the right word, as it didn't appear to be human flesh. The deflected cello case banged straight into the giant bell.

Hearing the bell chime at such a close proximity was almost enough to break Saya's eardrums.

Saya covered her ears like her life depended on it.

"This has to be it for tonight—"

Saya saw the retreating man's mouth move, but couldn't hear what he was saying.

Before she knew it, he dove out the window of the belfry with his back to the moon.

Saya ran to the window to follow the path of the cloak-winged man, but by the time she got to the window and looked down, she couldn't see anything.

The Phantom had disappeared.

+

Hanoi was hot.

It didn't matter what season it was, the sun beat down on this country all year long.

Raised in Okinawa, Riku was used to hot and humid weather, but the differences between Vietnam and home were enough to feel like torture.

For example, of all the shops and restaurants facing the street they were on, not one had an air conditioner. Some places had an electric fan in a corner of the shop, but that had about as much meaning as pouring water into a live volcano.

One redeeming factor was that all the restaurants and fruit and vegetable shops had mostly open fronts, allowing for ventilation.

But along with the breeze came swarms of flies, which was even more annoying.

"Damn . . . What a pain in the ass."

Sitting across from Riku was Kai, who batted at the flies with one hand as he scooped *pho* noodles in his mouth using chopsticks in the other.

He then tried to catch a fly using his chopsticks like the master swordsmen from the old days.

As noble as his efforts were, Riku hoped that he wasn't successful in his self-appointed mission.

"You can't eat with chopsticks that have touched a fly. That's dirty."

"I guarantee you this shop's kitchen is a nest of cockroaches at night. Clean, dirty, it's all the same."

"Kai-niichan!"

Riku immediately looked over at the group of regular-looking customers who could have heard Kai, but they were intently watching a soccer match on TV with the older lady that was the noodle shop's owner, and took no mind to Kai's comment.

It was a good thing none of them understood Japanese. As Riku turned back to Kai he lifted up the black American Express credit card lying on the table.

"I wonder how much money is in here."

More than gold or platinum cards, black credit cards were a measure of not only the holder's economic status, but his social status. Or so Riku had heard.

"The note said that it was enough to buy a tank."

"A tank? So that's like five million yen?"

"More like ten million, I'm guessing. But what do I know?"

"Why did they give us all this money, all of a sudden?"

"Gee. I wonder."

Kai was playing stupid, but Riku caught on to what he was saying.

This was more than enough to get back to Japan. This was for the parentless brothers to live stress-free lives back home. David had arranged this.

Kai set his bowl down and leaned back.

"Shall we?"

"Where to?"

"Where do you think? To look for Saya."

"..."

The black flies flew in spirals near his bowl, but Riku didn't move.

"What's wrong?"

"I don't think Saya-neechan is in this country anymore," said Riku as he stared at the clear soup in his bowl.

He didn't have to look up to know that Kai's expression had changed.

"What makes you think that?"

"I mean, we looked this hard already, and we haven't found anything."

They'd spent the first day-and-a-half at the Hyphong Port city, then spread the search for the last six days to all the hotels on the map in Hanoi, Vietnam's largest city. They had come up with nothing.

What Riku was afraid of wasn't that they would never find Saya. He would spend all the time in the world if it meant finding her safe. However—

"Neechan left without saying anything to us, right? It just makes me think that she didn't want to be with us anymore . . . that she wanted to keep us out of danger."

"So, what do you want to do? Are you saying we should go home without her? Leave Saya here?"

As he tried to consider an answer Riku felt something rub lightly against his foot.

When he peeked under the table, he saw a strange brown-colored baseball. He picked it up and looked at it closely before realizing who it belonged to.

The hemp-colored summer dress contrasted nicely with her cocoa-colored shoulders and limbs.

The gracefully featured girl looked to be about Riku's age, and she smiled at him from the near side of the sidewalk.

"Heeya!"

At the same time he heard Kai's yell, Riku saw the boy carrying a wooden baseball bat and another boy, the catcher, run away. What looked to be a young umpire ran off the other direction. The baseball he pitched hit the wall behind the batter box and bounced into the dirt rolling almost all the way back to the pitcher's mound.

"C'mon! C'mon! That's no way to catch!"

"So childish sometimes," commented Riku, sitting on a slope facing the playing field.

It appeared that the young girl sitting next to him had a different impression.

"Your brother is really amazing."

"Well, yeah. He was an ace pitcher at his high school."

"I heard that baseball is really popular in Japan. That's so cool."

The owner of the baseball was a girl named Mui.

"Nobody around here even knows the rules. And they don't sell the equipment. It's a real pain. The only people we have to play against are the students from the Japanese school."

She told him that the balls and bats they had were hand-me-downs from that Japanese school.

Despite her unnatural rhythm, her Japanese was excellent, and it appeared that Riku had made an international exchange through a shared enjoyment of sports.

"I thought they played baseball everywhere."

"The Japanese school teacher told me that it's mostly played in North America, the Caribbean, and then in Japan, Korea, and Taiwan, and those are about all. France and England don't know anything about baseball . . . just like here, all the kids play soccer."

So that was why Mui was staring so intently at Kai on the pitcher's mound.

"To tell you the truth, I think we are very happy to have met someone who plays baseball."

"Just a lucky coincidence."

Riku watched Kai's super fastball send the other kids scattering in every direction and tilted his head in confusion.

"If my body was in better condition, I would definitely be playing, too."

"Huh?"

"The doctor told me I can't overextend myself."

"Oh. Really . . . ?"

More surprising than the sad statement by Mui was the fact that she didn't seem all that bothered by it.

In Riku's elementary school class there was a girl who had asthma who couldn't participate in gym class. Like Mui, she seemed perfectly healthy from the outside.

"Riku, don't you play baseball, too?"

"I am not good at sports like my brother. I spend more time reading and playing video games, I guess."

"You have a game system? You must be rich!"

"No, not at all . . . Well, actually now that you mention it, right now maybe we are rich."

Riku patted the pocket with the credit card in it and corrected his words. Mui's expression didn't change to one of envy.

A shadow unexpectedly fell over their backs.

"What is this? Usually Mui is stuck watching baseball all by herself."

A Vietnamese man, about thirty years old, came down the slope grinning.

"They're our new friends. This is Riku. Over there is Kai."

"*Konnichiwa*. I am guessing you are Japanese."

His Japanese was flawless. Maybe he was a member of Mui's family. But he seemed too young to be her father.

"Mui, did you remember to take your medicine?"

"Oops, I forgot."

"That's not good, Mui. That medicine is donated to you."

"Can I wait until this game is over? I'll take it right after."

The man smiled and patted Mui's head lovingly.

"Take it right when you get home."

"Okay."

Mui smiled and turned her attention back to the playing field. The man then looked at Riku.

"Are you two traveling on vacation?"

"Ah, yes. Basically."

"How about your parents?"

"It's just the two of us."

"Oh, that is . . . Two brothers traveling alone. Quite impressive."

It seemed like he understood there was another reason they couldn't go back to their home country. For a moment his face looked very serious, then it returned to his friendly smile.

"Well, if you aren't in any hurry, I am sure Mui would love to have you two join us in our home for dinner."

"Riku, I bet everyone would love to hear Kai talk about baseball, too . . ."

Mui placed a hand on Riku's shoulder, and her face came so close to Riku's his cheeks turned red. He couldn't help but accept the invitation.

"Yeah, sure, okay . . ."

Mui and all the boys made it home during the slow-moving dusk, and Riku was a little surprised by what he saw.

It wasn't a house, and it wasn't an apartment building. It looked more like a school.

"This is my home. We all live here."

It was a private, volunteer-run juvenile protection facility. Mui and the others were orphans who had been abandoned by their parents.

Riku didn't have parents anymore, either. George, who was his father after his real father, was gone now. His only family was Kai and Saya. But now Saya was somewhere else, and Riku realized that as they had been wandering around this foreign country, he hadn't had much to smile about.

Walking out of the kitchen carrying a large pot, Riku saw Kai, who was brandishing a ladle, being surrounded by younger kids.

"You never give up! I told you, we'll play baseball again tomorrow. If you don't eat, you won't even make it to first base."

Kai looked stern-faced, but the kids saw through that and were sensitive to his true kindness. They didn't seem the least bit afraid of him.

"I'm sorry. It sounds like you guys were forced to come here."

Riku turned around to see a volunteer lady bring a pile of plates to the table. She spoke in a mix of Japanese and English.

"Oh, no! Not at all. I haven't seen Kai having this much fun in a long time."

"The kids are happy, too."

"But, you made us dinner, and are giving us a place to stay . . ."

"Don't think twice about it."

She told him children shouldn't worry so much and then chuckled to herself.

"We get support from a company that receives donations from places like Japan and Europe. We have plenty to go around."

"Like for Mui's medicine?"

"That's right. A French drug company supplies her medicine at no cost—oh, over there. It's that guy."

The lady quickly set the plates on the table and looked at the doorway.

Standing with his back to the hallway was an Asian man in a business suit. He bowed and entered the room.

"Here's today's supply."

The man took a sealed medicine bottle out of his briefcase.


After her first night, Saya went to the classroom and was met with a surprise.

When she walked into her third-floor classroom the entire room full of girls turned and looked at her.

"Umm. . .What's wrong?" Saya asked Min as she stood frozen in the doorway.

"Look," said Alison, a close friend of Min's. She pointed to Saya's desk as she eyed Saya curiously.

The girls turned back to their desks one by one. So here was what everyone was worked up about.

On top of the desk someone had placed a rose. Its petals were opened up facing the ceiling.

It was a deep blue, the color of sapphire.

The fresh perfume of the rose wafted up her nostrils.

"What's this? A blue rose! Could it be a proposal of love from the Phantom?!"

Min's excited declaration caused the entire class to go into a shrieking uproar.

However, not everyone was enthusiastic about this bizarre turn of events.

"The Phantom? And her?"

"So this means she is the most beautiful girl in the school?"

"Impossible. How could someone say that it wasn't Anna-Marie?"

These slanderous exchanges were coming from different parts of the room, and as much as Saya preferred not to hear them, they were purposely meant for her ears.

Anna-Marie herself didn't interject any comments, but simply stared intently at Saya. The moment their eyes met, Anna-Marie quickly looked the other way. Saya smiled meekly at her honest predictability. Maybe she wasn't such a bad person at heart.

No matter how beautiful someone was, and how good their grades were or how powerful their parents were, someone who truly had a poor character wouldn't be fawned on by her classmates, and wouldn't be trusted by the teachers.

However, what surprised Saya the most was the attention they gave to the blue rose.

Once it was break time the classroom door became flooded with students from other classrooms.

It was as if she were a red panda walking on its hind legs at the zoo.

"I wouldn't overthink this, Saya. It could just be someone's idea of a joke."

"Yeah."

Saya nodded at Alison's logic, but she couldn't simply laugh it off.

She'd seen the Phantom with her own eyes just the night before.

He's a Chiropteran. This rose was his provocation.

"But still, I wonder where someone would get their hands on a blue rose."

"It must be from that place."

"That place?"

Min and Alison glanced at each other, as did the other girls within earshot.

Apparently there were some things about this school that Saya hadn't learned yet.

"On the side of the church is an off-limits rose garden."

"Rose garden . . ."

Saya tried to imagine a bird's-eye view of the campus.

The cathedral was built facing the garden at the entrance of campus. Facing the cathedral on the right side was the central garden, so the off-limits rose garden, as they called it, must have been on the other side. That would be the left-hand side, where the bell tower sprouted up.

Thinking about it, none of the walkways led past that side of the cathedral.

There was no path there.

On the other side there was a sheer cliff, so it was likely no accident that the pathways leading that way had crumbled away.

"Ms. Lee told us to stay away from there because it was too dangerous, so no one has ever tried to get in there.

Even on a school campus, this rose garden was completely isolated.

It's possible that the blue roses were grown there.

✝

Saya waited until the sun went down, and everyone in the dorm was in bed before slipping out of her room.

She left to meet Hagi in the central garden.

Saya looked up at the silhouette of the bell tower in the night sky.

It was the tallest structure on the campus. She was told that it was possible to see into the rose garden from there.

Saya noticed the soft sound of someone walking on the grass behind her.

"Hagi."

The moonlight peeking through the clouds lightly brushed down on his beautiful features.

"I received a blue rose today."

"Blue rose . . ."

"I was told on the other side of this cathedral there is a secret rose garden. Everyone thinks the blue roses are grown there. Did you hear anything from the old gardener?"

"No."

"Hmm. Well, you aren't exactly the talkative type."

" . . ."

"If there really are blue roses growing there, it must be the work of the Phantom—it will lead us to the Chiropteran from yesterday, I am pretty sure. I want to check it out, but . . . look."

Saya pointed to where the gravel path would have continued if it hadn't been interrupted by a cliff.

A rope had been put up to prevent accidents, but it was the chasm, not the rope, that was preventing Saya from getting to the rose garden.

"If only there was some way to get across . . ."

As Saya scratched her head she suddenly lost her balance, and let out a yelp.

"Whoa-whoa!"

She was swooped up into the air, a passenger of Hagi's, who had leapt into the sky.

He had wrapped his left arm around her waist and sprung toward the stars. Riding the night wind like a wave, a moment later she took in the sweet smell of her surroundings.

Bent on one knee, Hagi set Saya down feet first. She immediately looked around, taking in the place.

"Roses . . ."

The moon snuck between the thick clouds, delicately illuminating the garden below.

There were roses everywhere, clumped in groups, big and small, adorning the garden.

The aristocratic color of blood—blue.

It appeared that the garden hadn't been maintained in some time. The stone arbor was covered in moss, and ivy and weeds had run rampant.

In one hand, it was sad to see a botanical garden go unkempt, but on the other hand, it could be seen as ruins revitalized by the mysterious blue bloom spread throughout.

Like orchids, the tending of roses is a time-honored tradition, and human coddling has made the rose a finicky and weak plant. Without perfect temperature, humidity, and sunlight conditions, the rose bush would likely live a very short life.

These blue roses in no way fit the typical reputation, and had thrived with no outside assistance.

"Hagi?"

Saya gradually sensed a great sadness had happened here.

He brought his bandaged right hand up to his face and stared at it intently.

Saya saw a ripple of bewilderment spread over Hagi's normally icy expression.

"Is something wrong?"

"No."

Without shaking his head, Hagi's gaze returned to the garden. It seemed there was nothing to worry about. The collapse of the earth had left cracks in stone walkway where weeds had now taken root. Saya began to walk down this path.

Visible from the entrance of the garden was a cylindrical walled gazebo surrounded by trees in the rear of the garden. It appeared to have been unaffected by whatever seismic activity had caused the crevasse to open between the cathedral and the rose garden.

The rusted gate emitted a high-pitched squeak when Saya pushed it, letting them know that it wasn't locked.

"Let's take a look."

She expected to see water pipes and equipment inside the gazebo, but it was just an empty space. In the floor was an open pit with an iron ladder leading underground. Saya made her way down.

The light Hagi handed to her wasn't necessary. The slightly illuminated room looked like a box-shaped cavern.

"There's no one here."

There was nothing particularly eye-catching in the room.

Saya saw a doorway.

The source of the limited lighting was on the other side of the iron-bar double doors.

The air flowing in between the bars was icy cold. The opposite of the warm night breezes above ground.

The large arched ceiling and lines of stone pillars implied that it was a large open space. Probably in order to keep the temperature down, the lights installed in the support beams were very soft.

Piles of wooden barrels were stacked like mountains from just beyond the bars in the door to as far as the eye could see. A faint acidic smell seemed to rise from the stone-paved floor.

"Alcohol . . . could this be a storehouse for wine?"

Saying the words out loud reminded her of something David had said.

According to him, of the list of items delivered to the Yanbaru Nature Conservation Center, only one was imported by someone other than the U.S. Army: French wine. It had come from this school, which was the reason Saya was here, pretending to be an exchange student.

These barrels must have been filled with the very wine in question.

Saya pressed her face between the bars in order to get a better look inside. She quickly noticed something other than the barrels.

It was certainly something that didn't belong here.

An enormous cube-shaped metal cargo container.

". . . Seventy-two, twelve, twenty-six."

Saya said the ID number printed on the door of the container out loud.

If they could get closer they could investigate further, but this barred door wasn't as generous as the door to the gazebo.

It was tightly secured with a lock.

Crack detective Saya rattled the door in a fruitless effort to get it to cooperate, but then something caused her to heart to skip a beat.

"Is there someone down there?"

The voice calling down from above belonged to Ms. Lee.

The sound must have carried out of the gazebo.

The light from the lantern carried by the female teacher flowed down the shaft. Saya anticipated running into the Phantom, but never would have expected Ms. Lee to appear. They said even the patience of a saint has its limits, and saint or not, Saya was sure she had reached Ms. Lee's limit. Saya imagined that if she were to get caught breaking the rules again, she would be sent to the detention room, and probably receive a beating.

"Wha-wha-what're we gonna do?"

As Saya glanced right and left searching for something she knew wasn't there, Hagi grabbed her arm and pulled her.

Saya fell into his chest, and together they glued themselves to the wall.

It was the wall directly under the door to the gazebo. The room opened up from the shaft like a bottle, so the wall would be in a blind-spot from the opening above.

Saya held her breath as she prayed that Ms. Lee's enthusiasm for her work wasn't so great that she would actually attempt to climb down the ladder to see what was going on.

The lamp light from above which flickered on the stone floor suddenly went dark.

Ms. Lee had given up her investigation.

After waiting several minutes, Saya climbed up the ladder and exited the gazebo. From the shade of the grove of trees, Saya confirmed that there was no one else in the rose garden before taking another look at the blue roses.

"She got here through the cathedral."

There must have been a rear entrance to the rose garden, which was supposedly isolated due to the giant fissure in the ground. To enter from there one would have to come out from some door in the left-hand transept inside the church leading outside. If that door remained locked, regular students would never have the chance to discover the secret path.

It might have been the mental strain from unraveling the mystery, but Saya felt like the roses did not approve.

Under the moonlight the rose garden was gorgeous.

"But, there is something about this place that isn't right . . ."

It wasn't the same as déjà vu, but somewhere a bell was ringing inside her head, and she pulled her cell phone out from her pocket.

She called David's phone.

After three rings he answered in a clear voice.

"It's me. What's wrong?"

He was awake, even at this hour.

"Well, right now, I just checked out an underground storage room at school."

"There's a storeroom under Lycee?"

"Yes. The entrance is in the rose garden where the Phantom gets his blue roses."

"Are we sure the Phantom is a Chiropteran?"

"Well, maybe . . . but this Phantom looks different than the Chiropterans I saw in Okinawa. It's like it is smarter, or something . . ."


"'Chevalier.'"

The information from Saya caused David to stand up from his chair and stiffen his back.

Julia, standing on the other side of the room, stopped pouring coffee and quickly turned around, but Louis, who was sitting on the bed using his laptop computer and eating snacks, stuck his hand in the air to keep her from interrupting.

For a half-second, this high-class hotel room in the middle of Hanoi was as cold as a polar icecap.

"Chevalier?"

Saya, who must have been calling from the rose garden, repeated the word mysteriously.

". . . What did you see in the basement?"

"Let's see. There were big barrels that looked like they held some kind of alcohol, and then there was a shipping container . . . It had the numbers seventy-two, twelve, twenty-six written on it."

David was able to decipher the significance of the numbers.

No member of Red Shield could ever forget them.

Saya mistakenly took David's silence as disapproval.

"Uhh . . . I will go take another look. Next time I will get into the storage room . . ."

"No. We must proceed with extreme caution. We have to think of the Chiropteran. You have our support."

If that container was what he thought it was, David concluded that this might be too much for Saya, at least until she had a full return of her abilities.

"Don't let anyone find out that you know of that container's existence. The Phantom could be a teacher, or even a student."

"Okay. So I shouldn't do anything now?"

"Right. We need to figure out a way to get someone else into the school."

"You could become a gardener's apprentice like Hagi . . ."

"What?! He is there? A gardener?"

The reserved tone of Saya's suggestion caught David off-guard.

While David was so focused on Saya's infiltration, Hagi must have taken advantage of the distraction and, despite the lack of logic, traveled to Lycee.

"He's become really popular on campus."

"I don't want to . . . well, it's too late now. Can you tell him not to bring too much attention to himself?"

David sighed as he pressed one finger into the spot between his eyebrows.

Hagi had positioned himself near Saya, as he had become Saya's Chevalier once again. It was his only aspiration.

"I will contact you again tomorrow morning. For now, hurry and get back to the dormitory."

"Umm . . ."

The tension in Saya's voice kept David from hitting the END CALL button.

"How are Kai and Riku doing?"

". . . Same as usual."

Telling lies and manipulations was a familiar part of David's work, but having to lie to a child wasn't painless.

"Really? Okay. I need to get back."

David could hear the smile in her energized voice.

Even after hanging up the phone, the sour look on David's face remained.

Setting her coffee cup to the side, Julia smiled in her usual way.

"Pangs of guilt?"

"There is no reason for me to feel guilty. She needs to be focused on battling the Chiropterans."

If Kai and Riku were allowed to tag along, Saya's sword would dull from emotion.

It wasn't strictly to advance the goal of Chiropteran elimination, but also with Saya's personal safety in mind.

The brothers were George's sons. Those two surely could survive on their own, even without parents.

"The important thing now is to put together a plan of how to proceed from here. If the Chiropteran Saya encountered was truly a Chevalier, then it is not hard to believe the container lost thirty years ago is in a storage room under Lycee."

"'Chevalier'. . . According to Joel's diary, the high-ranking Chiropterans who protected the 'Diva' were called 'Chevalier.' In Russia, Germany, and also here—"

"Delta 67, Cinq Flèche, Chevalier," said Louis, typing on his laptop at the same rhythm of his words.

David took a sip of the coffee Julia had poured for him before he spoke again.

"I need to see if the container is real or not with my own eyes."

"You aren't going to request reinforcements?"

"Headquarters is not going to move on a hunch. We need to find a way to get into Lycee on our own."

"In that case, we may have the perfect opportunity."

The overworked springs under Louis's rear creaked as he turned the laptop's LCD screen to the others.

Louis has brought up Lycee du Cinq Flèche's official homepage.

In the information section was an announcement regarding a yearly event.

"It's a dance."

And it was to be held in two days.

It was a hot and humid night.

However, if this had been Brooklyn, and not Hanoi, the night breeze would have been blocked by the tall buildings, and the heat rising from the ground due to all the people and machines running would have made feel even more like a steam bath.

Thankfully, the air conditioner inside the late-model German auto was working perfectly.

"Okinawa reeked completely of America. Hamburgers on the menus at restaurants, U.S. Marine uniforms in windows of used clothes stores, baseball on TV . . . How the locals could stand it was the real mystery."

Van's mouth remained in constant motion as he sat calmly in the back seat of the car.

He was sucking on a piece of hard candy from Okinawa, in fact. This one contained real pineapple juice.

"I hope I wasn't being rude. I know you worked for the U.S. Army there."

"No, no."

The young researcher from the Yanbaru Nature Conservation Center was hand picked by Van, and sat next to him in the back seat. A polite smile was glued to his face.

"I get the feeling that the leftover remnants of my home country, France, don't run as uncomfortably deep here as they do in Okinawa. Without taking the humidity into account, of course."

"Monsieur Argeno. The target is on the move."

The Asian man in the business suit turned from the front passenger seat and looked at Van.

Van wondered what someone working for the volunteer organization would think of this man's face. Here this seemingly well-meaning gentleman comes by with precious medicine for the sick orphans. What would they think if they found out he didn't have a charitable bone in his body?

It could only be called a tragedy—well, perhaps it was more of a comedy.

"The cruelty of this world truly is laughable."

"Huh?"

"It's nothing. Now what was it you were saying?"

"The target is starting to respond."

"Who did you give it to?"

"To one fourteen-year-old female."

"Hnn? This girl?"

Looking out the window of the car, Van saw a slender orphan in a white one-piece dress step out the front gate of the protection facility.

From the other side of the street, he could clearly see her face. He wasn't sure if it was the nature of the Vietnamese race or a nourishment issue, but overall she looked younger than her years. However, Van noticed she had delicate and graceful elements in her features.

The night wasn't as thick in more developed nations, and Van took a look around to try and grasp how dark it really got here at this hour.

She was responding.

Across the street stowed in a parked truck, was much of the same equipment that was used in Okinawa. What they were doing was broadcasting the voice of a "mouse" in the immediate vicinity. This was a sound that was out of the range of a normal person's hearing.

Van bit down on the shrunken candy in his mouth in satisfaction of these results, but then noticed something curious.

"What about that?"

From behind the girl came someone else. It was the figure of a boy who was about the same age as the girl.

For a moment Van thought it was another girl, he had such a cute face. However the clothes he wore were definitely those of a boy. He was Asian, but looked more Far East. His skin tone wasn't dark like one who lived closer to the equator.

"Two of them? That shouldn't be . . . Our target was only the girl on the right. Our reports say this boy is traveling, and is just spending the night at the facilities."

"Maybe so, but doesn't it seem like he can hear it, too?"

Simply looking at the boy's behavior, it was the only conclusion Van could come to.

He wasn't acting like someone that had followed the girl outside simply because he was concerned about her.

Resting his elbow on the door handle and his chin on his fist, Van observed the actions of the young girl and young boy for several seconds before looking over at the researcher sitting next to him.

"There is no doubt about it."

The researcher pushed up his glasses and squinted as he looked outside, and then nodded in assent.

This one was a real find, too. He had to acknowledge that. The goddess of good luck was feeling generous tonight.

A grin leaked out the corners of Van's mouth and he swallowed the rice-grain-sized remaining piece of candy.

"Well then, shall we initiate collection procedures?"

"But . . ."

"It's fine. You are not troubled by having too much raw material to work with, are you?"

"Check."

The man in the suit pulled out his cell phone to contact the team in the truck.

But that hand froze in midair.

What stopped him was seeing a third person step outside the front of the gate.

He might have been in his late teens. He had red streaks in his hair and a fearless look. Above all, he looked prepared to protect himself.

"We have an additional individual. Please take care of this before any more decide to join the party."

The last boy was an added bonus.

This one didn't come outside from the call of the "mouse," but to check on the younger two. It wasn't only a matter of timing. This one would get to join the boy and girl, like it or not.

Even if he didn't have the acquired skills, this child might be useful in an upcoming demonstration.

"Roger."

Three men jumped from the rear door of the truck he'd been in contact with.

Watching them follow the wall and stay in the shadows told Van that these men had experience in these sorts of things. He didn't know how they were hired, but it certainly wasn't from any legitimate business.

In each of their hands was a bottle of chloroform.

There was no need to verify the fate of the girl and two boys.

Van closed his eyes and leaned back into the headrest, releasing the tension from his shoulders and back. He listened as the course of events proceeded as he expected.

"Recovery completed."

"Nice work. Let's get them to the regular place."

Van reached over the seat in front of him and placed a candy in the man's breast pocket. He then unwrapped another piece of hard candy and popped it into his mouth.

## 02

THE PROBLEM WASN'T coming all this way to Vietnam, but that he didn't have anyone to blame for his not having any connections or contacts here.

If he could talk directly with someone at Lycee du Cinq Flèche then it would be perfect, but despite all of Akihiro Okamura's attempts, he couldn't furnish a personal connection or the proper funds. For what it was worth, he was able to arrange a meeting with a man from the export company who was in charge of the distribution of the wine from the school. His only condition was that they meet during his lunch break.

"What do you think of this *pho*? Pretty good, huh?"

"Sure . . ."

The waitress barely set the second bowl down before the man sitting across from him was slurping noodles into his mouth.

On the other side of the table was Okamura, who'd had a hard time finding his appetite since he had arrived here. The time change must have thrown off his stomach. Back in Okinawa, he would be up from his futon and out the door with his camera in moments, even at three in the morning, when Takeda called, so jet lag shouldn't have been an issue. It was most likely the sudden jump in temperature that had worn his body out.

"The noodles are made from rice, so it is even better than *udon* for your digestion."

"Yes, right. I actually want to hear about this dance that they hold there."

"It's a yearly tradition. The ball also serves as a social event for parents and sponsors."

"A ball . . . hmm."

This was something that didn't translate culturally.

Japanese high-school students did a school festival and a sports day, and that was about it.

"Do you think I would be able to attend?"

"You? That is one of Vietnam's most prominent all-girl schools."

He gave Okamura the once-over, but Okamura couldn't say anything to protest his obvious opinion.

"If I could, I would really like to get my hands on a bottle of the mysterious 1967 Chateau Duel."

"Unfortunately that would be impossible. You'd never get permission. Say, you should write an article about this shop's *pho*."

"Sure. I'll think about it."

Like the fly by his bowl that he swatted at, the man's usefulness was also being driven away.

In a roundabout way to get to talk about the wine, Okamura had presented himself as a reporter doing a travel journal on Vietnamese cuisine, but this was starting to turn into a waste of time.

"Your company exported the wine from Lycee to Okinawa, right?"

"We get an order and we move what we move from point A to point B. That's it."

"Can't you help me out?"

He couldn't ask to be invited to the dance, but if he could find a way to do some kind of odd job or assist with the food, or some way to get in to Lycee, it would really get his investigation moving.

"There's nothing I can do to help."

"Isn't there someone you could talk to?"

"The owner there, Karl-san, is well known among Vietnamese circles, but he is also in charge of the world-famous Cinq Flèche Pharmaceuticals, a drug manufacturing company."

"They are headquartered in France, right? . . . If you could—"

"—Cinq Flèche Gold. It's sold in Japan, too? It's the same Cinq Flèche."

As the Japanese TV commercial began to play in his head, Okamura wiped the sweat from his brow with the back of his chopsticks.

"Yes, now that you mention it. I have heard the theme song before."

"Me too. They play it all the time here."

"Yes, you're right . . ."

Okamura knew that in the crowded power-drink market in Japan, Cinq Flèche Gold actually had a positive effect on a person's performance.

How many times had there been when Takeda had patted his butt to go snap photos at three or even four scenes, and then come back to the office only to be dragged out all night drinking with writers and editors to soak in lessons from the veterans—and then get up and do it again the next day? The fact that he could go to get a physical and come out with a clean bill of health was completely thanks to the contents of that little bottle sitting in his refrigerator. Okamura was sure of it.

A lot of his coworkers swore by it, as well, but there were others who claimed it worked so well because narcotic drugs were among the ingredients.

"I mean it is such a huge corporation. It's one thing for them to contact us, but for us to try to get their attention. That would be pretty difficult . . . You've come all this way, how about some sightseeing? I will introduce you to an inexpensive tour guide."

"No, really, it's all right."

"So you are going to do an article on this *pho*, right?"

"Give it a rest, please."

Okamura had learned all that he was going to from this man.

At this point the only option left was to go directly to Lycee du Cinq Flèche. He didn't have a written invitation, but he did have a camera and a press ID. And his elegant power of persuasion.

The normal atmosphere of the cafeteria had been completely transformed into a dazzling ballroom. The tables had been replaced with a crowd of formally dressed parents, older brothers, sponsors, guardians, and other invited guests mingling and chatting.

The music from the orchestra flowed up to the arched high ceiling, gently encouraging guests to dance. The piece by the king of waltz, as he was called, Johann Strauss that was being played fit perfectly on this campus, this evening.

It was "The Emperor's Waltz." Saya had heard it before in music class.

The sounds of the strings were so beautiful, Saya instinctively searched the musicians to see if Hagi was among them.

"Of course, it couldn't be . . ."

If he had been here the other girls would have already made a scene.

Still, the room had a very luxurious feel to it.

Normally everyone wore their functional *ao dai*, so they all put a real effort into looking beautiful in their evening gowns this one time of year.

A spectacle like this at Koza Commercial High's school festival was unimaginable. If she and Kaori were to get dressed up like this at school, everyone would assume they were coming as a couple of Marie Antoinettes for a Halloween party. Of all the girls she knew, the only one that probably looked good in a dress was Mao Jahana.

And when around competitive girls, especially one like Anna-Marie, a fight would break out, for sure.

Saya giggled as she pictured in her head the sparks that would fly if those two were in the same room together.

Because of the reputation of her father's company, Jahana Industries (Jahana Syndicate!) Saya thought that Mao would be a difficult person to be around, but she was actually very kind to Saya. She wondered what Mao was up to now. Mao and Kai had been good friends, so she was probably a little sad.

"Saya, over here."

Min waved to Saya from her spot near a corner.

She was joined by her close friends Beni, Chen, and Alison.

Naturally, all of the girls were in dresses and the ones with long locks had put their hair up.

"You're late!"

"Sorry. I've never had to put on clothes like this before . . ."

"Yeah, 'cause in Japan you wear kimonos, like geisha."

"Well, I haven't really worn one of those, either."

Saya suddenly had a desire to check herself in a mirror. She looked around in every direction. She'd done her best to make herself look nice in her room, but she had lost all confidence in her work.

"I feel kinda silly."

"What are you talking about? You look great."

"Thanks."

The low-cut white dress Saya was wearing was one of the ten or so formal gowns Min had in her closet that Saya had tried out and finally settled on. The ornamentation was minimal and the conservative design of the organdy dress appealed to Saya's tastes. The panier hoop skirt over the ruffled underskirt went below her knees, and was surprisingly easy to move around in.

And being able to move easily was a factor she was concerned about.

It wasn't because of the dancing, either. It was because she was Phantom-Chiropteran hunting.

"For a girl who got a blue rose from the Phantom, she sure picked a bland dress to wear."

Min's eyebrows pinched together at the purposely loudly stated comment.

"How dare you make fun of the dress I loaned her!"

"Oh, that's not what I meant at all. So sorry you are so sensitive about it."

The harsh critic was one of Anna-Marie's minions.

Even among the students they stuck out, wearing the most expensive and eye-catching eveningwear. They were getting a lot of glances from the male guests among the crowd.

Above all, Princess Anna-Marie looked absolutely royal. Her dress was glowing, and she wore an embroidered silver choker, as well as an anklet, rings, and earrings, so her entire body seemed to sparkle in unison.

"Let's remain calm, ladies. Tonight, our guests are watching us."

It was the final word from the head swan.

After an Anna-Marie tongue-lashing, none of the other girls had the guts to say anything in defense of Saya and Min.

"You really should try and make yourself look nice, Otonashi-san. Let's fix this . . ."

Anna-Marie extended her right hand to Saya's head and removed a hair clip Saya had put on and moved it closer to her ear.

"This looks much better."

Like an artist using charcoal, she swiped at Saya's bangs, moving them to the side, and then lifted Saya's chin slightly. She looked satisfied with her achievement.

Having just been treated like a child by her classmate, Saya felt more than a little embarrassed.

"Thank you . . ."

"Now, let's all enjoy ourselves."

Without a smile Anna-Marie turned on her heels the other direction.

Anna-Marie headed toward a more lively section of the room, and her cronies followed suit. Min and Alison and the others watched them walk off, looking as if a wet blanket had been thrown over them.

"Anna-Marie is worried how the men will see her. She'll surely find some handsome guy . . ."

"Are you trying to help the enemy?"

"Are you declaring war? Like, which of these girls is most appropriate for the Phantom?"

"Ple-please, stop it."

Before Min and her friends stirred things up too much, the flustered Saya tried to put an end to it.

Right then they heard some sort of disturbance taking place in another part of the ballroom.

The orchestra stopped playing, and an announcement was being made to the attendees. The comments of surprise replaced the music and idle chatter quickly subsided.

In a single moment, Lycee's cafeteria turned into the newest extension of Hofburg Imperial Palace.

"It's started. Time to find a partner."

"See you later, Saya."

Based on the manners established in Vienna, it was now a woman's chance to ask a man to dance, and Min and the other girls were going to follow it to a tee.

As the girls walked through the masses in twos and threes, a tall man hovered over Saya.

Her back stiffened as Saya wondered if he was going to ask her to dance. Her heart beat faster, and she set all discouraging thoughts aside to relish in the moment.

"This looks like a smaller version of the Viennese Opera Ball."

It was David.

Instead of his usual undertaker's suit, he wore a tuxedo.

Saya actually thought he looked a little handsome. He usually came across like a strict teacher, but seeing him now, he looked like a Hollywood movie actor on the red carpet.

But that wasn't the only surprise. The moment Saya laid eyes on the woman David was with, her eyes immediately shot up to the chandelier.

"It's smaller than I expected, but the orchestra is quite good. I heard they call on the music union to perform every year. "

". . . Julia-san?"

Saya's draw dropped open and she stared at the woman.

She wore a very revealing dress that had a neckline that plunged almost to her navel, showing off not only her white skin. Her smooth limbs flowed from the thin evening gown seamlessly, and every movement she made was graceful and refined. Someone who had the least bit of doubt about the beauty of her own legs would have a slit that high in her dress only if something had torn it.

A nervous smile formed on Julia's glossy lips.

"Clothes like this don't look good on me, so I don't like to have to wear them . . . but to get in here a guardian needs a companion."

So David and Julia were acting as if they were married and came here in the role of Saya's guardians. They were too young to be her parents, not to mention clearly not Japanese, but there was no shortage of successful people who had adopted, or were at least sponsoring, gifted girls and placed them at this school.

Thinking Julia's dress didn't look nice on her wasn't right. People that didn't appreciate their own natural merits could bring the scorn of others onto themselves on occasions like this.

Saya then felt very self-conscious about her own dress.

She would never look as beautiful as Anna-Marie or Julia. She wasn't like Min and the others who could simply enjoy themselves at the party. She felt like the ugly duckling stuck with the swans.

"And the Phantom?"

"Ye-yes?"

"The Phantom."

Heavy-hearted as she was, Saya looked at David's glowering face, and forced herself to remember the mission.

She hadn't come here to dance.

"Since I last talked to you I haven't seen him. Probably tonight, too . . ."

"If he is indeed connected with Lycee, as I suspect, then it will be hard for him to avoid an important social event like this. He'll be here tonight. The problem is identifying him in the crowd."

"Hagi is also standing guard in the bell tower."

"I see."

Looking out the French window at the tower, David nodded his head.

"Saya, if you see the Phantom, kill him."

"I understand. But, he's a person . . ."

"It doesn't matter. The mission is to eliminate this Chiropteran. We don't intend for you to be here any longer than you need to be."

So that's how it was.

Saya put a hand to her chest and hid her face. The fabric of the dress she had borrowed from Min felt nice. She was not meant to be here for the long term, and as soon as the mission was complete, the curtain would fall on her friendships and school life here.

"He is among regular people, so he won't try to create a disturbance, I believe . . . but if it seems like he might try and escape, you must not hesitate."

"Understood."

"I am going check out the underground storage room and see if the container you told me about is what I think it is. Julia, if I don't come back at the appointed time, you know what to do—"

Despite saying she didn't look good in that dress, Julia seemed like she enjoyed being David's temporary wife, yet at his words she returned to being a cool-headed member of Red Shield.

"Got it."

"I'll leave the rest to you," said David as he turned away in a hurry.

David walked along the wall to avoid running into the other guests, and Julia waited until he disappeared out the entrance before turning to Saya.

Saya heard a small moan from behind Julia's gentle and mature but lonely smile.

"Are you nervous?"

"Wha—? Me? I have never been in this sort of situation . . . And I am not beautiful like you are, Julia-san."

"That's nice of you to say, but you are very beautiful, Saya."

Julia smiled and placed her hand on Saya's shoulder.

"You need to stay loose. If you get too tense then you won't be able to do anything. Try to relax."

"I'm sorry."

"I'm going to take a look around the campus. Just try to act naturally. And don't just be a wallflower."

"Uh, okay."

Saya had the impression Julia was encouraging her to dance.

After Julia disappeared into the crowd of black tuxedos and multicolored dresses Saya's gaze moved to the back of the ballroom.

A countless number of couples were dancing in circles to the lively rhythm of the waltz.

The guests were mostly Southeast Asian and Chinese, it appeared, but there were quite a few Westerners, as well.

The Phantom was probably among the people here.

The mask-wearing man she'd encountered in the bell tower that night had long black hair, more popular with women than with men. In fact, she couldn't be totally sure that the person wasn't a woman. It was dark up there, and they were only together for a few moments. The voice was deep, if Saya remembered correctly, but she shouldn't just toss out the idea that it might not have been a male.

Could it be that gentleman fiddling with his cigar? If he undid his ponytail, it would be about the same length as the Phantom's.

Then there was the young woman with her back to Saya who was placing an empty glass on a waiter's tray. If she were to dress as a man, she may have looked a lot like the Phantom from behind.

Anybody in the room could be hiding the fangs of a Chiropteran behind their smiles.

That must have been what Julia meant. But it was impossible to not be nervous in a situation like this. Saya reminded herself about the dagger hidden in her skirt as she continued to scour the crowd with her eyes.

Applause echoed off the ceiling.

The first song had finished.

The volume of chatter rose. Some people, tired from dancing, walked off the dance floor to take a break while other married couples remained in each other's arms to enjoy the moment. Boys scurried about looking for new partners for the next number, and girls hiked up their skirts and bowed in greeting.

Among the young people rose a burst of squeals and Saya quickly moved to investigate.

"Look there. It's a blue rose!"

The most excited chatter was coming from the group of girls which included Min, Chen, and Alison.

There must have been about ten girls who had formed a loose circle, keeping the subject of their attention in constant view. Even the tall Anna-Marie glanced over to see what the ruckus was about.

What this growing number of girls was staring at, could it be—

"The Phantom?"

In her flats, Saya tried to see by standing on her toes to no avail. She began to quickly move closer in, but then caught herself. She mustn't draw attention. It was best to move naturally.

Saya walked to the rear of the crowd and peeked between the other students' heads.

Blue rose.

It was tucked into the lapel of a snow-white double-breasted suit jacket, making a clean background for the brilliant blue of the flower.

It was a young man in his early twenties.

"Nope."

It wasn't the Phantom.

He was the wrong age, wrong physique, and had the wrong air about him. There was nothing in common with the Phantom.

Frankly, he was too pretty.

His wavy blond hair framed his soft-looking face. There were only a few times in life one got to lay eyes on perfect specimens of the human race, but it was fair to say this was probably one of those times.

If Hagi's beauty was like that of the moon at night, then this man's beauty was like that of the sunlight in spring.

The appearance of this charming man caused all the cheeks of the nearby girls to turn the color of cherry blossoms. The young man seemed more embarrassed than proud, but still carried himself elegantly as he smiled and walked deeper into the ballroom.

As if it was on cue, the second number started, cutting off the buzzing chatter.

It was clear the girls were a bit nervous about what would happen next.

With timing like this, there was no way the guy could just stand by the window and do nothing.

He surely knew the proper way to act in high society events, and doing nothing on a night like this wouldn't be accepted by these young women.

With that in mind, all the girls were thinking one thing. Who would he ask to be his dance partner? The anticipation of his decision was causing a physical and mental strain unique to females at this age, on the brink of womanhood.

For a man trying to retain his honor, situations like this could be hell.

In order to play it safe, he began by slowly walking through the crowd, stopping here and there to smile and nod.

Saya could see each individual girl's heart melt as he laid eyes on them one by one.

She understood how they felt. However, she had more important things than dancing to worry about this night.

She needed to be looking for the Phantom's bloodshot eyeballs, not this young man's gaze.

She realized she shouldn't be so close. She had to be sure not to stick out.

Just as she walked back to the wall to keep an eye on the ballroom, the blond man started walking again.

In his path was a tall and especially beautiful girl among the crowd of well-dressed maidens.

As he passed one girl after another he left a trail of disappointed sighs.

"He's heading toward Anna-Marie."

"Of course. Who else could he ask?"

"They would make a picture-perfect gorgeous couple."

Saya couldn't see her face, but from the way Anna-Marie straightened her back, Saya sensed her expression was one of haughtiness mixed with pure femininity.

Thinking they would make a nice duo, Saya's attention turned to other parts of the party.

Her examination was interrupted by a hand thrust out before her chest.

The hand that extended from the white sleeve was soft and feminine.

"May I have the honor of this dance?"

". . . Wha—?"

What was the meaning of this?

She looked up to see the young man's smile, and then looked around again.

All eyes were on Saya. There was no envy or jealousy. Every face showed a look of disbelief. Min raised her clasped hands together, giving Saya the message, "Congratulations."

The only exception was Anna-Marie.

". . ."

She kept her back to Saya—Or more clearly, she hadn't moved a muscle since Saya had looked away from her. Overcome with shock, it was as if she was frozen.

"Umm . . ."

"Give me your hand."

"Excuse me?"

Completely caught off-guard, Saya initially wasn't sure how to respond. At a loss, she followed his directions.

Like a dog being commanded to shake hands, she put her right hand into his outstretched palm. Immediately his warm fingers wrapped around hers.

"Thank you."

As her smiling partner tugged her arm, Saya realized her drastic mistake.

"Ho-hold on . . ."

The look on his face was gentle, but he had a firm grip on her hand.

Unable to put up a fight, Saya allowed herself to be pulled to the center of the dance floor.

The young man turned with a spin, and suddenly his chest was close to hers.

His left hand planted itself on her exposed back.

"Oh!"

Not having wings wasn't the only reason she wasn't able to fly away from the ballroom floor.

Dozens of couples joined in to the rhythm of the Viennese waltz, and everyone seemed to dance in unison.

The beautiful "Blue Danube."

Saya knew the tune, but had no idea how to dance a waltz.

She was very aware that she had given up control of her own movements to her partner. She couldn't remember ever being this nervous before. She realized that the muscles honed to do a high jump were completely different than the muscles needed to do a waltz.

Her biggest worry was making sure she didn't step on his feet. She looked up at him with her face bright red, and made her appeal.

"I-I mean-I have never done this before . . ."

"I'll lead you. My older brother told me I am a good dancer."

In no way was he exaggerating about his dancing abilities.

Saya gripped his hand tight, and let him direct how her body moved. Without second guessing his lead, she was somehow able to keep up with him.

It was clear that her body was remembering how to dance.

"You are doing very well. Are you sure this is your first time?"

"No—I mean yes. It's true."

Even if he was just being polite, Saya sensed no negative feelings from him.

Her face felt hot.

From up close it was no exaggeration to say he had the face of an angel. There may have been other men out there this handsome, but none had the honest smile of this one, especially with someone he had never met before.

"When dancing a waltz, you should not look at your partner's face."

"Oh . . ."

Saya looked away from him.

She detected a roguish chuckle under his breath.

"If this is your first time, and we are doing this well, it must mean we are very compatible."

"Hn?"

It sounded like a pickup line, but considering the transparency of his expression, she took the words at their literal meaning.

Saya felt ashamed of her racing heart rate.

Time seemed to speed up.

Their musical journey from the black forest to the black sea along a beloved Eastern European river carrying them in triple time had come to an end.

The air was filled with the sound of applause and compliments.

The young man's hand still held Saya's.

"I should apologize. I couldn't stand the gazes from all those girls, so I asked you to dance to avoid trouble. It was because you seemed different from the other girls."

He wasn't trying to make excuses, and his eyes grew narrow.

"And for that, I am very sorry. But I will also tell you that I am truly very glad I invited you to dance with me."

Saya found nothing about this confession disagreeable.

He hadn't been trying to be diplomatic, it was a heartfelt apology for an impolite act he felt he had committed.

She had to respond somehow. But what was an appropriate reply?

Saya scorned herself for not paying attention to high society manners, and when she opened her mouth . . .

"So this is where you are?"

The irritated man's voice came from behind the young man.

It was a white man in his late twenties. He seemed high-strung, but at the same time, his eyes had a slight lascivious twinkle. The spectacled man carried himself like an intellectual, and Saya guessed he might be a medical researcher, like Julia.

"I was looking for you."

"Oh, Van. I could say the same. Where were you?"

They obviously knew each other. From what Saya could guess, the young man was the son of a large corporation's president, and the older man was his manager, of sorts.

"I wanted to be able to ask for one more dance, but my carriage has already arrived. It is a true shame."

Their hands separated from each other.

Losing the warmth from his palm, her hand momentarily grasped for his before falling back to its place at her side.

"Enjoy the rest of the dance."

The young man pulled the blue rose from his lapel and set it in Saya's hair above her ear.

With a slight hesitation, the young man smiled and turned away from Saya.

The man with glasses he called Van grabbed the young man's arm and pulled him away irritated.

"Solomon, we don't have time for this. If you have free time to waste messing around the campus, I would rather you spent it looking at some of the experiment results."

"Yes, I understand. I have already met with Karl, so my work is finished. And I met someone nice, too."

What caused the young man to stop once on his way to the exit was Saya.

It wasn't Saya herself, but Min's calling of her name.

"Saya!"

Min came over to her as fast as she could, but still respecting the manners of the elite guests, she didn't run.

"How was it? Was he the Phantom?"

"Uh . . . I don't think so."

"Really? You two looked so natural together when you were dancing, I thought it must be him."

"You really thought so?"

Saya reminded herself that they didn't see the Phantom as a Chiropteran, but as a rose-delivering youthful nobleman of legend.

Saya looked one more time at the young man.

The man had turned and looked surprised to catch Saya's glance.

"Saya . . . ?"

He was able to hear Min call her name. Seeing him repeat her name to himself surprised and confused her. Maybe to a European it sounded like a strange name.

His lips then broke into a bittersweet smile.

"Solomon?"

"Yes . . . Karl is really too much, isn't he?"

Prodded by the man pulling him, he bowed a final salutation and began walking toward the entrance again.

She heard him say the name "Karl." That was the same name as Lycee's chairman of the board. No doubt many of the guests tonight had some kind of personal connection with the chairman, and the young man might have been a family member of one of those attendees.

"And I didn't tell you, a nice guy came up to me earlier. I'll introduce you to him."

As Min happily tugged on her wrist, Saya's gaze landed on a window behind Min that looked out onto a wall facing the central garden.

The giant arched French windows mostly reflected the light from inside the room like a mirror, but within the shadows of people moving along the glass, the view outside was visible.

As Min scanned the ballroom for her new boyfriend, Saya's gaze was planted over her shoulder.

On the other side of the French window she saw a figure in a black cloak.

He wore a mask that looked like a bat's wing, and a sneer that looked like a crescent moon.

"Saya."

Min's voice whipped into Saya's ears like a cold chill, and she pretended not to hear her.

The glass of the window rattled ever so faintly.

It was the call of the Chiropteran, a sound normal people couldn't detect.

"The Phantom."

"Saya?"

"Min, I'm sorry."

Waving her hand goodbye might have been a rude gesture, but she didn't have time for regrets.

Saya took off running as fast as she could toward the window.

As if he has been waiting, the Phantom's cloak fluttered.

If she ran to the entrance and back around to the other side of the window, then he would get away. Saya cut through the center of the ballroom, passing guests and other students and grabbed the handle on the window. It wasn't locked, but was much tighter than she expected.

"You have to pull it."

The girl standing next her gave Saya a hand.

Saya looked up, and saw that it was Anna-Marie.

"Ah . . . about before . . ."

"No need to worry about it . . . Your dancing, it was very good."

It didn't seem like she had made a complete reversal of her attitude until now, but for Anna-Marie to do anything nice was incredible progress. For a single moment Saya forgot she was in a hurry, and smiled.

Although it seemed to sting a little, Anna-Marie returned the gesture.

"Thank you."

That's all she said before she bolted outside.

But the figure was gone.

From the passageway leading to the teacher housing on the right stepped out Julia.

"Saya, what's wrong?"

"The Phantom was just . . ."

"You saw him?"

"Yes."

Only a few seconds earlier he had been standing on this very spot.

He couldn't have gotten far.

Scanning the darkness, Saya looked in every possible direction.

She heard a heavy creak.

It was the door to the cathedral.

Basked in the moonlight she saw the silhouette along the façade.

Even from that distance, the Phantom's sneer was crystal clear. He then disappeared into the interior of the cathedral.

"From there he can get into the rose garden, and then into the underground storage . . ."

"No! That's where David is now!"

If they didn't do something, the Phantom might get David in a sneak attack as he investigated the container.

An attempt to contact David only validated their fear; David's cell phone didn't get reception underground.

"Hagi!"

The wind gusted high in the night sky.

A tall figure swooped down from the bell tower and landed in front of them without making a sound.

He knelt like a knight bowing to his lord.

"I saw the Phantom. Come on, let's go!"

Hagi propped the cello case onto his shoulder and stood without saying a word.

+

Even in Vietnam, there were prominent schools full of rich kids from big-name families.

The doormen knew courtesy, but not flexibility.

"Excuse me for asking, but can you please show us your invitation?"

"You know what? It looks like I forgot it . . ."

"I am sorry for the inconvenience, but we can only allow guests with invitations to enter. We are going to have to ask you to leave."

". . ."

At the very least he probably should have arrived in a tuxedo, but nothing like that fit inside his travel bag.

As Okamura and the doormen smiled impudently at each other a black limousine pulled up next to them.

The driver's window opened and David saw an overweight black man behind the wheel. He passed one of the doormen a gold-fringed piece of paper.

Without even looking at it the doorman put his hand to his chest and bowed.

"Allow me to be the first to welcome you to Lycee du Cinq Flèche."

The limousine traveled forward almost silently, and Okamura noticed the couple sitting in the back seat. It was just a habit of his profession.

It was a white man and woman. Probably a married couple.

The man was probably in his mid-forties. His cheeks were sullen and the ill-natured crease running between his eyebrows showed signs of a very callousness individual. Okamura wouldn't have been surprised to hear that he made a living as an assassin.

On the other hand, the woman sitting next to the man was an absolute knockout.

She was younger, more like in her early thirties, and she had a nice-looking profile, but Okamura could also see a clear intelligence. He also took note of the sugar-white tone of her chest and shoulders barely covered by her dress.

They looked like a couple in a movie. Okamura clicked his tongue as he watched the limo carrying the foreign spy and the gifted scientist toward the entrance of the school.

"Judging people by how there are dressed . . ."

Clearly it wasn't the invitation but your clothes and car that got you into high society shindigs like this one.

He couldn't just go back to his hotel now empty-handed, having taken an auto-cyclo taxi and made it as far as the outside gate of Lycee.

This sour sting in his gut wasn't going to go away unless he found a way in, despite the feelings of those in charge. But still, he couldn't get past the guards at the gate, and wasn't even going to try to scale the tall wall surrounding the campus.

As Okamura put the gate behind him and walked back down the road along a canal, something caught his attention. It was a large-sized trailer truck coming from the direction of the city.

Okamura saw it pouring out exhaust as it passed him, and then made a turn into the woods. He didn't miss the Cinq Flèche company logo printed on the side of the wall of the flatbed.

"Worth checking out . . ."

No doubt about it.

This side road led to the back of the school, and was the perfect entryway for uninvited guests. The road actually went down and into what looked like the side of a cliff. The trailer truck had driven into the rear of the excavated sheer wall below the campus.

It was an underground warehouse—a storeroom for maturing wine.

"So this is where the wine came from."

He tried to get an idea of how big the storeroom was, and just how many casks of wine were in there. As wine productions go, it was definitely on the large end of the scale.

Members of the upper echelons of society were known for their expensive tastes, was this kind of volume necessary, especially at a school?

One area appeared to house wine waiting to be shipped. Okamura could see the wine already in bottles.

"Chateau Duel, 1967 . . ."

He recognized the dark green glass of the bottles.

They were the same bottles he'd found among the medical garbage at the dump in Okinawa.

He picked up a bottle, but it was lighter than expected. Empty. So was the bottle next to it, and the one after that. All empty.

"So they haven't filled them yet . . . but, wait a minute."

That didn't make sense. These bottles should have been filled decades ago in France. That's at least what it says on the label. Is it possible they planned to fill these bottles now? Obviously this wasn't 1967 and they weren't in Bordeaux.

Only the bottles would be the real thing. The wine inside would be fake.

"What is going on here? . . . There is more to this than simply exporting French wine from Vietnam to Okinawa."

On another shelf were heavier bottles. These were full. But they didn't contain wine of the noble rot Bordeaux fruit.

After taking a few pictures, Okamura looked over the flatbed truck. It had been empty earlier, but now carried a large container. The crane attached to the ceiling was too big for carrying barrels of wine, but was likely installed for a container like this one.

It appeared that this container was about to be moved somewhere.

Okamura wondered if it was full of the same bottles of wine.

"Seventy-two . . . twelve, twenty-six . . . ?"

Okamura didn't think the numbers inscribed on the container had any particular meaning, but his journalistic instincts told him to snap photos of everything he could.

In the dark basement the flash of his camera popped again and again.

He was lucky enough to come in when the driver's seat of the truck was empty and no one was around. There was the party going on up there, so the guards from the storage room were likely working the gate and the ballroom. That made his job a lot easier.

The self-congratulations ended when a bright light flashed.

It was hundreds of times more powerful than a strobe light, and Okamura was temporarily blinded.

"You there, come out!"

Apparently his calculation of the number of people in the storeroom was off.

From the rear of the storeroom came a Vietnamese man in uniform slowly coming toward Okamura, who had snuck into the shadow of some wine casks. There was one other man behind him.

"We know you are there. Come on out where we can see you."

No matter what, they would come find him.

Okamura's stomach twisted into knots.

They could bust him for trespassing, but he clearly hadn't stolen anything. He would have been completely lost if they were calling to him in Vietnamese, but they were speaking English. Just in case, he pulled some bills from his wallet to see if he could buy his way out.

"Okay, you got me. I come out."

Replying in broken English, Okamura stepped out into the open. He held up his hands to show he wasn't a threat.

However, one of the men had a pistol pointed at him, causing Okamura's spine muscles to stiffen.

He wasn't in Japan anymore. He realized a little too late that there was no guarantee he would be able to talk his way out of this one. A cold sweat formed on his brow.

"Don't worry. I am not a strange man. I am a Japanese journalist. I work for Ryukyu Daily Newspaper."

He waved the press ID he held between his fingers so they could see it.

The one with the gun held it up higher, indicating he wasn't going to fall for anything, as he came closer to Okamura. He nabbed the ID with the hand also holding the flashlight and looked it over.

The other man looked a little more like a Japanese and Southeast Asian mix, and he dressed like a typical salary man. Not wanting to get mixed up in the situation, he jumped up into the truck's driver's seat.

"I came to cover the party, but I guess I got lost. Can't we just forget about it? I'll be out of your way in no time."

The man didn't respond.

First he tossed Okamura's ID on the ground like a piece of trash, and then he snatched his camera. The single-lens reflex camera followed the same fate as the ID.

"Hey!"

The response to his protest came in the form of a single blow.

The stunned Okamura grabbed his head and fell to his knees, only to watch his camera get progressively destroyed under the heel of the man's boot.

"Don-don't . . ."

"Hey! We're in a hurry. Finish up and let's go!"

"I know," replied the man to his partner, and he slipped his index finger over the trigger.

Okamura was about to die—

The executioner's expression didn't change as he looked down upon the scared-stiff Okamura, but suddenly his eyes wavered.

The gun and flashlight fell to the ground. The light rolled away, causing the surrounding barrels and pillars to flicker like film on a movie screen.

Struck dumb with fear, the wide-eyed Okamura couldn't pull his shaking legs out of the way of the collapsing man. From his seated position on the ground, Okamura looked up to see the figure of a blond-haired man in a tuxedo.

He had whacked the Vietnamese man in the back of the head, knocking him out.

Okamura recognized him. He was the passenger in the limousine when Okamura was trying to get in the front gate.

"You . . ."

"Get out of the way."

His Japanese was clear, and he didn't waste any words as he headed toward the truck.

"Diva."

His sputtering dripped with hatred, and he sounded like a man about to rip the heart out of his enemy.

The high-beams of the truck switched on, bleaching the interior of the storeroom.

Okamura could feel the growl of the truck's engine in his gut.

The man raised a pistol he held with both hands.

The revolver he carried was bigger than the pistol the Vietnamese man had held.

"Cut the engine!"

The man behind the wheel didn't follow the blond man's directions. He gripped the wheel with a real look of terror on his face.

The pistol roared.

Okamura expected to see the spray of blood hit the inside of the shattered windshield, but it didn't happen.

"Wha-what the . . . ?"

The driver was still able to shriek, despite looking death in the eye.

What stopped the bullet from turning the driver's head into a burst tomato was what looked like the outstretched wing of a black phantom.

It was the cloak-like tailcoat of a longhaired man. He wore a weird mask on his face.

"Hee hee hee . . ."

As the strange man chuckled, his left arm crossed in front of the truck's windshield.

A thin line of smoke rose from the bullet hole in his arm.

"So naïve . . ."

Both the gun-wielding blond man and Okamura stared in shock.

He hadn't fired a peashooter like the pistols the Japanese police carry around. It was a "Dirty Harry" Callahan–caliber bad-guy-blasting, hand-cannon. It should have exploded his arm like a twig.

It had torn through the sleeve of his cloak.

The muscles of his arm swelled, tearing through the seams in the cloth. As it still was taking a form, the metal-looking arm, part reptile, part carnivore rejected the bullet sunk into the surface of its flesh, and squeezed it out. The bullet dropped and rolled after hitting the floor.

"Chiropteran . . . The Phantom!"

The man readied his gun again. Okamura was amazed at not only how brave and calm he was, but also at the skillful way he moved.

In a moment's time the black shadow dove toward the man and swiped at him with his beastly left hand, sending him in to the air as if he were light as a feather.

He landed at the base of a stone pillar and coughed violently into his hands as the black-cloaked mysterious man gave an order to the truck driver.

"Get this truck out of here."

"Ye-yessir."

Probably less out of a sense of duty and more out of a sense of terror, the business-suit man pressed down hard on the gas.

The engine roared and exhaust sputtered out as the truck traveled back up the road to the surface, ignoring Okamura as it passed.

At this point, he needed to keep his attention focused on the young man in the cloak.

His left arm was clearly inhuman.

Okamura crawled into the shadow of one of the giant racks and rummaged through his bag.

"Camera . . . camera . . ."

He nervously advanced the film for his dead father's classic Leica M4 and looked through the finder.

"Is it too dark to get a shot?"

Despite the fact the Leica M-series was made a half-century ago, they were still amazing cameras. He had no choice but to put his faith in the talents of Oskar Barnack's engineering.

Licking his lips, he snapped the shutter.

In this case, the dignified click of the shutter's wink would be painful to his subject's ears.

"Your evil disguise is about to be exposed."

"David!"

"Waa!"

It was then that two different voices echoed through the storeroom.


"David!"

In pursuit of the Phantom, Julia had come down the ladder in the rose garden gazebo and was lifting the hem of her dress as she ran off.

"Waa!"

Saya was still coming down the ladder, and not used to her outfit, she missed a step, and fell into the dependable arms of her trustworthy attendant standing at the bottom of the ladder.

She probably wanted to blame it on her fierce courage and enthusiasm in her new role, but the truth was she was a clumsy girl.

"Ah, thank you . . ."

Embarrassed, her eyebrows rose up, and without a word, Hagi stood her up onto the ground as Julia ran onto the big room with all the wine barrels.

The door that was bolted closed earlier now stood wide open. No doubt David had found a way to open the lock when he infiltrated earlier.

The room was like a magnificent catacomb, but was highly structured and laid out like a chessboard. She saw a truck carrying a large container drive away toward what must have been the exit.

On this side of the truck was a man hunched against a pillar trying to stand up. It was David.

In front of the gun-toting David stood a calm figure dressed in black.

Julia was the first to notice that his left hand looked like that of a Chiropteran.

"The Phantom?!"

Her right hand pulled up the hem of her skirt as her left pulled out the Derringer strapped to her inner thigh. She raised the pistol with both hands.

"Julia! Diva is inside that container! Hurry and tell Louis!"

Louis, who was waiting with the limousine needed to follow that truck.

Without hesitation, Julia turned and bolted right.

With only his gun as a weapon, there was no telling how long he could hold off the Chiropteran. On top of that, his enemy was a Chevalier.

If this had been typical combat, Julia would have done her best to fight along with David, without hesitation.

But this time, she had Diva right in front of her nose.

Red Shield existed to eliminate Diva. It was the priority far above protecting other agents and protecting one's own self. Without hesitation.

"Julia-san!"

Julia ran into Saya and Hagi on her way back down the path she came.

"Saya, turn around! Go back to Louis!"

In order to bring down Diva, Saya's power was indispensable.

However, the Chevalier was not stupid. Confusing him with typical Chiropterans was a mistake.

Julia raised her chin to see a dark shadow zip up into the air, but by that time he had already landed in front of her, his arms spreading velvet wings.

"What do we have here?"

He grinned at the transparency of their objectives, but when he saw Saya's face his eyes and smile lit up even further.

The flick of his claws resounded like blades sliding against each other.

"Julia-san, please step back."

Saya took a step forward, and was gripping the handle and sheath of the katana she was just handed from Hagi.

"It's all right. Hagi is here, too."

Understanding what Saya meant by her instruction, Julia felt a pain in her chest.

When she said "all right" she wasn't talking about her own personal safety. She was telling Julia that she would protect her.

This was coming from a paper-thin waif of a girl brandishing an ancient weapon.

She slid her thumb across the heel of the blade, and a thin stream of her blood ran down the length of the sword like a vein.

As this happened, Julia saw Saya's eyes adjust to a devilish hue. She had learned how to consciously shift to her other self. On the other hand, it was also possible somehow the circumstances initiated her transformation.

+

Saya realized the Phantom wasn't looking at her eyes, but was looking above and to the side.

His gaze focused on the blue rose tucked above her ear. His eyes looked intensely for a few moments, but then relaxed. His bitter smile told her that he either understood something or was perplexed by something.

"I know I shouldn't, but I just can't help myself . . . So is this the taste of the forbidden fruit?"

Behind the beautiful young tenor of his voice was the enthusiasm of a madman.

His long hair flipped around.

A line of silver flashes streaked through the air where his head had been only a moment before.

Hagi's daggers lodged themselves into a stone pillar, and Hagi himself closed in on the Phantom at high speed.

The Phantom crossed his arms in front of himself to block the impact of the cello case coming straight at him, but he still was sent flying straight back like a straw in the wind.

No. He hadn't been sent flying back, he jumped back in order to avoid being killed by the impact of Hagi's attack.

The Phantom pushed off the ground with one hand and with the flair of an acrobat kicked off a pillar to come back and counter Hagi's attack.

His sharp claws squealed across the lid of the cello case.

Pressing back and forth, the two men stared straight at each other.

"You're putting up quite a fight. I wouldn't expect any less from Saya's—"

His words were interrupted as he parried a blow from Hagi.

"—Chevalier."

Hagi continued swinging the cello case. But the man was called the Phantom for a reason. Like a willow in the wind, he avoided the attacks with ease.

"However—"

From below his mask a muffled laugh spilled out.

It was the first time the Phantom had moved forward.

He slipped around the giant iron-like cello case and was right before the tall, young man's face.

Hagi showed no fear. He allowed himself to be pulled around by the force of the swinging case to catch the Phantom's head with his knee.

Thud—the sound of a man's kneecaps crashing on the floor. The other man's legs went limp.

Yet just as the knee met his temple, the Phantom deftly swung his arms around Hagi's body.

The Phantom then spun his body around and threw his prey like a shotput.

"Hagi!"

Hagi crash-landed into a mountain of barrels, which then buried him. The disappointed looking human-shaped Chiropteran then turned toward Saya.

Her body felt light. She could fight. Saya screamed.

"Kyaaa!"

A high arching leap and he came down with flash.

Her blade should have sliced through the crown of his head, but instead swooshed a dry ring and hit the floor.

The sly beast had slid backward. He lifted his head.

There was a crackling sound and at the Phantom's feet fell his mask, cut into two.

"Saya."

"You are—"

Through the gaps in the long hair drooping over his face the Phantom smiled, and Saya could see childlike traces in his features. He was a young man, and it wasn't the first time she had laid eyes on this face.

"Karl Fei-Ong . . ."

"Chairman-san?" muttered Julia with nervous surprise.

He was the other man in the cathedral when Ms. Lee scolded Saya for trying to go into the bell tower. He ran Lycee du Cinq Flèche, and was a well-known executive at a drug company.

But why had he said his own name . . . A campus administrator had mountains of responsibility. To imagine a person of that social status . . . a Chiropteran?

Did the girls that were killed at this school in the past die by his hand?

"Saya, you danced beautifully tonight."

His fiery eyes were fixated on the blue rose in Saya's hair. He must have seen her dance with the young gentleman, Solomon.

Hearing about her own private life from a stranger, a peeping Tom, caused Saya to grind her teeth nervously.

With the tip of her katana aimed at his eye, Saya brought her blade down at an angle.

"Eeya!"

Her blade only ended up clipping off the edge of his cloak. Saya was trying to mount an attack on her enemy, who had turned his chest to avoid the swipe of her sword.

Saya couldn't get blade to meet flesh. Slash, slice, slash, the Phantom rotated his body, escaping the blade, and soared up into the air.

Karl kicked one of the stacked barrels and it came flying at Saya like a cannon ball. Instead of dodging it, Saya advanced.

Slice, slash, her bare blade drew a bright cross in the dark.

The empty barrel was quartered, breaking the hoop holding it together, and the barrel disintegrated into splinters. Through the shards the mysterious black bird came into view.

Oops.

The distraction of the barrel allowed him time to close the gap between them. She swung her katana sideways.

But the enemy was faster.

The Chiropteran's left hand was like an arrow, and came straight at her.

The claws that cut Saya's cheek also sliced through the blue flower, sending the petals into the air.

With her body thrown back, Saya used all her energy to bring her long blade around again. The darkness was sliced in two. His cloak split down the middle, the Phantom leapt behind Saya.

Spinning around, the tear in Saya's skirt was obvious.

"Spin!"

As Karl's claws fluttered through the air, a guttural voice regurgitated from his throat.

"Dance!"

One of her puffy sleeves collapsed in shreds, and a shallow cut split a line across her stomach.

"For me!"

"Aa—"

A clump of Saya's clipped bangs flew away in the wind. Every cut was just across the surface of Saya's skin. He was playing with her. Saya's brow creased and she took a step backward, and then forward again with her blade raised.

Slashing down and across from her shoulder wasn't enough to get the Phantom to move.

The phantom caught the handle of Saya's blade midair with the hard, cold palm of his left hand just above hers.

"Le-let go!"

Saya's voice was almost pleading. The grip in the sword was incredible, and no matter how hard Saya pushed or pulled the sword wouldn't budge.

"Saya, you are . . ."

He lifted her chin with his gloved right hand.

He forcefully turned her head one way, then the next. He came close enough for her to feel his breath, but she was confused by the look on his face.

"You haven't awakened yet?"

His face was elegant but something was missing, and Saya stared as his face went through rapid changes.

Dissatisfaction, dejection, anger, irritation—and finally sorrow.

"Don't you remember? The things that you did . . . were they all lost as you slept? Not like this . . . not like this . . ."

After convulsing with laughter, the Phantom's expression turned to that of a child on the verge of sobbing. A trickle of tears ran down his face.

"I can't kill you like this, can I?"

Saya's spine ran cold and her shoulders shook.

This man knew Saya's past. What did her former self do that she didn't remember? Was what she did the reason he hated her so much?

A thunderous roar shattered Saya's anxiety.

A blossom of fresh blood exploded in the air, and Karl's face, which had filled Saya's vision, was suddenly pulled to the side.

"How unrefined."

He rose back up, revealing that half his head was exposed flesh. He looked to the rear of the passageway as if he were glaring at a howling stray dog.

David stood in front of Julia and steadily readied his pistol straight out from his shoulders.

The gun roared again.

Two bullets entered the Phantom's chest, and his entire body rolled back. But, as he slid across the ground he rose on his knees and lifted his head.

From the young man's blood-soaked head a single bullet wormed its way out.

"Saya, it's really too bad. You are not yet complete. Your anger and sadness were at their peak. But look at you now. You are just a normal little girl."

As he spoke those dense and gloomy words, there was an eruption from the pile of barrels behind him.

Among the wood shards flying through the air Saya saw the arm of a Chiropteran. Karl spun around in time for that arm to wrap its claws around his neck.

"That hand . . ."

The captured Karl was slammed into a pillar by Hagi, but at the same time landed a swing into Hagi's abdomen, sending him up, backward into the crane.

Rubble fell from the ceiling, and the entire underground was in danger of collapsing.

As he released the cylinder and reloaded his pistol, David yelled out.

"Julia, now's your chance! Go to Louis!"

"All right."

As Julia made her way to the exit, she was not hindered by the Phantom.

The truck had at least a five-minute head start. The chances of catching up with it were pretty low.

On the other side of the countless rolling barrels, Hagi and the Phantom continued their battle. Hagi swept the Phantom's legs out from under him, slamming him onto the ground. A crack opened in the stone floor, and pieces of rock flew through the air.

However, it was as if Karl had anticipated this, and he laughed, kicking up from below. Hagi's lanky body went careening though the air, only to be buried, again, in a pile of barrels.

In one swift move Karl was airborne. As nimble as an insect, he danced through the air. From the stone floor David fired his revolver, shattering bottles lined up on shelves.

Saya gripped her katana with all her might, ignoring the pain of her nails driving into the heels of her palms.

This was no time to be afraid.

The Phantom soared, avoiding the bullets from David's gun. The moment his foot hit the ground again would be her chance.

Now!

"Hyaa!"

Her scream sounded like she was breathing fire, and Saya planted her right foot into the earth.

Saya swung her blade with everything she had, yet her katana only touched the damned air.

He had disappeared.

That was the only explanation. He was faster than common sense allowed. There was no comparing with the Chiropterans she had fought until now.

"Nice swordsmanship."

The words rained down from above.

The Phantom was hanging upside-down from the crane's rebar. He looked exactly like a bat.

Both his legs were wrapped around the steel frame in the ceiling.

"However, your eyes are not fully opened yet . . . And this is the night of the party. I regret we didn't get to share a dance, but I have some things I need to tend to."

His face hidden behind his long hair, the Phantom retreated into the darkness.

David fired his pistol again, but the bullet only sparked up the steel girders.

"Until we meet again. Promise me a dance then."

From the darkness of the vaulted ceiling fell a precious gem.

A blue rose.

The Phantom's psychotic laughter echoed through the chamber.


Outside the assembly hall she sensed the feeling, especially tonight.

The heat from all the people dancing might have made her high. It also might have been her excitement from meeting a handsome boy.

Min considered for a moment that it was possible her temporary light-headedness was her own fault.

If she had asked Alison or Anna-Marie they would have told her to think about it harder.

"I wonder where Saya ran off to."

Sitting on the stone steps of the cathedral, Min sighed to her outstretched feet.

"Wanna bite?"

"Nope."

Min's refusal to the young lad that stood behind her with a plate of food from inside was clear. She wasn't hungry and she was on a diet, anyway.

She wanted to introduce this boy to Saya, but she'd run off in such a hurry, Min didn't see where she went.

"Maybe she wasn't feeling well. She did say she wasn't accustomed to events like this . . ."

"Maybe she went back in through another door."

"I hope that's what happened."

Just as she reconsidered the idea, the half-cracked door to the cathedral spread wide open.

A blond gentleman in a tuxedo came out talking into a cell phone.

"That's right. Hurry and pull the car around to the front of the church. We may still be able to catch up. We need to follow that truck."

Following the man was a gorgeous woman in a very revealing dress. She sped past Min down the stairs. They were in a real hurry.

It was the girl that came out next that put Min into shock.

"Saya! Where were you? What were you doing?"

Saya turned toward her, surprised.

Min's usually moving lips were frozen.

Was this really Saya? It looked like her, but Min didn't recognize her eyes.

Her dress was torn apart, and was she covered in . . . blood?

The dark stains on the sword she carried in her right hand looked like dried blood, too.

What was going on?

"Saya . . . ?"

Her voice was weak from fear.

Min could see by the look on Saya's face that she could feel her pain.

A limousine screeched up to the front of the church and the man in the tuxedo opened the rear door and yelled at her.

"Saya! What are you doing?!"

Saya looked confused and a tall man placed his hand on her shoulder.

"Saya."

His voice was monotone, but carried a certain loving affection.

The man's hand seemed to melt Saya's frozen gaze.

Without a word, Saya turned and was guided down the stairs by the tall man and led through the open door into the back of the limousine.

The door closed.

Saya turned and looked out the window at Min.

The limousine took off quickly.

Min didn't take a step. She couldn't move. She could only watch the car speed away.

As the limousine sped through the front gate, from the rear window Min saw Saya turn and look at her, anguished.

She looked like a lost child, and her lips seemed to be saying something, but Min couldn't make out the words.

I'm sorry? Goodbye? Thank you?

Surely they were sad words. Min realized that much.

## 03

THE WHITE MOON peeked from behind the clouds. It had been about twenty-four hours since the party at Lycee du Cinq Flèche and the night sky hadn't changed.

It was another beautiful evening.

As Solomon stood on the balcony with his palms resting on the guardrail, his attention turned to the surroundings below.

When compared to the rubber plantations that surrounded them, the rear garden of this mansion looked about as natural and organic as a golf course. Stone-paved paths wound through the manicured lawns, and something even more inorganic rested on the grass. It was a very old container.

To anyone else it probably looked like a typical box you see being moved around at a harbor, hundreds coming in and going out every day. However, Solomon gazed at this one with a very special affection.

"..."

On the ground there was someone else looking at the container in the same manner.

It was Karl.

His long coattails looked out of place here, and he had an anxious look of reverence on his face. If someone who knew the normal Karl Fei-Ong saw him in this state, they would probably be struck speechless.

His eyes didn't have the sparkle of someone who could have a coherent conversation.

He fawned on the inanimate box like clergy used to stare at statuettes of the Virgin Mary received by the Vatican.

Since his arrival after daybreak with the container in the truck, he had spent most of his day with the container.

Sensing someone behind him, Solomon turn his head.

"Solomon."

The lights inside went out, and Van Argeno stepped into the moonlight.

Solomon noticed a sullen look in his thin bespectacled eyes.

"It's a nice night tonight, isn't it, Van?"

"What is your intention for Karl? I am in charge of the strategy planning for this project, but have received no instructions and no information."

"Are you worried?"

"Everything that happens is my responsibility."

He could say that if he pleased, but he was not only overstepping his authority with a superior—Solomon—but was showing dissatisfaction in not knowing all the details. The discomfort in Solomon's brow was not seen by Van, but should have been obvious.

Van couldn't wait if Solomon expected him to do all he wanted. His perfectionism to the point of selfishness was one of the underlying motivators in his work.

He also had a sweet tooth, and even if it was a childish trait, Solomon didn't hate it.

"What is that old container that was sent here? We went all the way to Karl's place yesterday for that? I want you to hurry and approve my research and also I have been waiting to give you a demonstration of phase two."

"A demonstration, you say?"

"Yes. We did some dosage comparisons of Delta 67 from phase one, but we couldn't confirm zoanthropy. Our experiments are still limited to 'mice' in children, but I would like to show you the fruits of our labor."

"When you are the one rushing me, I know I can expect some wonderful results. I leave it all to you."

"Thank you very much."

His tone said he wasn't interested in flattery, but his facial expression said otherwise.

"So, how about this demonstration . . . ?"

"Before that, Van, there was something I wanted to ask you."

"What is it?"

"Tell me about the samurai man."


The floor was cold, and as Kai inhaled the smell of dirt in the humid air while he waited as the sound of footsteps came closer.

The sounds of the shoes and frequency of steps told him there were two people.

The lock was undone and the barred door creaked as it opened.

Kai was laid out on the floor and didn't move as much as a finger.

"Hey, wake up!"

The voice which gave the order in bored-sounding Vietnamese was that of a man.

Not getting any reaction, the same order came again in clumsy Japanese.

"Wake up!"

At the same time something hard tapped him in the back of the head. It came down pretty hard. Kai realized it was the bottom of someone's heel, but swallowed back the rage in his gut. If he were to explode now, he would never get out of this jail.

"Is this the one they are using for the demo?"

"Yeah—I am telling you to wake up!"

His head was scraped against the stone floor. Tiny sharp rocks pierced his skin, and just as Kai was at the breaking point the two men gave in.

"He ain't getting up. Let's carry him on a stretcher."

They must have thought he'd passed out from weakness. To ensure that conclusion would be made, Kai hadn't touched the breakfast placed in his cell this morning.

They must have been getting the stretcher ready, as the two men who had entered the cell both had their backs to Kai. He could tell by the shuffling of their feet.

It was in that instant Kai rose up.

With one hand on the ground he spun his body to clip one guy with a kick into the back of his knee.

"Owaa!"

As the man fell backward, Kai cleared the metal tray he'd grabbed with his right hand.

Surprised by his partner's shout, the other guy turned around right into the swinging tray. Blood shot from his nose and a tooth hit the ground before his back crashed into the bars of the door.

Kai quickly jumped to his feet, and as the first guard stood back up again, Kai kicked him in the back of the neck with all his strength.

His head shot up and as he fell again to the ground Kai saw his eyes roll back into his head.

"Have a nice rest, geezers."

A quick search of the knocked out men uncovered, as Kai expected, a set of keys.

If only there was more time. Kai grabbed a piece of bread that had fallen onto the floor and quickly stepped out of his cell.

He was in an old structure. Looking down the corridor, Kai saw there were countless cells just like the one he'd spent the night in.

After planning on sleeping at the volunteer orphanage with Mui and the others, the last thing he would have expected was being tossed into a place like this. The orphanage may have had hard mattresses, and the kids were a little obnoxious, but compared to this prison, that place was like the royal suite at a fancy hotel.

"What the hell is going on?"

Setting aside the question of where he was, Kai had no idea why he was here.

It was obvious that someone ratted them out, but he had a hard time believing it could have been one of the volunteers at the orphanage. It was clearly a separate group. Kai had forgotten that this was a country with an imperfect system of law and order, and an organization which abducted children wasn't unthinkable. He recalled hearing stories of Japanese being targets for kidnappings and ransoms by local mafia organizations.

This prison had around thirty cells, and many of them were occupied.

They held children wearing solid red or yellow raincoat-like ponchos. They mostly appeared to be early elementary-school-aged.

"Could this be for real?"

They must be part of the human slave trade. The owner of this operation was evil and insane, Kai was sure of that.

As Kai clenched his teeth, he carefully searched the hallway for his younger brother.

"Nnh!"

After a jar of pickles has been left in the refrigerator for a long time, it takes all of one's strength to get the lid off. That's what the groan Kai heard reminded him of.

It quickly changed to a defeated panting.

"It's no use. I can't get out."

"I think they might try and sell us."

It was Riku and Mui. And they sounded close.

Kai turned a corner, and their temporary residences faced each other at the end of the hall.

"Yo!"

"Niichan!"

Riku had gotten quiet when he'd heard Kai's footsteps, but hearing his brother's voice made his face light up. Riku was wearing a white top and was strapped to a bed with cloth belts.

"Keep quiet. I'll untie you."

The keys he'd snatched were already becoming useful.

He opened the cell door, and once he loosened the restraints Riku grabbed the keys and headed for the cell across the hall.

"Mui, are you okay?"

"Yeah. I should be asking you. You were the one strapped down."

"Nothing to worry about."

Riku laughed nervously and covered the marks on his wrists from the straps. This made Kai smile.

Considering that Riku was the only kid in the prison who was tied up told Kai he must have given those men earlier a hard time. Kai was sure he was restrained because he'd tried to fight off those guys to help Mui. Kai was proud of his little brother for sticking up for the girl.

"Say, Niichan, we need to let the other kids out, too."

"Yeah, don't worry. We will."

Trying to escape this place with all these kids was not an ideal plan, but it wasn't as if they could just leave them in their cells.

If George were here right now, he would make sure that every child got out.

It didn't take nearly as long as Kai had expected to get the kids out of their cells.

None of the children showed any fear and none of them were crying.

They obediently exited their cages and followed their liberators like chicks following a mother hen. Kai noticed that the children didn't say a word, but maybe that was because they were so happy to be relieved from the unimaginable stress they had been through, they didn't want to say anything to jeopardize it. For now the important point was simply getting out of here.

It appeared their holding cells were underground.

There were no stairs going down, but they found a staircase leading up to the only way out.

As Kai examined their options, from the narrow corridor a barrage of voices rang out, causing Kai to spin around in confusion.

Were there still guards on this floor? That was Kai's first reaction, but he soon realized that wasn't the case.

It was singing—and at a time like this—and it came from under the hoods of the children following him.

"Hey, what are you guys doing?"

The children didn't seem to hear him.

This was because their collective song filled up the underground space, drowning out any sound that competed with it.

All the children were hooded in red ponchos, and they sang emphatically in perfect rhythm with each other. It wasn't clear what the gently flowing tune meant.

"C'mon you guys. Keep it down. They are going to catch us if you don't."

His words were completely ignored. It didn't seem to be because he was speaking in Japanese, either. Grabbing kids by the arms and trying to sit them down had zero effect.

"Everybody, I am begging you. Please just calm down and be quiet," said Mui in Vietnamese, but with the exact same results.

"I can hear it."

"Huh? Hear what?"

"The song! Kai-niichan, can't you hear it, too?"

"Song? You're damn right I can hear it. They are singing at the top of their lungs . . ."

"That's not what I mean!"

It was rare to hear Riku respond in such a frustrated tone.

"I can hear the song . . . It's a woman singing . . ."

"A woman?"

Kai held up an ear and listened carefully.

However the only thing banging his eardrums was the song sung by these children.

"Riku, it's just those kids!"

Mui directed Riku's attention to a few kids who'd started their way up the stairs.

Mui had tried to block them, but their little bodies, which didn't come up much past Mui's waist, easily ducked her attempt to restrain them. The children weren't moving particularly fast, but did have a strong collective determination.

"Mui!"

Knowing she had a weak constitution, Riku rushed to her side.

Kai also went to lend a hand.

Groups of clean-shaven cherubs made their way up the stairs in the meantime. The youngsters walked uniformly to the surface, and there was nothing they could do to stop them.

They weren't escaping. They were being called to something aboveground.


Not many people knew about the secret attics inside the magnificent structures built during the French occupation.

The designers and workers were as buried as the plans they had designed.

The woody smell of the room brought back ancient memories for Karl.

He carefully wiped the dust from a paper globe with the tips of his gloved fingers, and then faced the desk in front of the window. It was littered with framed photographs.

These pictures also held many memories.

There was one of the two brothers standing next to a young woman—the men in the picture were Solomon and Karl.

The inscription on the edge of the frame read "November 8, 1920."

The face of Karl in the picture was a mirror image of his face today. Only his right arm was visible in the photo.

The next was a wartime photo from 1943 and was taken in Allied territory.

At that time Karl and Solomon were officers in the Allied forces.

In the picture the two of them were in military uniforms, and posed with one brother in a business suit, and there was also another older brother in a high-ranking Third Reich Nazi uniform.

This brother's name was Martin Bormann and he was no longer living.

Among the proud Chevaliers, he was the second one to quit, and his loss was rather difficult for Karl.

The last photo he looked at was the most recent.

"December 24, 1972."

This was during the slow quagmire of fighting between the everyman farmer fighters and the capitalist American Army. He remembered the thick jungle, the mines, the bombings, the strewn arms and legs . . .

Standing among Solomon and Karl were a group of white-coat–wearing researchers posed in front of the very structure Karl was in at this moment.

This was just when their research had started, and Delta 67 was still in test-grade, being researched in fruits and vegetables.

After that—

Karl grabbed his left arm with his right hand and squeezed down hard on his sleeve.

"Saya . . ."

The katana-wielding goddess that had run about that burning village.

Her sword had left the ground red and blood-soaked with bodies.

Those angry crimson eyes—

The pain and hatred he felt then welled up in him now.

"It was two days after that picture when you lost your arm, wasn't it?"

Karl turned around to see the young blond man, smiling, but with a look of concern in his eyes.

"Solomon . . ."

"I heard about the samurai man from Van. There is only one person in the world that can kill Chiropterans by crystallizing their blood."

Solomon came to Karl's side and rubbed one of the picture frames lovingly before turning to him.

"Karl, I understand why you were in a hurry to get Diva transported."

It was to feel safe.

Every second counted in exposing Diva to their natural enemies.

And there was one more thing.

And this wasn't an anxiety. He was enthusiastically anticipating round two of the evening ball to begin.

"Karl."

His brother's sigh was as listless as his previous gesture with his hand.

"It's all right if you feel resentment. But you mustn't kill her. She is—"

"Is that the wish of a Chevalier, or just your personal desire?"

"Both."

The silence hung heavy in the still air of the room.

After a few moments, Solomon's voice revived the damp atmosphere.

"If our brother knew, what do you think he would say?"

"Don't tell Amshel."

"That completely depends on you."

The implied threat didn't fit with Solomon's soft features, and Karl glared into his dull eyes.

The rattle of the window broke his concentration.

They both looked outside at the same time.

Diva had begun her song.

Karl's pupils widened like a feline's.

Solomon walked out to the back garden with his younger brother and realized too late that they were not the first to arrive.

Van Argeno and his assistants were there. So they were able to hear the song, as well.

That meant she was in a good mood tonight.

Solomon listened to her pleasant song as he and Karl walked across the grass toward the container.

"For some reason my card won't open it . . ."

Van Argeno faced the security device on the container's door, looking at it like a despised toy as he condemned his Cinq Flèche Executive keycard.

There was no way he could open it. This door wasn't for company execs. It was more than that. It was sacred.

In the entire world there were five who had the ability to open it.

"Move."

Karl stood above the young Frenchman in hierarchy, and nudged him aside roughly as he produced a card of his own and slid it into the card reader.

There was a short beep, and the light on the reader went from red to green.

Fearing nothing but his siblings, Karl grabbed the handles and pulled the doors open.

From behind the opened twin doors flowed the light song and a sweet fragrance.

Van looked into the container's interior and his expression warped into one of shock and maybe even disgust.

"Wha-what is this?"

"Delta 67's raw materials."

The sweet-toothed executive's face looked like one of those marionettes that shows itself at the hourly chime of a city center clock tower. Solomon then turned his gaze to his little brother.

"It looks like Diva is having a nice dream."

"Diva?" asked Van, his throat dry, as Karl stared into the container, unable to turn around.

Solomon only answered with a silent smile, and looked back at the mansion.

This song would probably beckon them, wouldn't it?

A dozen or more children wearing hooded, dyed tops innocently made their way toward the container. From their tiny mouths flowed Diva's song in perfect harmony as they walked across the grass in the evening moonlight.

"Who let the 'mice' free? I ordered the phase two demonstration to be canceled."

The typical Van would have said these words, blaming someone else for something that was his responsibility as he sucked on a piece of candy, but that was not the case this time.

The tongue-lashed assistants did what they could to capture the tiny escapees, but there were too many of them. If an assistant grabbed one, more hands came to pull him free.

Karl closed the container doors and smiled sarcastically.

"What a kind reception these children have brought you."

"Karl, you were saying that . . ."

Van's voice trailed off.

He must have noticed the long-haired man he was talking with was now humming along with the children.

For a normal human like him, this must have been a very baffling situation.

Solomon broke his silence in sympathy.

"She is close."

"She?" Van asked dubiously.

"Solomon, I leave Diva to you," said Karl as he fluttered his tailcoat. "Now you all come with me."

Summoned by the young man, the children obediently followed behind. Like the Pied Piper of Hamelin, his tailcoat became their refuge.

"Wait a minute. We need them for our experiments . . . Where do you think you are taking them?! This is outside your authority!"

Van's sudden outburst fell on deaf ears.

As Van stepped forward to stop him, Solomon placed his hand on Van's chest. No one had the power to stop Karl. No one besides Amshel.

"Karl."

Birthplace and race were important, but none of that was more important than the bond of brothers.

"Be careful."

"I'll give you a magnificent show."

Karl slid a strange-looking mask over the top half of his grinning face.

The slightest hint of a smile appeared at the corners of Solomon's mouth.

"He truly cannot be helped."


At night, the water's surface and the sky were the same.

Stars floated on the glassy surface of this river which cut a line into the dense forest.

The reflections tried to escape the spiraling ripple in the water. They had been going upstream for about two hours. The bow of their disguised wood fishing boat came in to find a resting place on the river's bank.

"Uwaa . . . oof."

A tree branch jutting out from the land hanging over the water whacked Saya in the chin, and she almost fell over the side of the boat.

Hagi, who had been standing behind her, grabbed her before she ended up soaking wet, but David, wearing his field uniform, still scowled.

"Be more careful!"

"Sorry . . ."

Little incidents like these did not build David's confidence in her. Saya was constantly reminding herself of this.

The four other people who had just boarded their boat also had the same serious expressions.

These were Red Shield combat professionals who had experience fighting Chiropterans. The four of them were dispatched by Headquarters after David put in a request. They were all probably anxious about the upcoming battle. Saya had no doubt the group was trying to decide if Saya was a dependable member of the team or not.

"I hear she hasn't completely regained her memory. Is she going to be all right?"

This question from their leader, Clara, was directed at David, not Saya.

Her long rifle rested on her shoulders and at that moment, the distinguished features of her African heritage looked not quite suspicious, but more distrusting.

"She will be no hindrance in combat. Saya's memory isn't what is needed for killing Chiropterans, it's her blood."

"If that's the case, can't we just prepare our bullets with her blood?" stated the sunglass-wearing, goateed Rogers with no expression.

"We would if that worked," answered Julia from the deck of the boat.

Both Julia and Saya wore the same khaki green uniforms as David. The exceptions were the fisherman's garb Louis wore in the pilot house and Hagi, who was in his same formal jacket accessorized with the cello case.

"You know what is written in 'Joel's diary,' correct? Still, we couldn't be sure without trying it in actually combat."

"If we had some live Chiropteran samples we could test out that theory, and things might be different, huh?"

This time it wasn't the hunched over Rogers, but the nearly two-meter-tall giant, McCoy, who spoke earnestly, asking his question to no one in particular. It sounded like arrangements could be made, if necessary.

"Is that what you're asking us to do? That's pretty big for a Christmas present."

The short, but charming Spencer added his comment in as a joke.

Julia sighed in frustration. Spencer and Rogers gave each other high-fives.

They were bold and fearless men, but the thought of actually capturing a Chiropteran, rather than killing it, would have made their bones rattle.

On the other hand, maybe killing them was more difficult.

"Regardless, the fact remains that Saya is the only one who can kill Chiropterans."

To put an end to this argument, David turned to Saya.

"You can do it. Right, Saya?"

Realizing a negative answer was not an option, Saya hesitated a half-second before she responded.

"I can."

To solidify her determination, she nodded her head up and down.

She had to fight. She had to put these painful days behind her so she could go home and be with Kai and Riku.

As they were traveling up the river, David had told her about Diva.

Thirty years earlier they'd lost track of the whereabouts of Diva, the leader of the Chiropterans, but she was supposedly housed inside that container.

The main purpose of Red Shield was to find that iron cradle the queen of the monsters slept in and destroy her, according to David.

That mission would be completed tonight.

They jumped off the boat. As she trudged through the mud in her boots, Saya repeated to herself the detailed instructions.

Non-combatants Julia and Louis were to wait with the boat. Saya, along with David, Clara, Rogers, Spencer, McCoy, and, of course, Hagi, progressed through the greenery.

Before long Saya noticed the thick, chaotic jungle turned into a more organized, manicured plantation.

The morning mist created a haze around them, and there were many kinds of plants that Saya didn't recognize from Japan. However, she knew the stalks lined up perfectly like high-school students at morning assembly were rubber plants.

During the prosperous "afterglow," as it is called, of the French occupation, this plantation had been a Cinq Flèche Pharmaceuticals property. Louis had determined that the container had been delivered there, and less than twenty-four hours later plans of attack were prepared and were being executed, as if Red Shield was really the high-grade elite organization that they said they were. Saya truly felt this could really be happening.

David and the others walked quickly.

Even carrying those gigantic heavy-looking guns, they advanced along the uneven ground without comment. On top of that, each member of their team vigilantly was on lookout and covered a specific direction as they advanced.

The only other female, Clara, carried a gun that looked like it could honeycomb a car—Saya had assumed it was simply some sort of large-scale machine gun, but had then heard it was called a MINIMI, apparently a Belgian light machine gun.

Saya only carried her katana, and felt ashamed that that alone contributed to her fatigue.

"Aa . . ."

As Saya started to lose the pace of the rest of the team, Hagi's hand came to help her along.

"It's all right."

If she needed help now, what good would she be when things got really tough? She pushed his hand to his side, and pushed herself to keep up the pace.

After that about ten minutes passed.

Slowly Rogers raised his bearded chin and looked into the growing foggy mist.

Clara's brow wrinkled.

"What is it?"

"The chirping stopped."

Hearing it said, Saya noticed that he was right.

"The birds stopped . . ."

The singing of the birds had filled their ears ever since they were on the boat, but suddenly the wild fowl chose to be silent. Even a few moments earlier she'd seen a beautifully colored parrot flying between the trees.

The happy-go-lucky look on Spencer's face disappeared as he cocked his shotgun. David and Clara also raised their weapons.

Complete silence seemed to stir uneasiness in people.

Suddenly a sound broke through Saya's frozen tension.

"Singing . . ."

"Saya?"

"I hear a song."

Looking at David she realized that he couldn't hear the song.

Everyone's eyes followed the sound of a dense boom.

Hagi's cello case dropped to his feet.

That seemed to be an order to the plantation to emit another thunderous roar.

This time it was the mismatched sound of helicopters over the dense forest.

"Seahawks!"

"They might be going to take the container."

To Karl Fei-Ong and the other Chiropterans, Diva's survival was more important than their own.

Are they being careful after the recent confrontations with Saya at Lycee? It seemed obvious that they had kept the container here as long as they could, but now were going to transport it to the next safe place.

"We can still make it in time!"

What kept David's legs from breaking into a run was the sound of a song being sung.

Saya could hear this one, too.

It was the same song she'd heard moments earlier, but now was a collective humming from many voices. It wasn't clear if the source was the moon or the fog as the tune permeated the night.

"Diva . . ."

In very non-Hagi fashion his left hand held his trembling right hand, which rested atop the cello case. His right hand shook as if it was freezing.

However, at that point Saya and the other members of the team were too preoccupied to worry about Hagi's condition.

They focused on the breaks in the thick fog that had formed ahead of them.

Coming through the mist, they saw red ponchos.

Children. Judging from their height, they were five, maybe six years old. From under their hoods the song continued.

"Why? Why are there children in a place like this?" asked Rogers as he readied his weapon. He quickly determined there were more than ten children hooded in brightly colored polyethylene ponchos.

One native-looking boy moved toward him, walking as if he were stepping on cotton. Suddenly from his forehead stuck a silver flash.

It was a cross-shaped dagger.

The fog in front of him turned red and his small body fell backward.

"Hey, they're just kids—"

Eyes wide open, Clara immediately hurled blame at Hagi, whose expression hadn't changed at all.

Another child leapt like a monkey from Rogers's side and attached its jaws to his neck.

He tore out a piece of his throat and chewed it like a piece of meat.

Bright red blood splattered the rubber plants.

"Wha—?"

Saya didn't understand what had just happened.

Rogers's head leaned back, staring straight up at the night sky, and his body collapsed.

At the same time David shot down a small red figure that jumped at him, sending it rolling onto the ground.

Saya saw the child who had been struck down with the dagger rise as if he was being pulled up by a string.

He was laughing.

He laughed to show friendship to his new playmate, and then the dagger ejected from his forehead like he was spitting a watermelon seed.

After that the hole in his head split open, tore through the length of his body, splitting it into two.

Like a cicada shedding its larvae shell, the skin of the boy broke away to reveal its new form, which appeared like an alien or some kind of goblin.

"Chiropterans!"

Saya's scream was drowned out by a barrage of gunfire.

As all the children began a similar molting process, the soldiers of Red Shield blasted them with their guns.

"Get to the mansion!"

"But . . ."

"Get it together! Run!"

Saya could not tear her eyes off of Rogers's body as it went into post-mortem convulsions. Clara grabbed her by the arm, and that finally set her legs in motion.

She heard a strange cry rain down from above the rubber trees.

The light coming from the large mansion about 300 meters away reflected the slimy body of the creature, which previously had the hilt of a dagger sticking out of its forehead, attacking from above.

A swinging cello case found the ugly head of the assailant and planted it into the earth below.

Besides the Chiropterans, there was nothing in their way.

However, it may have been easier to deal with a hundred armed soldiers and a compound surrounded with electrified razor wire. As the troupe approached the entrance to the mansion, they were still surrounded by the tiny hyperactive killers.

"There's no end to them. Even if we blow their legs apart, there are still too many."

David was using the same SPAS shotgun he had at the nature conservatory in Okinawa, and was blowing holes in nearby enemies, but McCoy looked at his technique disparagingly.

The Chiropterans blew back onto the paved driveway leading up to the front lawn of the mansion and put out their claws to stop their bodies from rolling. Fresh flesh quickly filled the holes from the shotgun blasts.

David grabbed the handle of the wooden door at the entrance, but realizing it was locked, turned the muzzle of his weapon to it.

"Get back!" commanded David to Saya as he fired his gun.

Destroying the lock and hinges with shotgun fire, David kicked in the door, and slid into the front opening of the mansion.

After a quick check of the interior, Saya and Hagi followed.

There were no signs of life in the giant entryway which opened up to the second floor.

Within the chorus of gunfire Saya heard going on still outside, she also heard shouting and turned back around with a deep sense of dread about what she might see.

"McCoy!"

"Don't worry 'bout me!"

The giant man tried to suppress Spencer's concern.

McCoy twisted the barrel of a pistol into the mouth of a pint-sized Chiropteran that had attached itself to his knee, and pulled the trigger. The back of its head exploded outward and sent the Chiropteran flying to the ground, and McCoy fired one more round for good measure before turning his sweaty brow to Spencer.

"Go on ahead."

Spencer couldn't acknowledge the instruction in words. He didn't let McCoy see him hesitate before entering the building.

Clara and David were speechless.

Spencer moved backward toward the doorway, blasting his gun at the Chiropterans, and nodded to his colleague's bravery before running to join his colleagues inside.

" . . ."

Saya was essentially in a state of shock. Only her legs knew to follow the men as they went into the depths of the mansion.

How much deeper could the bonds of people go? Together they had sacrificed their own lives to destroy the Chiropterans, to destroy the one called "Diva."

*Could I ever be that strong?*

Saya asked herself this as she ran under the giant chandelier in the entry hall.

The song she had heard since entering the rubber plantation got louder inside her ears.

It was her fault.

Everything felt heavy, like she was running underwater.

Clara's machine gun roared and the handrail to the stairway to the right exploded in splinters.

Her bullets tore through the Chiropterans flying through the air, putting bullet holes in the wall and sending a storm of blood to rain down on them.

It wasn't any safer inside the mansion.

"On the other side of this open area should be the rear garden. That's where the helicopters went."

"So that's where the container is?"

Bringing up the rear, Spencer blasted a boy still in his red poncho, instantly painting a crimson-colored flower on the wall.

Saya watched intently.

From the pool of his own blood, the blasted boy pulled himself up.

This was a Chiropteran, but its body still looked human.

"Saya! What are you thinking? Fight!"

David's commands fell on deaf ears.

From a side hallway a child walked toward Saya.

"Kill it! They will never be a human again!"

"I can't . . ."

She couldn't pull the katana from its sheath.

At first the hooded little figure walked slowly, barefoot towards her, but then he broke into a sprint.

The hood fell back, revealing his face.

The skin of his Southeast Asian face hid the simian monster-like creature below its surface.

"Aa . . ."

The quick-stepping mini-Chiropteran vomited blood just before her.

Blade-like claws—Hagi's right hand, bore through the thin chest of the creature from behind.

"Aa . . . AAH!"

Saya expressed her irrational terror with a guttural scream.

The sliced-up child rolled across the floor. He had no expression on his face.

This scene was overlapped by a memory Saya had seen before.

A girl.

Her back was to Saya, and she was running frantically.

She splashed through puddles of blood and mud.

She turned around, and showed her face.

She didn't appear to be afraid as much as she didn't know what to do. She showed a quiet tone on her dark, calm face.

An explosion-like burst of blood painted her field of vision red.

She smelled fresh blood and iron.

"Saya! Saya!"

Hagi was yelling her name uncharacteristically loudly.

She saw the ceiling behind him, and his beautiful face looked deeply concerned.

She faintly realized she was being carried in his arms.

Her body was sapped of all strength. Her joints felt broken. She could see, but it was taking an inordinate amount of time to comprehend what she was looking at. Her mind seemed to be on the verge of losing consciousness.

What seemed to be preventing that was the growing sound of the singing in her ear.

"What's wrong?"

"I don't know. We don't have time for this."

"Roger. Let's go!"

The density in the sound of the machine gun fire intensified.

Within her vague comprehension of her surroundings, she felt the sensation of floating on a breeze.

The walls of the hallway flowed past her at a great speed. Hagi must have been running as he carried her.

If felt like a long time passed, but was really maybe less than a minute.

She sensed Hagi had stopped.

He passed through the door at the end of the hallway.

This was a very spacious inner room.

There were stairs inside this room as well, and it had a very tall ceiling. The large dignified desk and chairs with their wide legs stood on top of what appeared to be a Muslim-influenced, densely dyed Spanish rug. A second-floor balcony encircled the room.

From behind them Saya heard Spencer's shotgun blasts and pump loading over and over again until he got in and closed the door. David and Clara pushed a long sofa to block the door. The carpet bunched up looked like a layered Napoleon pastry.

Making sure everything was covered, Spencer explored the room to ensure there were no hidden enemies.

The constant din ended a few seconds earlier, and the smell from the haze of gunpowder spoke finally registered in Saya's nostrils. Hagi laid Saya onto the carpet.

The worried look on his face couldn't be a good sign. Just as it entered her head, that emotional thought was dissipated into the gunsmoke-filled air. Just thinking was exhausting.

Hagi was on his knees and looking at Saya when suddenly his head looked up.

Spencer had noticed something at the same time.

"Above us!"

A number of quick-moving figures jumped from the second-floor balcony.

Once again, the three guns repeated their chorus of fire.

The tiny Chiropterans hit by the gunfire fell to the carpet in varying sizes of slabs of flesh.

The sounds of battle seemed like noise from a television as Saya calmly gazed up at the ceiling as she lay on her back.

"I am so happy we could meet again, Saya."

From this angle she had a commanding view of a dark figure in an ominous-looking mask.

The Phantom.

"Doesn't this kind of remind you of that day? Naturally the actors on both sides are different, but it still brings it all back."

He leaned back in a deep laugh.

"It's a reenactment of our own Vietnam War!"

War—

Clara's machinegun roared. The sound was like iron balls being smashed against a concrete wall.

Thump. Saya heard a heavy sound near her ear.

She turned her head to see a bloodstained body part lying on the floor.

It was a child's right forearm.

The face-up palm grasping at the air with its tiny claws showed it was clearly Chiropteran, yet still, at some point, it was human.

All other sound was drowned out by the song.

The willowy echo of the young girl's voice bundled itself in the air and penetrated into Saya's eardrums, completely holding her consciousness hostage.

"No. Make the singing stop."

"Saya."

"Please. Somebody help me . . . Father . . . Kai."

She covered her ears with her hands and rolled onto her side, but the song only came in on a stronger frequency, and her brain felt like it might snap. It wasn't that the voice was so loud, but it was penetrating in the way that sound was accentuated when heard deep underwater.

"The song . . . stop it . . . stop."

From the base of her neck she felt blood swell painfully to her cranium.

A door opened.

"No!"

Saya's back bent like a bow and from that moment what she saw until now was lost, and she was now looking at a different scene.

She saw the bodies of young children.

The wet ground around the human bodies were soaked in blood.

They looked like garbage tossed out on collection day.

There were men, women, children, infants. All their bodies had sections cut out, exposing their organs, pink muscle and white bones.

There were bodies of Vietnamese girls.

Bodies of people she didn't know.

Bodies of Chiropterans.

George's body.

Bodies, corpses, dead, death . . . Kai's . . . corpse.

"Kai."

*Kai, help me.*

A tear swelled in her eye and ran down her cheek.


The "mice" froze.

In fear.

Fighting an enemy for the very first time, it wasn't unexpected that they might lose their abilities from shock.

The end of the "mouse" attack also resulted a cease of gunfire.

The humans were bewildered by the peaceful state that came without warning.

One member of the troupe, a healthy-looking white man, seemed to sense something, and looked over his shoulder.

"Saya . . ."

Everyone in the large room was focused on one point in the room.

"Beautiful."

Karl kept the rumbling he felt inside his body in check. His lips trembled.

He looked upon the girl who stood up with the katana in her hand.

Her eyes hadn't changed in thirty years. They still burned the color of combat.

"At long last, my lovely, we meet again."

He plucked the blue rose from his lapel and held it out to her.

"Welcome back, Saya—"

The roar to the heavens was enough to rattle the chandelier.

Saya leaned her head far back as she released her battle cry, and then her beautifully murderous face turned to her trophies.


Kai could not fathom why the tremors and sounds of gunfire from the top of the stairs didn't send the children into a panic.

And Riku had said that he could hear a song.

Kai couldn't hear anything like that, but it seemed to be sending some of the children rolling on the floor. Mui along with two other kids wearing yellow raincoats moaned in pain as they groveled on the ground.

As a high-school student, Kai was stunned at how much strength these children had as he tried to calm them down.

"Please, you guys need to be quiet."

They didn't seem to hear a single word he said.

Riku, who was desperately trying to calm the children down, looked into his older brother's eyes.

"What's happening?"

Kai wanted to ask the same question.

At this moment, what was going on inside this building?

Leaving Mui and the other two behind, the other children went up the stairs, despite Kai's attempts to stop them. Those kids were all wearing red hooded tops. Mui and the two others were in yellow. Riku was in white. Obviously, the color of their clothes had some sort of meaning.

Only Riku, who had no abnormal reactions, was in white. For some reason the other three were in yellow. It was the children in red who feverishly sang that song and marched up the stairs. There was something between the white and the red that had to do with that song.

If only somehow he could get a handle on what they were singing . . .

"Riku, wait here with them."

"Niichan, where are you going?!"

"Up here to see what's going on."

Kai left Riku with the others, and raced up the stairs. He checked to make sure there was no gunfire before he turned the corner.

As far as he could see, there was nobody.

The first floor was different from the basement. It was incredibly clean. It looked like the elegant interior of a European millionaire's home.

As he was running down the long straight hallway, Kai suddenly heard the sound of gunfire close by.

This was a mansion above the cells for the kidnapped young children. He thought he might be hearing a gunfight between rival mafia gangs.

As quickly as it started, the sounds of gunfire stopped.

It was as if the sound had been sliced off by a blade.

Then, during that peaceful interlude, a high-pitched roar ripped thought the building.

Kai legs froze out of instinctual fear.

"Saya?"

It couldn't possibly be.

Kai couldn't imagine how Saya, whom they hadn't seen in over a week after separating at Hyphong Port, could have made her way to this mysterious place. His ears must have been playing tricks on him.

No. He couldn't mistake the sound of his sister's voice.

Despite how improbable it sounded, it was she.

Kai turned left in front of the staircase leading to the second floor, and turned left again as the hallway led him. He opened the door to the room at the end of the corridor.

It was a giant room with the ceiling two floors up.

The heat and humidity combined with the horrid stench blown against his face forced Kai to cover his mouth.

There was only one word to describe the condition of the room. Death.

Death in the shape of a black-and-red mountain piled in the center of the room.

They were now completely smeared with blood, but Kai recognized the red raincoats. The shapes of the bodies . . . there was no mistaking they were the bodies of the children of what David called Chiropterans.

And they were in pieces.

Kai could hear the repetitive and disgusting sound of something wet.

These boys and girls, their ages still in single digits, were being sliced apart, limb by limb, and pieces were tossed onto the growing pile . . . and the person cutting and tossing and cutting again repeatedly, dripping in dark red blood was—

"Saya?"

Frozen in place, Kai was unable to do as much as blink as his shoes became soaked with blood.

Near her was a short-statured young man laid out on the floor.

As he gripped a heavy-looking shotgun, his eyes were fogged over and focused on nothing.

He was dead. Seeing the deep cut from his throat to the base of his abdomen, it wasn't a difficult conclusion to come to.

Identically, there was a taller woman holding a machine gun with her back propped up against the wall.

Her military uniform was soaked black in blood across her chest and stomach. Her face was as white as a sheet, and her eyes had already clearly given up hope for survival.

Along the opposite wall knelt a man applying pressure to a cut on his shoulder. Kai had never seen Hagi in this condition before.

David was there, too.

He looked like he was all right, but he held his pistol with both hands pointed to the ground. Seeing his back heave up and down and realizing that David hadn't noticed that he had entered the room told Kai that he was on the brink of complete mental and physical exhaustion. Considering David's seemingly endless reserves, Kai was shocked once again.

"What . . . what the hell is going on . . . ?"

Still unable to process what was happening before him, Kai could only mutter the thoughts shooting through his head.

But she must have heard him.

Saya turned from her hill of flesh and looked back at him.

Her eyes sparkled the same thirst for blood as her dripping red sword.

Every pore in his body expanded, soaking him with sweat as he stared at the face of Death.

It was just like the last time. At the school at night, the first time the monster came and she sliced it open. It was that look—No . . . this time it was more intense.

"Fantastic. What a performance."

The proud compliment from an overly enthusiastic member of the audience came from above.

"Phantom . . . Karl! You son of a . . . !"

David raised his pistol to the ceiling to see the upside-down image of the young man in tailcoats and mask looking down at him.

As the gunfire rained from David's pistol, the giant bat seemed to vanish in thin air.

His bullets only broke the chain holding the giant chandelier, which fell onto the table in the center of the room with an enormous crash.

The man in the weird cape jumped to the balcony on the second floor.

As David kept firing his pistol up, from behind him came the figure of a girl.

And she walked defiantly.

Precisely, and not in a hurry. More like a lion that was about to put its fangs into the neck of a cornered gazelle.

Saya's arm spun around like it was carried by the wind.

It wasn't clear whether the leaping Chiropteran had intended to attack or escape, but either way, it was cut in half, and sent in two pieces onto the floor.

Saya ignored the crystallization of the monster's blood, ensuring its true annihilation, and moved forward.

"What's she doing?"

The crease in her true target, David's, forehead already showed prominently as he pulled the trigger.

At the same moment Saya cocked her katana over her head.

From out of nowhere slid in Hagi, who grabbed David and pushed him out of the way.

The blade aimed at David's cranium was warded off by Hagi's dagger.

Sparks flew and Saya's sword was pushed back.

However, with a surge of tremendous force Saya's sword broke through the dagger, smashing it to pieces. Always prepared for misfortune, Hagi grabbed Saya's waist, pulled her to him, and crashed onto the floor. When they finally stopped rolling, the person on top was the young girl.

Unfortunately for her, Hagi had a firm grasp on both her hands, so she was unable to use her sword.

"Saya . . ."

Hagi's pleading voice evoked a smile from Saya in response.

What looked like a smile was really her exposing her carnivore fangs as she prepared to strike.

Hagi's pale waxy throat was penetrated by the white lupine teeth. His exquisite face leaned back in order to breathe.

Hagi's throat gurgled as his neck was stripped apart, and despite being hidden relatively far back, Kai heard every moment.

"You . . ."

After being pushed away by Hagi, David had turned and noticed Kai.

It had been a while since they had seen each other, but this wasn't a time for greetings and small talk.

An enthusiastic laughter echoed throughout the room.

"Very nice, Saya. More . . . More!"

A black clad young-looking man stepped up on the guardrail that surrounded the balcony a floor above. The man—the Phantom, as David called him, spread out his arms and jumped to the first floor.

Reacting to the sound of his feet hitting the ground, Saya lifted her head up.

Her lips and teeth were dripping with strings of blood mixed with saliva.

Saya sat up on Hagi's chest. Her expression was rapturous—suddenly her eyes opened wide burning red, and she snapped a bite of the air just before her.

Her beastly roar electrified the room before dying out.

Before the echo of her cry completely faded away her limbs had come together and she flew up like a leathery-winged bat.

After pushing off the ground, in one fluid motion Saya turned toward the Phantom as she bent her knees back and reared the sword behind her head, only to swing it back down in front in her.

A moment later, the sharp clank of metal rang out.

Saya somersaulted back into the air and landed on her hands and feet like a four-legged monster.

Kai had no understanding of what was happening.

The young man should have been split in half from his head through to the floor, but there he stood, without a mark on him.

"Hee-hee."

From the tips of the Phantom's fingers extended the blades that had blocked Saya's attack faster than the eye could see. They were not of forged steel, but were hardened claws of a wild beast.

A Chiropteran.

"Shall we dance, Saya?"

The mouth of his sleeve to the shoulder of his tailcoat suddenly swelled under the pressure of the monstrous arm underneath.

So angry she was shaking, Saya opened her mouth and let out a fiery hiss, like a cat.

She stood up and held her sword loosely as she ran in for another strike.

"Saya!" screamed Kai.

He couldn't do anything. He couldn't fight and he couldn't stop them.

All he could do was shout at the top of his lungs.

That's why he'd screamed. At the moment the cry left his lips, it didn't matter to Kai if he lived or if he died.

His voice poured down and the room became completely silent.

David turned and looked at Kai, and even Hagi had regained enough strength to sit up, but Kai ignored them. He poured all of his energy into focusing on his sister.

Come back. Saya—

Saya's legs stopped in mid-sprint.

The tip of her katana rested on the floor and her face looked to the source of the shout.

"Kai?"

At first she looked surprised and confused, but then her lips curled into a smile.

It was Saya.

Kai had come to her rescue.

Just like he had done so many times before. Like the first time she'd seen the Chiropteran at the school, and at sundown at the beach, whenever things were scary, whenever things were difficult, Kai always showed up.

*I've wanted to see you so badly, Kai.*

As Saya was about to voice this thought, she caught a glimpse of her right hand, and her heart sank.

The katana she held was dripping wet.

With blood.

She felt as if cold insects had slipped under her skin and were crawling up her back, biting her nerve endings.

Timidly, Saya's head turned to examine her surroundings.

The vaguely familiar smell was almost enough to make her retch.

The large room was soaked red, splattered in blood.

The blood flowing from the large pile of body parts had permeated the carpet, creating a dark red bog, and the air was thick with the stench of exposed bowels and sliced-open intestines.

The room was littered with red chunks of flesh.

Her eyes crossed over the bodies of tiny Chiropterans that would never be human again, and then the dead body of poor Spencer. And then along the wall was the barely breathing Clara. Hagi, who was attempting to stand, held one hand to his neck to close a wound, and it was dripping red with blood.

David's steel expression suddenly relaxed, almost halfway looking relieved.

"Did I do . . . all this . . .?

Her limbs felt like foreign objects.

Her katana fell from her right hand and crashed next to her foot with a clang.

"What is this?!" Karl shouted, cursing in resentment, and Saya's chest felt tight.

His arm had transformed into a monster's claw. His entire body shook with anger and hatred.

"You! What did you do?!"

Saya shivered realizing that this sudden bolt of unrestrained anger, clearly visible through his mask, was directed not at her, but at Kai.

"What did you do to Saya?!"

Karl took a step toward Kai, who was crouched near the doorway, yet that approach was stopped by some invisible bond.

Karl focused on an empty space in the air, and exhaled an irritated huff.

"Telling me to stand down?"

It wasn't obvious who he was communicating with, but it was obviously not someone in the room. It may have been the call of the Chiropteran, or the voice from the song.

Soon after there was a violent blast that filled the air, drowning out his murmurs.

A storm of bullets honeycombed the opposite wall.

The gunfire should have torn through Karl, but suddenly, he wasn't there.

With incredible strength, he had jumped back up to the handrail above and the gunfire soon followed, creating a trail of holes in the ceiling and walls behind him.

The rail and balcony were engulfed in bullets, and a small explosion clouded the area.

But Karl had already dashed across the second-floor balcony and slipped through a doorway.

There was a pause in the booming barrage of gunfire.

As the last empty shell hit the floor, the gun-wielding Clara who had been shooting while sitting propped against a wall, tipped over to the side.

"Clara-san!"

Saya ran to her to help prop her up but then noticed the deep gash in her chest exposing her ribs. Saya couldn't speak.

Saya had done this.

She had slashed open Clara, hurt Hagi, and killed Spencer.

"Say, you are back to your normal self."

Her normally dark skin had turned a pallid shade.

"I wish you would have revealed your secret . . . a little earlier . . ."

Clara turned to Saya trying to smile, and a clot of blood spilled from out of her mouth.

Saying nothing, Saya put a hand on her shoulder and looked into Clara's eyes. The tears dripping off her cheeks mixed in with Clara's blood.

"David, hurry . . . Diva . . ."

"I know."

Those were the only words David had for his dying comrade.

This large mansion did not leave room for sentimentality.

From the other side of the door that Kai had come through entered the cry of a Chiropteran. It sounded close.

"Saya."

Clara gripped Saya's arm stronger than she would have expected from the woman.

"Go. Get the bastards that turned these children into monsters . . . before they get away . . . Only you . . . can save . . . can save our tomorrow."

"Tomorrow . . ."

It was similar to George's dying words.

Live today for the sake of tomorrow.

That's right.

Moaning and crying and doing nothing was unforgivable.

What she had to do now was stand and fight.

It was the only thing she could do in legacy of Spencer and Clara.

Clara coughed and hacked up another giant glob of blood.

"Clara-san!"

"Hurry . . . You are the only one who can do it!"

Saya couldn't respond to Clara's angry words meant to get her moving, and she looked at Clara one more time before quickly lifting her head.

Saya laid Clara back onto the floor to keep her from sliding and then stood up. She picked up her katana, and she turned around one last time to smile and bow to Clara.

In her hand was a grenade, and Saya turned to avert her eyes.

Without looking back, Saya began to run.

She looked straight ahead through the door and into the corridor leading to the rear garden. Less than ten seconds later a loud explosion blasted behind her.

The shock pulsed through the floor under her feet.

". . ."

Saya stopped and turned around. She wanted to scream Clara's name as loud as she could, but she resisted, biting her lip so hard a drop of blood formed.

David, who was a little further ahead of Saya, yelled to her without turning around.

"This is something only you can do. It's the reason we are here. It's the reason Red Shield was formed."

There was no need to feel sorrow or self-pity. That's what he was saying.

It would be hard for her to fight if her vision was clouded by tears.

"Kai, take care of Riku."

David turned to her big brother and gave the orders leaving no room for argument. Kai was the only one who knew where Riku was inside this giant mansion.

"Saya . . ."

"I'm okay."

Looking straight ahead, Saya couldn't let Kai's pitiful tone get to her.

"I have to do this . . . I have no choice but to fight."

"I know."

It was there that Saya watched Kai turn and go back the way they'd just come.

"We'll come find you soon!"

Saya nodded to Kai without a word and turned to continue her dash down the hallway.

David opened both double-doors at the rear entrance to the mansion.

A sudden burst of wind ruffled Saya's short hair.

Saya stepped out into the rear garden, which was even bigger than the garden in the front of the house. Sitting on the grass with their rotors spinning were two Seahawk helicopters.

Preparations to transport the container had already begun.

Karl looked in their direction. He had already removed his mask.

There were other men with him.

One man, in particular, grasped Saya's attention.

"I know him . . ."

It was the noble-looking young man from the ball at Lycee who'd taught Saya how to dance.

Sensing her presence, he glanced in their direction. His blond locks danced in the wind like a field of wheat.


Now was a crucial time.

The cancelation of the demonstration was up to CEO Solomon's discretion, so there was nothing he could do, though now that the research farm was under attack, Van thought that the response should be led by Karl Fei-Ong.

The unauthorized release of the "mice" along with the armed assault from some who-knows-where assailants would lead to delays and unnecessary horseplay.

"Karl, what in the hell are you doing? Who is attacking us?"

Karl completely ignored Van's inquiry.

"Why? Why did you stop me?"

Such an audacious attitude when addressing the head of the company.

"We had a promise, remember?"

The white-suit-wearing young executive brushed his flaxen hair blown from the helicopters away from his eyes and turned away. It didn't appear this man of such high social status was off-put by the impudent words of a man far his subordinate. Van sensed a certain level of intimacy between them that went beyond labels and status.

"Even if I did play with her, she would put up a good fight."

"It isn't wise to take her too lightly. Brother said as much, too."

"Well then, get Diva away from here as soon as possible!"

That being said, Karl turned and looked toward the rear entrance to the mansion.

Like a starving wolf sensing fresh meat, his vision fell on the single figure of a young girl.

Her strong legs began to carry her to their position, and Van thought it might have been his imagination, but her eyes seemed to glow red like two buckets of molten iron.

Not finding the words to express himself, Van could only cough out a grunt.

The large sword pointing down from her right hand glinted a silver reflection.

So the sword that cut apart the "mice" inside the mansion had found its way here? This was unbelievable.

That sword—that silver reflection, the memory soared to the front of his mind.

It couldn't be . . . the samurai man?

On one side of the girl was a mercenary-looking man in military garb, and on the other was a tall, handsome man with a coffin-shaped box strapped to his shoulder. This one appeared to be her personal guardian.

Solomon looked at the girl over Karl's shoulder, and looked down before turning his back to him.

"Take care of yourself . . ."

"I will."

Walking away from Karl's quick response, Solomon ducked his head to enter one of the helicopter's hatches.

"Hold—hold on a minute, Solomon. Is it all right to leave like this?"

"Perfectly all right."

He must have meant that he was leaving the resolution of this situation to Karl.

Bewildered, Van followed Solomon into the helicopter.

The bespectacled researcher in his business suit who had come with Van from Okinawa in the hopes of procuring a "mouse" specimen also crawled in.

Van held out a hand, pushing the man back outside the Seahawk.

"Your seat is in the other helicopter. Stay here for now and tell me what happens between Karl and that girl."

"But, Monsieur Argeno . . ."

"That is an order by the strategic commander."

Van placed two candies in the breast pocket of the man's mouse-colored suit.

It was a little bonus for staying behind and risking his life.

These were top-of-the-line chocolate candies specially ordered from the Bon Marché in Paris, but under the circumstances, just one seemed a bit stingy.


His name was Solomon, if she remembered correctly.

But Saya had no idea what that young blond-haired man could be doing here. As it looked, there was little question he was somehow connected with Karl.

There was also the man called Van, who was also at the ball. With them was a white man dressed liked a researcher also getting into the rear door of one of the helicopters.

A middle-aged Asian man in a suit exchanged a few words with Van, and then stooped down to run to the other helicopter.

The heated exchange going on behind him seemed to be of absolutely no concern to the unmasked Phantom.

"For leaving the stage before the final act, I humbly apologize."

Karl grinned as he walked straight at her.

His long, serpentine hair got shorter, swallowed up into his growing, ashen-colored scalp.

His tailcoat split open at the seams, revealing a hard skin covering a giant, muscular physique.

He lifted his head and roared in joy, shaking the night sky. What stood before them was larger than anticipated, a king among the monsters. What he had become was different than any Chiropteran she had seen before. His face had the features of a skull. His right arm looked as if it had been molded from a machine.

The claws of his left arm grew long, giving him a handful of blades.

"Saya, we can't let that chopper get into the air!"

"Right!"

Saya responded to David's scolding tone of an order directly. She lifted her blade pointed diagonally at the ground.

She stepped onto the grass and advanced toward the beast.

She made his glowing eyes her target and lowered her hips as she focused her assault.

She then showed a sudden shift in behavior.

In the middle of her course she spun on her high-laced boots in the grass and turned at a right angle.

From right behind her Hagi swung his right arm.

It was the silver blades that flew from Hagi's hand that slid gracefully into the monster's throat.

"Grk!"

The silver falcons continued to fly, entering Karl's head and chest.

As Saya ran low like the wind across the grass, she pressed her thumb against the rear base of her sword, releasing her blood into its veins.

Without a word, Saya flew into the air.

She raised her iron blade high above and brought it down right on target.

There was an unexpected clang and fireworks sparked off her blade.

"Amazing!"

Barely blocking the strike with his claws, Karl assessed the scene in one trembling word.

He dropped to the ground like a four-legged beast with an extra joint in each of its rear limbs, and made a lunge toward Saya's abdomen.

"Oof!"

The wind was knocked out of her and she flew backward, but turned her body to avoid the swing of his hammer-like arm.

At that moment the rotors of one helicopter increased in pitch and it successfully lifted its ten-ton body and attached container into the air.

"Can't let it get away!"

David leveled the aim of his large-caliber pistol at the cockpit as shots came at him from the other helicopter's hatch.

Cursing under his breath, David shifted his aim to the machine-gunner at the other helicopter's abdomen. He fired two shots, which sent the soldier at the machine-gun careening backward inside.

A man in a business suit recording the scene with a video camera howled like a fox as the gunner fell against him.

As this was going on, the first helicopter lifted off, carrying the container below it with a thick cable.

David assessed the situation as it came, and decided to jump into the second chopper. No doubt he commanded the pilot to follow the first helicopter.

Unfortunately, that part of the plan didn't end there.

"I will do more than just stop you."

To a normal person like David, the Chiropteran's threats would have sounded like animalistic screams, but his actions spoke towards his intentions.

The bullet-like strike of Saya's blade didn't cut through the first layer of skin, but the blow from Hagi's cello case took Karl by surprise, sending him flying next to the second helicopter, and blocking its path.

"Chevalier . . ."

"Ha ha. You are well-informed."

Diva's protector swung over David with his thick left arm.

His blades extended further, slicing through thick steel.

The shriek of the collapsing sound of metal filled Saya's ears and the helicopter's cockpit sunk while the windshield shattered white. The body slanted at an abnormal angle, and one of the runners bent underneath.

The sixteen-meter-diameter rotors dug into the ground spilling up a tremendous amount of dirt and debris.

"David-san!"

The impact sent David flying like a rag doll out the helicopter's hatch and onto the ground.

Hagi landed on top of the impacted pile of dirt and grass.

The cello case he carried landed right on the monster's arm.

However, that wasn't the end of his efforts.

"Gyu . . . !"

Karl slipped backward and retreated, his grotesque face showing pain.

It was at the same moment that the main rotor of the helicopter stuck into Karl's spine.

"Enough with the kid games!"

The brutally strong Chiropteran pushed back against Hagi.

His long claws met his neck and dove through his chest.

"Hagi!"

Saya leapt just after she screamed.

Through the thick dust, she aimed the edge of her blade straight at his head.

Karl blocked with his left hand and he took a deep breath as he responded.

"Don't use the same trick twice. Even thespians have to be original."

The claws of his left hand grew longer and twisted together to form a single long blade.

Saya jumped, and spun eloquently through the air toward her enemy's chest.

Saya landed with one knee to the ground. With a dry swish, the quick-moving blade was perfectly still.

Her blade had stopped halfway through the hard, thick material of Karl's right forearm.

"I have been waiting so long for you to awaken."

There was no sneer or cynicism. The words leaking from the monster's palate were sincere.

Before Saya could take another swing at Karl she was scooped up in his fleshless arm.

"Don't forget that."

The loving affection in his whisper tickled the downy hairs on her ear.

A bat-wing–like membrane engulfed Saya's face and body as Karl wrapped his arms around her violently.

"Aa . . ."

The only oxygen she had was in her lungs. Her throat wheezed and she could feel brain cells dying. Her vision was dim and foggy.

"Saya"

Through her cloudy eyes she could see the image of Hagi sprawled onto the ground, blood from his hand staining the earth.

He was always sacrificing himself to protect her.

*Forgive me . . .*

Along with her failing eyesight, her fingers were losing sensation, and she hadn't realized she had dropped her katana.

Suddenly the sound of gunfire was overlapped by the peculiar sound of flesh ripping.

The next moment her body was released.

Suddenly freed from Karl's deadly embrace, Saya fell headfirst onto the ground, and her lungs automatically inhaled, her nostrils filled with the thick smell of the lawn. She breathed in some dust, and her throat closed, causing her to cough spastically.

Saya sensed someone glancing at her from behind.

Looking up Saya saw Karl looking at the rear entrance of the mansion.

"Wha-what is that . . . ?" cried Riku, his voice cracking as he laid eyes on Karl.

A girl in a yellow poncho was leaning on his shoulder.

Next to them stood Kai.

He carried a thuggish-looking shotgun with both hands. It might have been left behind by Spencer. White smoke lingered from the shotgun's barrel.

On either side of him stood boys wearing the same yellow tops as the girl leaning on Riku. They looked as if they were in a trance.

"Saya! You all right?"

"Kai . . . Get awa—"

A Chiropteran could not be fought with a gun. Countless numbers of tiny silver balls were thrust from the monster's back, and it only took ten or so seconds for him to be back to his previous state.

"A comrade who knows no restraint."

A tremor-like growl reverberated from Karl's throat.

At the same time Riku screamed out.

"Ow! . . . Mui?"

The brown-skinned girl had gripped Riku's pale arm, and it looked like she was squeezing it pretty hard.

Her naïve, but graceful-looking face showed absolutely no signs of emotion.

The two boys grabbed Kai's hands holding the gun, preventing him from moving.

"Le-let me go!"

The physically powerful Kai couldn't budge his arms, no matter how hard he twisted his body. Theirs was not the strength of normal children.

They were also victims of the experiments that took place here.

"Eat your fill."

Karl's words were used as a signal, again.

The three children used their fingernails to dig into Kai and Riku's skin, and blood began to seep down their arms.

No!

Saya completely woke up.

She was going to turn them into three statues.

Karl looked her way, but didn't move.

Without a word Saya used her dropped sword to prop herself up to her knees.

"I killed you here, before. I am sure of it."

A look of shock slowly spread across Karl's face.

Saya's eyes locked onto Karl's.

"I don't know why I am here . . . and there are many things I cannot remember. There are also many things I do not want to remember. But one thing I do know is nothing can prevent me from stopping what you are doing to these children."

It felt like her knees were broken, and Saya used all that she had to struggle to her feet.

She lifted the sword with her right hand, and grabbed the blade with her left.

Hot pain.

"Even if it means losing myself, I will stop you."

Saya pulled the blade to her side, leaving a red mist trailing between her katana and her sliced left palm.

Saya dashed through the thin red cloud.

The Chiropteran's howl ripped through the still night.

Saya didn't wince as she sprinted. Straight forward.

Karl's right foot put a dent in the ground as he stepped toward her.

Saya had the drop on Karl and she swung her katana.

Karl moved forward, holding out his fleshless right arm to block the approaching blade.

The clang of metal rang out and her sword bounced off his arm and flew into the night sky, arcing for a moment like the crescent moon.

Saya jumped straight up and grabbed the hilt of her sword out of the air with her right hand.

Saya came down on his right arm once again, but this time gravity was on her side as she and her blade fell.

She came down from above his head, yet Karl was not flustered.

"This move again?"

Karl held up his inorganic arm, but this time the blade sliced all the way through without any resistance.

The floating forearm landed among the wreckage from the helicopter with a thud.

"Impossible!"

What was so special about Karl as a Chiropteran was nothing more than his body's ability to morph limbs made up of something other than flesh.

"The exact same spot?"

The spot on his arm where Saya had hit the first time had just begun to heal.

With surgical precision, Saya had sent her sword into the same hair-thin cut, successfully amputating his limb.

As the visibly shaken Karl watched the path of his left hand, Saya jumped to the side to avoid the swing of his left arm-blade.

Saya flew over the grass, and got a fair distance from Karl, turning and stopping on one knee. With Saya in his sights, the one-armed monster rushed forward.

In response, Saya followed suit.

Like a raging bull, Karl aimed his beastly pointed left arm forward.

The long, bayonet-like claw bore a hole through the air and drove its way toward Saya's head.

*Don't be afraid. Step into him!*

The precisely sighted, powerfully thrusted javelin of an arm barely met its target, slicing the shallowest of cuts along Saya's cheek.

At that moment Saya stepped into his gait and hunched low to the ground and pulled her blade down around to her enemy's legs.

Blood spurted from the monster's left shin.

It wasn't a particularly deep cut. But it was all that was needed.

"Grrwaarr . . . . !"

The pain that was unimaginable to a normal human sent Karl reeling backward. From the point of the cut the blood vessels began to harden into a stone-like condition and expanded outward.

Saya turned around, hearing the disturbing sound of bone and flesh being slashed.

She then put her arm in front of her eyes as a strong wind swept in like the one that had mussed up her hair earlier.

Karl's left arm had expanded into a giant wing, and the force from its flapping stirred up the air near the ground.

But with only one wing, the monster had difficulty getting off the ground.

It took all of his energy to get away into the dark sky.

An unexpected rainstorm soaked Saya's head and she squinted her eyes.

She wiped her hand across her face and saw that her fingers were painted red.

"Blood . . . ?"

Saya looked up and strained her eyes to see a downward spiraling Chiropteran.

She could clearly see that the lower half of his left leg was missing. He must have performed a self-amputation with his left arm-blade before the crystallization process reached further up his body.

The final blow had yet to be struck—

Saya broke off running to intercept the giant, misshapen, falling bird that had planted itself in the thick forest of rubber trees just beyond the garden.

It wasn't very far off, but chasing after him there would mean leaving the open area behind the mansion to go into a foreign and thick jungle. Saya wasn't a bird, and she was forced to abandon pursuit.

"..."

Saya looked at the plantation, scanning sternly in the dark, and then something caught her gaze on the bare ground.

What she found was the petrified left leg of the monster she was fighting planted firmly in the immaculately manicured lawn of the mansion's rear garden.

The three surviving children were housed on the lawn in cages supplied by Julia and Louis after communication from David.

Until they could be transported to a Red Shield medical facility, caging them was the only reasonable temporary solution, considering their mental condition.

"Mui."

Riku called to the girl on the other side of the iron bars, and she turned to look at his smiling face, giving him a sense of relief.

Suddenly she bared her fangs, and reached through the bars with her animal-like claws, sending Riku back, confused.

Mui growled menacingly, like a mountain lion. On part of her face was a web-like pattern of hairline cracks on her skin. Could there be a different creature just under the surface?

"Mui?"

Riku thought he could see some trace of reason, a break from her waking dream when had reached his hand to her.

However, that fleeting hint was gone from her face. Her eyes were muddied, once again. After a few tries it didn't take Riku long to understand that nothing would get through to her.

After the creature called Karl escaped from Saya's blade, Mui and the two other boys seemed to have calmed down. But since then they had fluctuated between violent and manic to near comatose states.

"When you get better, Mui, I'll buy you all the baseball equipment you want. And not used stuff, either. Brand new gear. We can make team uniforms . . . and I know! We can make that vacant lot look like Koshien Stadium. It's no problem. I have that much money now."

Even though he knew she wouldn't answer him, Riku couldn't help but continue talking.

His eyes stung, and he cut his monologue short. He couldn't take it anymore.

"She'll return to normal, right?"

"Yeah."

Kai's hand on Riku's shoulder felt reassuring.

Riku remembered something.

Whenever Kai was this nice, he was usually hiding something or not telling the truth.

He could no longer hold back his tears.

Boys don't cry. That's what his father had always said, but Kai didn't hold it against Riku now.

Saya stood off to the side near them and just stared at the ground.

"Tell me . . . whose fault is this?" asked Riku to Saya between sniffles.

". . ."

Saya didn't answer, but Riku could see the amount of guilt she carried in the way she wrung her hands together at the question.

"Why did this happen? Why does Saya-neechan have to fight?"

Her head hung low, Saya's shoulders began to shake.

But Riku wasn't trying to blame his sister in any way.

"I'll help, too."

Surprised, Saya lifted her head.

Riku had thought long about his statement before he said it.

"So, let's not keep any secrets."

Seeing the distorted look on her face, Riku wrapped both of his arms around her.

Riku sensed her fever and sobbing more than the blood and sweat that covered her.

Kai spread his arms and held both of them.

"You don't need to carry any burden on your own. We are a family, right?"

"Right!"

Like a young child, Saya was only able to nod in agreement, but then squeezed her arms around Riku tighter. It got harder for him to breathe, but when he felt the warmth of her tears, it somehow made him happy.

The edge of the night sky sparkled in a faint gold.

Dawn broke over the thick forest.

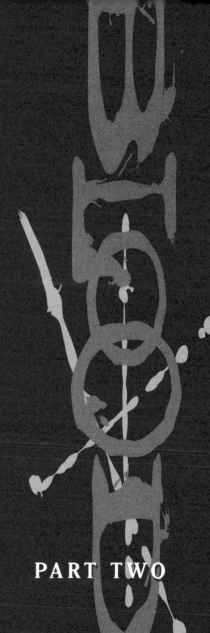

PART TWO

"I UNDERSTAND. I will track down Ted."

Standing in front of the window, thousands of miles from the Red Shield headquarters, David had given his report on the operations in Vietnam, and then hit the END CALL button on his cell phone.

As he turned around he looked to be in an even more sour mood than normal.

That's the look he had whenever comrades had been lost.

The more he fights, the more colleagues who fall, the deeper the crease on his brow grows, observed Julia analytically.

It was analytical, but the bottom of one's heart is best reached with a cold needle.

Julia was very self-conscious about the fact she couldn't deal with his suffering in anything other than a doctor's psychological approach.

The truth was the four people killed in Vietnam were superior Red Shield members.

Their deaths were not a minor blow to the organization.

"Headquarters still has no leads on Karl Fei-Ong's location."

"Yes."

The back of Julia's chair creaked as she leaned back. Her desk was covered with stacks of documents.

Julia clicked a few keys of her laptop and the human face of the Chevalier that had survived Saya's sword appeared on the screen.

"He has quit both his position as the Cinq Flèche Pharmaceuticals Vietnam head and his position as chairman of the board of Lycee du Cinq Flèche for personal reasons."

"Any information on that other man?"

"Solomon?"

It was just as easy looking him up in the Cinq Flèche Group database. A limited extent of information was available.

A very limited extent.

Two clicks later an image of the young and handsome blond appeared on the screen.

"Cinq Flèche used to be a French food manufacturer until they were purchased by an English investment firm. He was hired to be the CEO and president five years ago. Since then the company has rushed to become the world's leading pharmaceutical company. It might be faster to find a profile on him in a back issue of *Forbes* or *Time*."

A charismatic young executive with the world's economy at his fingertips.

"But, I can't find any information on him from before that time."

"Are you saying he's a Chevalier?"

"It's very clear Karl is a Chevalier, but . . . there's no proof to show Solomon is."

"We have to leave the tracking of Diva to Headquarters. Our job is to track down—"

"Ted A. Adams?" interrupted Julia.

As talented as Louis was at procuring information, their Far East location did cause sources to be limited. Tracking the Chiropterans and their queen, Diva, was too tall an order.

With Saya a part of their team now, their focus should be battle-prep, not info-gathering.

On the other hand, they couldn't just sit around waiting for deployment orders from Headquarters.

Even if tracking Diva was impossible, they could follow up on leads that might take them to her.

They were now docked at Naha Harbor, and were using a first-class stateroom as a branch office in a combined passenger/cargo ship. But more than likely they would be clearing out, soon.

Julia picked up a file from her desk. The name "Ted A. Adams" was written in her handwriting across the cover.

Among the documents and data that had been collected here from the experiment farm in Vietnam, almost all were marked with his signature.

The glacier-colored David allowed his eyes to follow the path of the pen in the letters in his name.

"Ted was a major player in the American Army's Chiropteran research."

"His name doesn't appear in the Army's deceased or MIA lists, David. He vanished from the Army records after the end of the Vietnam War in 1973.

"After Louis finds where he disappeared to in Vietnam after the war, we can then decide our next step. But even still . . ."

David's expression grew rigid.

He glared out over the turquoise-blue waves glistening in the sunlight like they were enemies in battle.

"We were so close to Diva, and now here we are, back where we started."

He felt his colleague's deaths were meaningless, and it was his responsibility.

Julia took off her glasses and set them on a pile of documents.

"Saya needs time to rest. If we push her until she breaks, we've lost our only counter-measure."

"Just as long as she doesn't get too used to being home."

Yet he had already let her return to her house and given her twenty-four hours off. Behind that hard exterior there was a warm heart in this man.

Julia hid a grin behind her fingers.

✝

"UWAAA!"

The scream was enough to nearly collapse the roof.

"Huh?!"

Saya's body sat straight up and her half-asleep eyeballs looked around in every direction. Once she was confident that she was, indeed, in her own room, she let out a sigh of relief.

She breathed in the familiar smell of her home. The air of Okinawa.

Saya then realized her left hand promptly searched for her beloved blade, canvassing her bed sheets, and she frowned, frustrated.

At that moment her katana was in same case as the cello, taking a rest after soaking in so much blood and grease. Since arriving in Okinawa, Hagi had separated from them, and she hadn't seen him since.

That scream . . . it had sounded like Riku's voice.

Worried about Riku she left her room and ran into Kai in the hallway.

"You can sleep more if you want."

"No, it's okay. I heard a scream."

"It came down from in the store."

They walked down the stairs to the first floor to find Riku inside OMORO.

"What's wrong?"

"Are you okay, Riku?"

He didn't answer.

Riku's graceful face was pale, and he stared at the floor, making no move to look up.

He pressed both hands against the refrigerator door, and was mumbling something to himself.

"Is there something wrong with the fridge?"

"It-it's awful."

Saya tried to open the refrigerator door, but the suddenly forceful Riku refused to budge.

"Do-don't look inside. Seriously . . ."

"What's gotten into you?"

"Listen, they turned the electricity off . . . How can I explain it? It's all green and brown. Things are all squishy or all dried out. It's a complete mess . . ."

"You don't need to give that much detail!"

Kai whacked his little brother in the head with the baseball glove he was carrying.

Saya remember clearly how the glove fit the hand of its owner so perfectly.

"That's, that's Father's."

"Yeah. We haven't done anything for Dad, so I thought we could at least put this in the family tomb."

George's remains had not made it back to the Miyagusuku family plot.

His body had burned in the rock-melting heat at the nature conservatory, and had been reduced to dust.

"Let's send Dad off together."

There was no sad or morose tone in Kai's voice.

George wouldn't have wanted a gloomy farewell, anyway.

"Yeah."

Saya grinned, showing her agreement.


It was her second time climbing this stone staircase.

The first time had been at night, and she'd walked over the stone steps with George. This time it was with her brothers, Kai and Riku.

In the moist morning air the trees and plants were painted with dew.

Even though it was autumn on the mainland, the last remnants of summer's humid heat still hid in the shadows.

From atop the hill looking out on the deep sea, Saya became more aware of the change in the seasons.

"Here we go."

Kai slid open the tortoise-shell–shaped tomb's door, and the blast of cold air from inside gave Saya a chill.

This was the first time she had entered the family tomb.

Graves in Okinawa were unlike those anywhere else in Japan. They were domed, hexagon-shaped tombs housing a room where people could enter to lay the ashes of deceased family members. This one was probably the size of a six-tatami mat room. The ceiling was typically low. So low, in fact, that Kai's hair rubbed against it.

"Is it really okay to set this stuff here?"

"Why not? It seems like something Dad would do."

Kai answered Riku's question as he held a cardboard box carrying the baseball glove, George's favorite frying pan, a *sanshin*, and other things that George had touched with his hands on a daily basis.

The sunlight on Saya's back leaked into the dim room as she entered, and the smell of the cool, moist ground was strong.

This was where she'd begun.

Putting it another way, this was where Saya Otonashi had been born.

"What's that? . . . Hey, what is that?"

Riku's eyes were stuck on the same place as hers.

It was in the back of the tomb.

It looked like a mass of white hair, a deteriorated bundle of white thread, resting on the ground.

"It looks like a spider's nest."

Riku's statement was partially questioning this curiosity and was partially disgusted by it.

Saya stared intently at the torn-up cocoon made of thread.

"He told me this is where I started."

"Where you started?"

"That's what Father told me once."

Until she had been accepted into his family, George said Saya slept inside this stone room. Saya had the sinking feeling this silkworm cocoon-like thing had something to do with her.

"There are so many things I need to learn more about . . . like, I wish I knew what I was."

It was possible she wasn't human.

Chiropterans—did it make sense for a human's blood to be able to destroy a creature that couldn't be killed by guns?

At first Kai was silently angered, but finally couldn't hold it in any longer.

"I told you before, didn't I? We are a family. No matter what happens to you."

The surliness in her brother's words made Saya strangely happy.

The aggressive and rough way he spoke dispersed Saya's anxiety, and she could see the true kindness in his heart. Kai stubbornly took nothing more serious than the concept of "family," and because of that, she imagined he would move mountains for her if he could.

"Dad would have said the same thing."

"That's right! Saya-neechan is Saya-neechan!"

Even Riku piped in sharply to alleviate his sister's fears.

Kai's face relaxed and he set the cardboard box on the ground.

"Well, shall we send Dad on his way?"

Saya put her hands together and closed her eyes.


For lunch they went to a noodle shop, Souki, in Koza.

It might have been because she was excited to have Okinawan food after so much Vietnamese *nuoc mam*, but the shop owner was visibly surprised to see her eat twice as much food as Kai.

"Saya, is there anywhere you want to go after this?" asked Kai as he stepped out of the restaurant after paying the bill.

Saya looked at the sidewalk.

"We visited Father's grave . . . I'll leave it up to you."

Maybe being given a full day from David to do whatever they wanted was too much.

She loved Okinawa and the view and people and everything, but knowing that tomorrow it could all be taken away again made it painful.

"Hey, Riku."

"Hm?"

"Didn't you say you needed to return a game you borrowed to your friend?"

"Yeah, Atsushi. His house isn't far from here."

"Since we're in the neighborhood, why don't you take care of your business now? My cell phone's service was cut off, though."

"Well, okay, but . . ."

Riku turned to get on the city bus to his friend's house, and Kai and Saya started walking home together.

A month ago she wouldn't have noticed anything special on this walk home, but now everything looked incredibly vivid and precious. Every step brought back memories, and as they continued Saya noticed that Kai had chosen the wrong road to head back to their house.

"Kai?"

"There's one place I'd like to stop at."

Saya was also familiar with the way they were headed.

It was a road they took every morning and every evening. It was an everyday, ordinary street with the typical shops, houses, telephone poles, mailboxes . . . the dog that always barked when you walked by, right on cue, barked at them as they walked by.

The front gate of Koza Commercial High School was closed. It was Sunday.

A young girl stood in front of the iron gate.

She wore faded jeans and a three-quarter-sleeved knit top. Her brown hair was tied back.

Next to her stood Riku. He was talking with her intimately, as if he was her younger sister.

At first Saya hadn't realized that her feet stopped moving.

Her ponytail spun to the side and the girl looked at Saya.

"Kaori . . ."

She must have dyed her hair, because the color was lighter than the last time Saya saw her, but her calm smile and gentle eyes hadn't changed one bit.

"Since we actually made it home, I figured you'd want to at least say 'hi.'"

The whole business with Riku and his friend was just so Riku could bring Kaori here.

Kaori stepped toward them to give thanks to Kai for arranging this meeting, but he just swatted away any attempt at gratitude.

Looking at Kaori's smiling face brought tears to Saya's eyes.

Kaori resisted the desire to run, and walked quickly over to Saya. She grabbed Saya's arms by the sleeves and gripped tightly.

"Welcome home."

Those softly spoken words, almost in a whisper, felt more precious in her ears than any screams of jubilation.

Saya couldn't hold back her tears.

"Kaori . . . I'm sorry . . . I'm so sorry . . ."

Saya didn't know how to look her in the eyes or what the right thing was to say.

All she could do was apologize.

She was sorry she had disappeared without saying anything. Sorry she couldn't see her smiling face again. Sorry she couldn't tell her the truth . . . There were so many things to apologize for.

Surprised that Saya was crying before she was, Kaori's eyes swelled with tears and she stood as she was, glued to Saya.

Kaori's hands moved to Saya's back, and she hugged her tightly.

Kaori's scent.

The warmth of her friend's hug and the sweet scent of the tropical air told her "welcome home" for a second time.

It took more than a few moments for the tears to stop flowing.

Saya noticed that recently she had turned into quite the crybaby.

For a while Kaori stroked Saya's back like a mother calming a baby, but then they both returned to being normal teenage girls.

"I was so worried about you."

"I'm sorry . . ."

Kaori didn't ask where she had been. Classmates knew not to ask about unexcused absences.

"I hear you don't have much time today."

"Yeah."

"How's George-ojisan?"

Saya's voice was caught in her throat.

"He's going to open the shop up again, right?"

Saya was unable to give Kaori the response she was hoping for.

Kai and Riku hadn't said anything.

The silence felt even heavier in the dull autumn atmosphere.

Kaori's chirping voice cleared the air of the sullen feeling.

"Oh, and you probably didn't hear that Kyoko started dating Yonamine-kun."

Saya was a little stunned by the sudden change of subject, but Kaori continued her report on the latest news of their schoolmates.

"And then I heard that they went on a date, and that Yonamine-kun's mom drove to pick her up."

"Wha—?"

"And they went to Chatan for their date, and his mom waited in the parking lot the whole time. Then she drove her them back home."

"You're kidding!"

Saya wasn't the only one to look surprised. Kai made a strange look, as well.

"Speaking of Chatan, a new jeans and clothes shop opened up, too. They sell some really cute tops. That's where I got this one."

"I really like that. That's my style."

"Then let's go there next time we meet up."

Kaori caught herself after she said this.

Saya didn't know how to reply.

The friendly chat had suddenly come to a full stop.

*Next time we meet up—*

Said so simply, yet it felt like that might be a very long time before that happened again. Saya couldn't promise this or anything to her.

What would be a normal activity for high school friends, Saya couldn't do.

Saya felt a pang in her heart. This was a mistake.

"I . . . I can't go back to who I used to be."

"Hm?"

"I was so happy to come back to Koza, but now everything reminds me of that fact. This town won't change. And it's better that way. But, I am the one changing . . ."

"That's not true! Saya, you are fine just as you are!"

Saya had known that's what Kaori would say.

Kaori's kind words used to make Saya feel better. But that simple thinking wouldn't work any longer.

"No, I have to change. If I don't change, I can't fight. I want to get stronger, so I have to go even further . . ."

She raised her chin and looked at the playing fields.

Confused by her friend's words, Kaori looked at Saya like she had lost her mind.

"Kaori, can you join me for a little while?"

"Huh?"

+

Kaori hesitated at first when she heard what Saya wanted to do, but soon nodded in agreement.

No matter what Saya needed, in the end Kaori was always willing to help with a smile on her face. Saya was stricken with a sort of amnesia, but it was thanks to Kaori that this past year at school was full of nothing but good memories.

Even on that night when Saya had gone back to school to get her shoes, it was Kaori who'd been nice enough to bring them all the way to her house.

That night—

The first time she'd run into a Chiropteran.

The American Army has torn down the thick shrubs next to the passageway where Inamine-sensei was chewed up by the monster, but new sprouts were already growing from the stumps.

Time changes living beings and the world.

*I have to change, too.*

"Saya! Ready!"

Kaori was waving from the field inside the track. They had jumped the fence without permission, and Kaori had set up the high jump and mat.

Naturally, they didn't have permission to take the equipment out of the clubroom, either.

Since it wasn't a school day, they were the only people standing on the red earth of the practice ground. None of the sports teams were practicing today, either.

"I hope we don't get into trouble, you know, coming in without permission . . ."

"It'll be all right. It's not like we're hurting anything."

Kai calmly cast aside his little brother's fears.

As a junior-high-school student, Riku was out of the question, and even though they weren't honor students, Saya and Kaori weren't well versed in school break-ins. Kai, on the other hand, had led many such excursions in his day, and had smugly taken on the role of leader of this adventure.

Borrowing the club room key from the teachers' office—again, without permission—seemed like second nature to Kai.

"You sure you want the bar this high up?"

"Yup."

This was a height that Saya had never been able to clear without knocking the bar down.

Saya walked all the way back to the far lane on the track. From there she looked at the bar just to her right.

It felt like ages since she had felt this nervous tension, and the oxygen entering her lungs turned cold.

The wind already carried a hint of winter.

She put her weight on her pivot leg, drew up her body, and turned.

She took in a breath of clear air, exhaled, and pushed off the ground.

Centrifugal force pulled her body in an arc-shaped path, her feet sprung with every step across the ground.

She sped up as she closed the distance to the bar, and right as she was going to hit it she leaned her weight into the wind.

With no fear, she gave all her strength.

Watching the blue float in the sky above, she felt her skirt flutter.

Like a fish in a mountain stream she arched her back as she swam up through the air.

Just as she registered the sensation of weightlessness, the mat caught her back.

The cloudless sky filled her view.

"Wow! That's better than just national meet levels!"

Kaori ran over to help Saya up.

The bar remained unmoved at the top of the stand. She hadn't touched it.

She had flown.

"From now on I'll only fly using all my strength. No matter what."

It was a challenge she was giving to her future self.

Hagi had said it before.

If she knew about her former self, she would lose her present self.

Ever since fighting with Karl in Vietnam, Saya had felt hollow inside, as pieces of her past were buried. His rage and delusional beliefs had been picking at her, even until now.

It wasn't going to be easy, but she needed to look to the future.

To jump and clear it.

Without forgetting to smile.

"Kai! There is somewhere I want to go!"

Even Saya was surprised how comfortable her voice came out. Standing with his hands at his sides laughing caused Saya to laugh as well.

She wanted to go to her favorite place in Koza, that beach.

The sky felt so high in the air.


The ocean was dyed crimson in the twilight, and the only sound was the waves crashing on the shore and pulling back. Crashing and pulling back. Again and again.

Even in the most southern islands of Japan, the sunset arrived earlier during this season.

But if you considered the temperature in Honshu at this time, Okinawa was nowhere near as cold. The smell of barbeque wasn't completely out of order.

"It's ready—"

Everyone gathered close to the barbeque as Kakimoto flipped meat and vegetables on the wire mesh over the coals.

The first one to stick his chopsticks in to grab some meat was Kato, whose love for food was no secret.

"Beef, beef, beef, only beef? An unbalanced diet will make you fat."

"She just kept putting more in the basket."

"It's okay. I have no problem with this menu."

"You haven't changed."

Kaori slowly lowered her chopstick from her mouth when she saw the stack of meat Saya was piling high on her paper plate. The diet-conscious Kaori's plate contained only green peppers and onions.

After they had left the store they'd run into Kakimoto and Kato—Kai's partners in crime—in the parking lot. After chastising Kai for being out of contact for a month, they gleefully accepted the invitation to the barbeque.

The two boys hadn't changed one bit, and Saya thought Kai was probably thankful for that, the same way she was about Kaori.

"Now that I think of it, you been in contact with Mao?"

Saya remembered something when Kakimoto mentioned her name.

The first thing Saya saw when they'd come home was a piece of paper slid into the doorjamb.

It was a handwritten note from Mao Jahana on a paper with her father's business address printed on it. For her to have communicated in such an archaic fashion meant that she had tried everything to get a hold of Kai, and there was little doubt the note was asking where he was and for him to call her.

Three quarters of the messages on the answering machine were from her. A lot were from Kaori, but the overwhelming frequency of Mao's calls had used up the entire message tape.

However, his answer was blunt.

"Enough of her."

"That's not right, man. She was real worried."

"I said it's fine."

He annoyingly waved his chopsticks to deflect any more prying questions, and called to Riku who came over to the grill.

"Give this to Hagi."

Riku took the paper plate of cooked meat and vegetables with both hands before Kai added a pair of disposable chopsticks and a paper cup of oolong tea.

Saya looked up at the top of the breakwater wall to see the tall man standing, staring out over the sea.

"Be right back."

"You got a ghost following you?"

Kai gave a sour look, but didn't stop his brother from delivering the food. Chomping on a mouthful of meat, Saya forced a smile. Kai gave his friends an earful, not willing to accept even a remotely negative comment about Hagi. This made Saya especially elated.


As he looked out at the sunset, Hagi met eyes with Saya.

Riku climbed the stairs to the top of the breaker wall, and noticed that Hagi's cool glare seemed softer than usual.

Back on the beach Kai was trying to force Saya to eat a green pepper while Kaori held her arms behind her back to keep her from getting away.

Riku wondered what Hagi thought when he saw high-schoolers playing around like that.

He was always there when Saya had to fight, and even when he got hurt, he still protected her. Without fail, he kept Riku's beloved sister alive. Probably since before Riku even knew Saya.

"Um . . . this tastes pretty good."

Hagi looked down upon the plate and cup offered to him.

His blue eyes looked purple as they reflected the sunset.

"It's more fun with everyone down on the beach. Saya-neechan would surely say the same thing."

Hagi's eyes moved again.

In the twilight Saya laughed loudly with her friends.

"Here is fine."

He must have felt like he would be in the way if he joined them.

Or it was possible that he didn't mingle with people unless they were fighting Chiropterans.

Riku felt a little discouraged until Hagi took the plate and cup from Riku's hands. He really wasn't being rejected.

"It seems like you always have that."

"Yes."

Hagi saw Riku eyeing the cello case set carefully on the ground, and responded abruptly.

"You are really good. You used to play by the bus stop on Park Avenue. I always listened to your performances."

Hagi's expression didn't change, and he responded by nodding.

Riku wasn't sure if he was nodding in appreciation or just acknowledging his existence, but the positive response from the tall man made Riku so happy his cheeks turned red.

Just as Riku was going to say something, the voice of his brother calling interrupted him.

"Hey! We are going to start lighting them off!"

"Wai-wait for me!"

He wanted to stay and talk to Hagi a little longer, but Kai had already opened the plastic bag holding the fireworks.

"Okay, well, see you later."

As he waved to Hagi, Riku ran down the stairs.


As could be expected this time of year, a lot of the fireworks were damp from the humidity.

"This one won't light."

"That's why they were on sale."

The first tri-color fountain didn't want to light at first, but once the fuse got going (and almost set Kai's hair on fire) the red and yellow sparks got Saya and everyone else excited.

The bucket full of seawater soon filled up with the burned up cardboard husks.

Kato and Kakimoto chased each other around shouting and swinging fountains from each hand. As they spun their arms in giant circles, they painted golden sunsets in the twilight.

Kaori and Riku crouched on the sound, their faces lit up by the sparklers they were holding. The sparks floated onto the sand like dandelion fluff.

As everyone was enjoying the fireworks, Saya found a spot closer to the water to sit and watch the sparks fly in the dark.

As she watched their gleaming smiles and listened to their loud laughter, the gunpowder smell of the smoke carried through the air didn't bother her one bit. It was the same smell as the smoke from the guns in Vietnam, and in this context, the smell was much less scary,

"Saya, don't you want to set any more off?"

"No . . ."

She didn't look at him as he sat down next to her while she answered him. His right hand scooped up a handful of sand and let it trickle through his fingers as his arm rested on his bent knee. The reflections of the orange and red and white streams beamed off his eyes.

"Saya—"

Kai spoke quietly, timing his words against the sound of the waves.

"You can stay here forever, if you want."

" . . ."

She watched as he slowly let his handful of sand slip between his fingers.

More than a little surprised by his words, she looked up to look at his eyes from the side.

In the night sky only lit by the fireworks, Kai's face looked very serious and mature. Saya's must have looked the same.

"I can protect you and Riku."

"Not yet."

Her voice felt very weak.

"I can't come back here. Not yet. There's something that I have to do."

She had already figured this much out.

And it wasn't because of David's encouragement. She chose on her own to continue to fight. She would no longer be afraid of her past, and with all her might she would look toward the future. That's how George would have wanted it.

She understood what Kai was trying to say so well, her chest ached, she was so happy.

But she couldn't let herself be the victim any longer. The warmth of his kind words troubled her, but couldn't deter her.

But if she left, there was no one she could depend on to take care of her.

There was one way she and her brother could both fulfill their wishes—

"Kai."

"Yeah?"

"Stay next to me, always."

That's all she wanted from him.

"Stay next to me, and never go away."

"Saya . . ."

"When I fight and fight, if you are close to me, I know I will never lose myself. You and Riku and George and I will still be a family."

She said this still not knowing for sure what she was.

But what she did feel was that there was something lying dormant in the depths of her self, and she had only had a peek at it, like looking through a keyhole.

What she didn't want most of all was a repeat of what had happened at the mansion in Vietnam. She didn't want to turn into that bloodthirsty beast ever again.

If she was close enough to hear his voice, she was sure she wouldn't lose herself again. Kai was the one who could keep her grounded and in control.

Kai's left hand held Saya's right and he gave it a squeeze.

"I promise. I will stay by your side. I will never leave you alone again. No matter where you are, I'll find you. Believe me."

"Yes."

Saya smiled.

It was a promise.

That's what Kai had said. And in the time since she and Kai first met, she'd never seen him once break a promise. Thanks to Kai's words, at least a part of Saya's anxiety had disappeared.

"You guys, come on! You'll miss all the fireworks!"

"Okay."

Saya also stood up in response to Kaori's call.

Still holding hands, she pulled Kai to his feet.

As she did her heart skipped a beat as the sea wind whipped through her hair carrying the unmistakable tone of a skilled hand rubbing a bow against strings.

On top of the breakwater she could see the silhouette of the young man pulling the bow over his cello.

Without words, he was able to set a comforting mood on the scene through his music. It was typical of the silent Hagi, keeping away but doing what he could. Saya was deeply moved.

+

The white dawn broke over the mountain ridge.

Morning.

"Hey, wake up."

"Hnn . . ."

"We're leaving."

Riku's eyes opened as Kai shook his shoulder.

During their hectic travels in Vietnam, Riku had developed the ability to sleep places besides his bed.

As Riku sat up and rubbed his eyelids, Kai's jacket, which had been covering him, slipped off into the sand.

"Already?"

"If you don't hurry up we'll leave without you."

Kai spoke quietly probably because he didn't want to wake his friends up.

The sunlight slowly revealed Kakimoto and Kato sharing a piece of driftwood as a pillow, snoring as they slept on the sand. Trying to explain everything to them would have been too much.

Surely Kai's anxiety wasn't necessary. Just looking at their co-matose faces told Saya that pouring buckets of water on them probably wouldn't wake them up. Saya bit her lip and looked out over the glistening ocean.

The giant rock jettisoning out from the sea basked in the sun-light.

To that stoic form rising from the water, this was goodbye.

Saya gave a long last look toward the ocean, and then turned and gazed on the sleeping Kaori.

She wished she could have heard her voice one more time.

Saya smiled as she turned away.

Kai and Riku started walking in silence.

"Saya."

Saya's step sunk in the sand.

She couldn't find the courage to turn back around.

If she turned around and looked at Kaori's face she would remember all her hesitations.

"Do your best."

Kaori spoke softly, but it had a huge impact on Saya's heart.

"It was really amazing. Your jump. I know you'll be okay, no matter what happens. So—"

Without looking, Saya could see Kaori's smiling face.

"—do your best!"

"I will . . . I have to go."

Without turning back, Saya continued walking forward.

Even as the curtain of night was lifted and the dawn lit up the beach brightly, Saya's vision was blurred.

She hadn't planned on crying.

She put on a smile and continued forward.

It was then she knew she would be back here someday. Back to the place where she'd started.

CONTINUED IN
VOLUME TWO

# BLOOD+

## Chevalier

## ABOUT THE AUTHOR

From his first book, *Everyone's (a) Bounty-hunter*, and subsequent releases, such as *The Calamity of a Zombie Girl*, and *Valkyrie of the Lightning Dragon*, to this four-volume adaptation of the *Blood+* television series, RYO IKEHATA has been gaining an audience for his fiction on both sides of the Pacific. Born in Shizuoka Prefecture, he currently resides in Yokohama, Japan.

## ABOUT THE ARTIST

A frequent contributor to Kadokawa's *Shonen Ace* magazine in Japan with such manga serials as *Detective Ritual*, CHIZU HASHII was the character designer for the animated *Blood+* television program, overseeing the conceptual design of all characters for the fifty-episode series. His illustrations also appear in the closing credits of many of the episodes of the television series. He lives in Tokyo.

ASUKA KATSURA

Set several decades after the events in the popular *Blood: The Last Vampire* anime film, an amnesiac Saya Otonashi lives as a seemingly normal high school student with her adoptive family in Okinawa. Horrible nightmares are the only hints at the violent life she once led, but her past is about to catch up with her and awaken the merciless warrior within. Chiropterans—powerful shape-changing creatures who need and crave blood—threaten humanity once more, and a mysterious organization called the Red Shield needs Saya's deadly sword skills and mysterious powers to aid in the fight against these beasts. Asuka Katsura's manga series successfully expands upon the original Production I.G/Aniplex feature, delivering moments of jarring violence and thrilling action in a tale that spans several centuries.

**MANGA VOLUME 1**
ISBN 978-7-59307-880-5

**MANGA VOLUME 2**
ISBN 978-1-59307-935-2
*Coming soon!*

**$10.95 each!**

**AVAILABLE AT YOUR LOCAL COMICS SHOP OR BOOKSTORE**
To find a comics shop in your area, call 1.888.266.4226. For more information or to order direct: •On the web: darkhorse.com •E-mail: mailorder@darkhorse.com •Phone: 1.800.862.0052 Mon.–Fri. 9 AM to 5 PM Pacific Time.

DARK
HORSE
MANGA

darkhorse.com

BLOOD+ © Asuka KATSURA © 2005, 2008. Production I.G • Aniplex • MBS • HAKUHODO First published in Japan in 2005 by KADO-KAWA SHOTEN PUBLISHING Co., Ltd., Tokyo. English Translation rights arranged with KADOKAWA SHOTEN PUBLISHING Co., Ltd., Tokyo through TOHAN CORPORATION, Tokyo. (BL7062)

The first book in a highly successful series of novels from Japan,
*Blood: The Last Vampire—Night of the Beasts*
is a startling, fast-paced thriller full of chilling surprises.

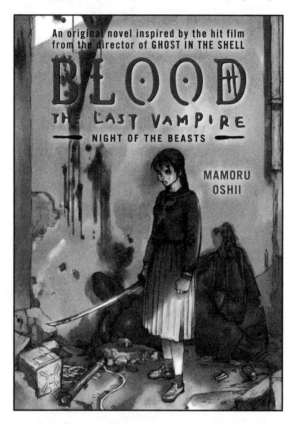

At Yokota Base in Japan, American soldiers stand guard at the brink of the Vietnam War. Although they fear the enemy outside their base, an even more dangerous enemy waits within—bloodthirsty vampires walk among them! Saya, a fierce and beautiful vampire hunter, leads a team of undercover agents who must wipe out the vampires before they can wipe out the base. But even though Saya is a powerful warrior, her ferocity may not be enough!

ISBN-10: 1-59582-029-9 / ISBN-13: 978-1-59582-029-7 | $8.95

AVAILABLE AT YOUR LOCAL COMICS SHOP OR BOOKSTORE
To find a comics shop in your area, call 1-888-266-4266
For more information or to order direct: •On the web: darkhorse.com •E-mail: mailorder@darkhorse.com
•Phone: 1-800-862-0052 Mon.-Fri. 9 A.M. to 5 P.M. Pacific Time.
BLOOD THE LAST VAMPIRE: NIGHT OF THE BEASTS (KEMONO TACHI NO YORU BLOOD THE LAST VAMPIRE) © Mamoru Oshii 2000. © Production I.G. 2000.
Originally published in Japan in 2000 by KADOKAWA SHOTEN PUBLISHING Co., Ltd., Tokyo. English Translation rights arranged with KADOKAWA SHOTEN
PUBLISHING Co., Ltd., Tokyo through TOHAN CORPORATION, Tokyo. DH Press™ is a trademark of Dark Horse Comics, Inc. All rights reserved. (BL7000)